A TOPOGRAPHICAL DESCRIPTION

AND

HISTORY

OF

ARKANSAS COUNTY

ARKANSAS

FROM

1541 TO 1875

BY

W. H. HALLI BURTON

Southern Historical Press, Inc.
Greenville, South Carolina

DEDICATION

*T*O the citizens of Arkansas County, amongst whom he has resided for more than a half century, these pages are dedicated by the author as an evidence of his appreciation of their friendship and ever abounding hospitality.

       W. H. HALLIBURTON

TABLE OF CONTENTS

	Page
Topographical Description	1

HISTORY

CHAPTER I.
From the Advent of De Soto in 1541 to the Departure of Moscoso in 1543 14

CHAPTER II.
From Marquette's Visit to Mouth of Arkansas River in 1673 to Settlement of Arkansas Post, 1686 26

CHAPTER III.
From Settlement of Arkansas Post in 1686 to Appearance of M. Pervier as Commandant in 1726 31

CHAPTER IV.
From M. Pervier's Advent in 1726 to Arrival of O'Reilly as Governor in 1769 38

CHAPTER V.
From O'Reilly's Arrival in 1769 to Settlement at St. Francis in 1797 . 43

CHAPTER VI.
From Philipps' Settlement at St. Francis in 1797 to the Establishment of the Territory of Orleans in 1804 . . . 51

CHAPTER VII.
From Organization of Territory of Orleans in 1804 to the Establishment of the Territory of Missouri in 1812 . . . 56

CHAPTER VIII
From the Organization of the Territory of Missouri in 1812 to the Establishment of the Territory of Arkansas in 1819 . . 68

CHAPTER IX.
From the Organization of the Territory of Arkansas in 1819 to the Removal of the Capital from Arkansas Post to Little Rock in 1821 . 81

CONTENTS—Continued

CHAPTER X
From the year 1821 to the year 1830 92

CHAPTER XI.
From the year 1830 to the year 1840 102

CHAPTER XII.
From the year 1840 to the year 1845 113

CHAPTER XIII.
From the year 1845 to the year 1850 117

CHAPTER XIV.
From the year 1850 to the year 1855 129

CHAPTER XV.
From the year 1855 to the year 1860 136

CHAPTER XVI.
From the year 1860 to the year 1865 141

CHAPTER XVII.
From the year 1865 to the year 1870 155

CHAPTER XVIII.
From the year 1870 to the year 1875 176

ARKANSAS COUNTY

Topographical Description

Ne Material Copyright 1978 by:
The Rev. Silas Emmett Lucas, Jr.

All rights reserved. No part of this publication may be
reproduced, stored in a retrieval system or transmitted
in any form or by any means without the
prior permission of the publisher.

SOUTHERN HISTORICAL PRESS, INC.
PO BOX 1267
Greenville, SC   29601

ISBN #978-0-89308-076-4

Printed in the United States of America

ARKANSAS COUNTY.

Topographical Description.

Arkansas County is located south and east of the center of the State of Arkansas and is bounded as follows: on the north by Monroe and Prairie counties; on the west by Prairie and Jefferson counties; on the south by the Arkansas river, which separates it from Lincoln and Desha counties; on the southeast by the cutoff that connects the Arkansas and White rivers; and on the east by White river, which separates it from the counties of Desha, Phillips and Monroe. From this it can readily be seen that at least two-thirds of its boundary is washed by navigable streams or waterways, to which may be added thirty miles of navigable waterways for small boats and timber rafts in Big Bayou Meto, for an average of six months in the year and an equal distance, for a like time, in Big Lagrue.

Bayou Meto flows through the northwest corner of the county, and continuing south, forms a portion of its western boundary. Big Lagrue, in the eastern part of the county, flows in a southeasterly direction from the northern boundary, emptying into White river a few miles above the southeast corner of the county.

The county embraces an area of about one thousand square miles; its mean length, from north to south, being about thirty miles and its width, from east to west, about twenty miles. The extreme southeast corner of the county is within six miles of the Mississippi river.

The surface is comparatively level, with sufficient depressions on the general surface to afford good drainage, but not such as to cause the washing of deep gullies through the land, after it is put in cultivation.

Seventy-five per cent of the land in the county is susceptible of cultivation.

There are but few hills, and those of but slight elevation above the common level of the general surface. The only lands, assuming the appearance of hills are on or near Big Lagrue, in the eastern part of the county and between Grand Prairie and Bayou Meto, in the western part.

Grand Prairie extends from about one mile west of Arkansas Post, northwest through the center of the country, to the northern boundary, with a width of from two to ten miles and with arms or branches in various directions and of various lengths.

Between these arms or branches are points of timber, from two to twenty miles in length, extending from the main forest surrounding the prairie and pointing mainly in a northern direction.

In these points of timber are streams of water: those on the west side of the prairie flowing into Bayou Meto and through it into Arkansas river, while those on the east side flow into Lagrue and through it into White river. These streams are not perpetual, but afford an abundance of water for ordinary purposes, except in seasons of protracted drouth.

The Bayous Meto and Lagrue furnish water, at all seasons, sufficient for ordinary purposes.

In addition to Grand Prairie there is, north of the town of DeWitt, between Big and Little Lagrue, Sassafras Prairie, which is from six to eight miles in length, from southeast to northwest, and from one to three miles in width.

East of Big Lagrue and west of Big Creek, is Lagrue prairie and between Big Creek and White river is White River prairie. These prairies are separated by the timber on Big Creek.

In the southeast corner of the county there is a belt or strip of country, varying in width from one to two miles, known or designated on the old plats of the public surveys as "The Cypress Swamp". This swamp extends from Lagrue, a few miles south of Lagrue Springs, first in a southwest course, then south and thence southeast to the Arkansas River about 8 miles south of Arkansas Post.

Through this swamp the flow of water alternates according to the stage of the water in the White and Arkansas rivers. If the Arkansas is high and the White low, the water in the swamp flows from the Arkansas to the White; and when the White is high and the Arkansas low, the flow is from the White to the Arkansas. White river is connected with this swamp by Lagrue and Arkansas river by Merrisack bayou.

East of this swamp is another prairie known as Little prairie, which is about ten miles in length, from north to south, while its width, east and west, varies from one to two miles.

Scattered promiscuously over all these prairies are groves of timber varying in size from one to four thousand acres. The largest of these is Big Island near the northern boundary of the county, east and southeast of and near the city of Stuttgart. Northeast of Big Island is Maple Island, through which the northern boundary line of the county passes, and southeast of the city of Stuttgart are Angelico and Mud Islands.

Notwithstanding the extent of the prairies, the area thereof approximating one-third the area of the whole county, there is no point within the same exceeding four miles from timber. This is in consequence of the numerous points jutting out from the main body of the timber surrounding the prairies and the number of islands of timber in the prairies.

The principal streams or water courses, enumerating from east to west, in the county, are Poplar Creek, Essie's Bayou, Tarlton's Creek, Big Creek, Big Lagrue, Little Lagrue, DeLuce and Cypress flowing east and southeast into White river; Mill Bayou or Longpoint, with its tributaries, flowing south through the center of Grand Prairie; Clearpoint, King's Bayou, Caney Bayou, Big and Little Bayou Meto and Crooked Creek, flowing south and southwest on the west side of Grand Prairie into Arkansas river.

All these streams except Big Lagrue, the two Metos, and Crooked Creek have their sources in the county.

TOPOGRAPHICAL DESCRIPTION.

The source of Big Lagrue is in Prairie County. Big Bayou Meto has its source in the high lands of Pulaski county, northeast of Little Rock, from where it flows southeast through Pulaski, Lonoke, Jefferson, and Arkansas counties, entering the Arkansas river a few miles above Thetford's old ferry, about seven miles west of Arkansas Post. It is the opinion of the writer that Bayou Meto originally entered the Arkansas river at Arkansas Post, but by means of cut offs, caving banks and consequent changes in the river's channel, the bank finally caved into the bayou, thus causing it to enter the river at the point of cut off.

This theory is supported by the fact that at what is now known as Thetford's Island (the point at which the bayou enters the river) there have been two cut offs and changes in the course of the river since 1849, causing this bayou to enter the river above and on the west side of the island, when in fact, before 1849 it entered the river and flowed east of the island.

At the time of the cut off in 1849 there was a large lake within one half mile of the point at which this cut off was made, showing that the river, at some anterior time, ran where this lake then was, and that the river had moved north, in the direction of the bayou, evidently cutting into it.

Within sight of the cut off of 1849, there was, and now is, a deep bayou or outlet of the river, with well defined banks and open channel about as high and wide as the banks and channel of the bayou before it enters the river. From this point the bayou continues its course between the river and the highlands adjoining the prairie, until it enters the river at Arkansas Post, which place is located at the upper end of the highlands abutting on the Arkansas river for a distance of about two miles.

There are a few small lakes within the limits of Arkansas County: two on White river—one just above the village of Mt. Adams and one between Crockett's Bluff and St. Charles—one or two in the lowlands south of Esses Bayou, one near the Arkansas river about five miles southeast of Arkansas Post, one between the Grand Prairie and Arkansas river, about four miles south of the village of Gillett, one at the mouth of Bayou Meto and one about three miles southwest of Arkansas Post. The last two mentioned were made by cut-offs and changes in the channel of the Arkansas river.

There are but few springs of water in the county, and such as have been found are located in districts subject to overflow in time of high water in the streams near which they are located.

The most noted of these are known as LaGrue Springs, located on LaGrue Bayou, about eight miles southeast from Dewitt. Their waters are said to possess medical virtues, and are resorted to frequently, when accessible, for the cure of various maladies, both by drinking the water and using it for baths. The sediment found on the sides of the openings through which these waters flow, is said to be a specific for inflammatory rheumatism and nearly all cutaneous diseases.

A number of springs issue from the banks out of the bed of Esses Bayou, the water from them being of various temperatures. One of them is known as the "Cold Spring", from the fact that the water issuing from it is of a temperature closely approximating that of ice water. These springs are located two or three miles east of LaGrue Springs, in a section of country fine for hunting and fishing in their seasons, and are visited by sportsmen in the latter part of the summer and through the fall and early winter.

Menard Mound.

In 1881 Edward Palmer, connected with the Ethnological Department of the Smithsonian Institution, visited Arkansas County for the purpose of examining and reporting upon the great mound located in the southeast corner of said county, together with a description of specimens of pottery found in and near the same.

This mound, with the collection of pottery it contained, was examined and catalogued by William H. Holmes, the result of this investigation being printed in Powell's third annual report in 1884, from which report the following descriptions, etc., are taken:

"A group of well known mounds is situated on the farm of the late Frank Menard, eight miles southeast of the village of Arkansas Post. The largest mound is nine hundred and sixty-five feet in circumference, at the top, and considerably larger at the base. The slopes are covered with trees and bushes." (The height of this mound is not given in the report, but it is at least sixty feet high, at this time.) "This mound had already been dug into quite extensively and it was thought useless to explore it further." Connected with this mound by a ridge of earth three hundred feet long and twenty feet wide, is a small circular mound fifteen feet high and forty-five feet in diameter, which bears evidence of having been occupied by houses.

Articles of Clay in Menard Mound.

Near the middle of the connecting ridge, just under the soil, a layer of burnt clay, about five or six feet in diameter, was found. At one side, imbedded in the debris of clay, a large quantity of fragments of earthen vessels was discovered. They comprise a number of bowls of various sizes, which are all quite new looking, and are of a type of ware quite distinct from that found in the field and graves of the same locality.

Restorations of a large number have been made and the collection proves to be extremely interesting.

The collector argues, from the position of the fragmentary vessels, that they had been placed, by their owners, upon the roof of the house which, he surmised, was destroyed by fire.

Plain bowls, of yellowish gray ware, restored from fragments described above, are wide and shallow, and somewhat conical. They are hand made, without polish, the material used being clay, tempered with pulverized shells. The walls are usually quite thin. Diameter, ten to thirteen inches. Height, three to six inches.

Other bowls corresponding in general character to those described above, have tasteful designs of incised lines and indentations on the exterior surface. The most interesting of these designs consists of a series of interlaced or festooned lines. The exterior margin is encircled,

TOPOGRAPHICAL DESCRIPTION

in all cases, by ornamentation consisting of parallel lines, groups of short incised lines or rows of indentations.

Articles of stone consisting of arrow points, spear points, knives and other articles are described.

Surrounding the Menard Mound is a field containing about twenty acres, which appears to have been, at one time, the site of a great number of dwellings, as layers of burnt clay are found at a depth of from one to two feet. This field seems also to have been a great cemetery, the remains of skeletons being found in great numbers.

Pottery is found in great abundance. It has, as a rule, been deposited near the heads of the dead, but no ornaments nor implements have been discovered with the remains. The frequent plowing of the field has destroyed many earthen vessels, the interments having been made quite near the surface. It is a noticeable fact that the pottery from these graves is of a character quite distinct from that of the Mound. This pottery is of the class of ware so common in this region.

There are eighty-five specimens of pottery, implements, etc., mentioned in the catalogue, with seventeen illustrations, given in this report of the Menard Mound and its surroundings.

There are other mounds located in various regions of the county, varying from one to ten feet in elevation. The most notable are as follows: One near the bank of White river, at the mouth of **Lagrue**; one between that and Little Prairie; one in Grand Prairie, near the head of Bob's Point; one on Point DeLuce; one near the east end of the bridge crossing Mill Bayou, on the road from DeWitt to Garrison's Ferry on Bayou Meto; and one in the town of DeWitt. There is also a mound on Col. Farrely's place, near the south end of Grand Prairie, about four miles west from Arkansas Post.

In digging for the foundation of a house which was built on the east side of this mound, great quantities of human bones, and pottery were found, showing that this mound had at some time been a burying place for builders.

There are three others of some notoriety, namely: One on the north bank of Menard Lake, five or six miles southeast of Arkansas Post; one between the south end of Grand Prairie and the Arkansas river, known as "Walnut Knoll"; and one on the north bank of Old River, near "Walnut Knoll" and southwest of and within two miles of Arkansas Post. These three are, in the opinion of the writer, of volcanic origin, all the others being, without doubt, the handiwork of the Mound Builders.

One of the peculiarities of this county is the absence of stone of all kinds, on the surface or cropping out of the hillsides or banks of streams. None has been found in digging, boring or driving wells anywhere in the county. In many places over the county, piping for wells has been driven a distance of more than one hundred feet without encountering stone.

There is a stratum of stone a few hundred yards long in the bed of a small, short bayou entering Bayou Meto, about sixteen miles west of DeWitt.

Water for domestic purposes is easily obtained in all parts of the

ARKANSAS COUNTY.

county by digging, boring or driving at depths varying from fifteen to one hundred feet.

In the forests of the county there is a great variety of timber for domestic and commercial purposes, such as white, red, Spanish, pin, post, willow or water, cow, overcup or burr and jack or black-jack—oak, three or four species of hickory, white and red or sweet gum, elm, maple, walnut, mulberry, hackberry, wild cherry, sweet and bitter pecan, poplar, dogwood, willow, ash, cottonwood, cypress, sycamore, tupelo gum, black and red hawthorn, sassafras, persimmon, honey locust, catalpa, redbud, wild plum and holly. A great variety of shrubs and flowering plants are to be found over the prairies and through the forests of the county.

The principal fruits grown in the county are apples, pears, peaches, plums and figs, with strawberries, blackberries, dewberries and raspberries, grapes, both domestic and wild, and muscadines, among the smaller fruits. The agricultural products are cotton, corn, wheat, oats, sweet and Irish potatoes, stock peas and melons of all kinds, the horticultural products, all vegetables usually cultivated in this latitude.

For the information of those desiring to know the constituents, productiveness, etc., of the soil of this county, the following extracts are copied from Dr. David Dale Owen's second report of his Geological Reconnoissance of the Middle and Southern Counties of the State of Arkansas: "The greater portion of Arkansas county between the Arkansas and White river bottoms is prairie land, derived, no doubt, from the clay bed which underlies the quarternary marl and sand, so well developed in Crowley's Ridge in Phillips and St. Frances counties.

"The prairie land is generally rolling and the valleys are from five to ten feet lower than the slight, ridge-like elevations. They are wet and spouty and the sub-soil, where thrown up by crawfish, is light-colored clay.

"Soils characteristic of this prairie land were collected near Col. Farrely's on Spanish Grant No. —

"(This grant is on the south end of Grand Prairie about four miles west of Arkansas Post.)

"The virgin soil was taken from land owned by James Moore on Section 18, Township 7 south, Range 3 west, and the cultivated soil and yellow ochre sub-soil, a few yards from the former, on Harold Stillwell's farm, which had been from forty to fifty years in cultivation. Virgin soil was also collected from a part of the prairie some four to six feet higher than that from which the above was taken. It is of a more porous quality.

The prairie land in this county has generally been looked upon as worthless, in comparison with the woodland which adjoins it, and the alluvial river land. The woodland is said to yield as much as 1,800 pounds of cotton, or from 30 to 40 bushels of corn to the acre.

On comparing, however, the analysis of its soil (No. 410 in Dr. Peter's Report) with that of the prairie soil, it will be seen that the latter possesses as much of the elements required for the nourishment of plants as the former.

The prairie soil is mainly deficient in lime, soda, potash and organic matter, in a soluble condition, as compared with the buckshot soil (No. 411 in Dr. Peter's Report) which contains these elements in an eminent degree.

By a good system of drainage, and the addition of lime in some form, the prairie soil may be made highly productive. Drainage will loosen the soil, permit the roots of the plants to penetrate to a proper depth, and correct the sour tendency which all standing or superfluous water exerts upon vegetation.

A set of soils, Nos. 1, 2 and 3, was collected from Col. Farrely's and James Moore's plantation as specimens of the cotton lands of the Arkansas river bottoms. No. 2, the cultivated soil, was collected with special reference to an investigation of the cause of rust in the cotton plant.

It was therefore taken from the parts of the field where that had most appeared, especially in the year 1857; the object being to ascertain whether rust is owing to the exhaustion of any of the ingredients required for the proper nourishment of the plant, or not. But it appears to be a local disease, only attacking certain plants on a ground; and as it is worse in some seasons than in others, it is more likely to be attributable to some other cause than a peculiarity in the proportion of mineral constituents of the soil.

The soil is a sandy loam, and the sub-soil, at a depth of from one to one and a half feet, is a dark gray, adhesive clay.

For the analysis of this soil see Dr. Robert Peter's Report, Nos. 414, 415 and 416, which folow:

No. 414.—Virgin Soil: Arkansas river bottom cotton soil. Col. Farrely's land, Spanish grant, Township 7 south, Range 4 west, Arkansas County, Arkansas. A sandy soil containing minute specks of mica of a warm brownish-gray color. No. 415—Soil from a cotton field in Arkansas river bottom on Col. Farrely's plantation, fifteen years in cultivation. (This sample was taken from a part of the field where the cotton was most liable to rust, especially in 1857, to learn whether it was caused by exhaustion of some of the ingredients of the soil requisite for the perfect growth of the plant.)" Dried soil darker than the preceding, of light powdered chocolate color. Sandy, containing small specks of mica. No. 416—"Sub-soil of the field fifteen years in cultivation, Col. Farrely's plantation, Arkansas river bottom, Arkansas County, Arkansas." Dried soil a little lighter color than the preceding; not so sandy; does not appear to contain mica.

Extracted from 1,000 grains of each of these soils, by digestion in water charged with Carbonic Acid Gas.

	No. 414 Virgin Soil	No. 415 Old Field Soil	No. 416 Subsoil
Organic and Volatile Matters	0.750	0.600	1.066
Alumina, and Oxides of Iron and Manganese and Phosphates	.703	.503	.830
Carbonate of Lime	1.117	1.420	2.747
Magnesia	.258	.367	.358
Sulphuric Acid	.022	.022	.027
Potash	.085	.064	.048
Soda	.046	.060	.057
Silica	.430	.380	.530
Total extract, dried at 212° F. Grains	3.414	3.416	5.633

ARKANSAS COUNTY.

Chemical Composition, dried at 400° F.

	No. 414 Virgin Soil	No. 415 Old Field Soil	No. 416 Subsoil
Organic and Volatile Matters	1.803	2.444	5.091
Alumina	2.185	2.260	6.085
Oxide of Iron	1.740	1.765	4.640
Carbonate of Lime	.380	.520	.970
Magnesia	.737	.664	1.555
Brown Oxide of Manganese	.170	.270	.245
Phosphoric Acid	.127	.143	.221
Sulphuric Acid	.050	.046	.084
Potash	.201	.295	.714
Soda	.100	.078	.080
Sand and Insoluble Silicates	93.415	92.215	81.240
Total	100.908	100.700	100.925
Moisture expelled at 400° F	1.550	1.800	4.925

'The soil of the old field is actually richer than the virgin surface soil, but the reason is obvious in the greatly richer sub-soil, some of which has doubtless been brought up and mixed with the surface soil of the cultivated field by action of the plough. The surface soil of this locality is sandy and only second-rate in fertility, but the sub-soil is very rich in potash, etc., etc., and by deep sub-soiling the land would be greatly improved in productiveness."

In addition to the foregoing, the following analysis of prairie and wood upland soils is given, which is extracted from the same report.

No. 406—"Virgin Soil: Prairie adjoining Spanish Grant on Section 18, Township 7 south, Range 3 west, owned by James Moore. An average of the prairie land of Arkansas County, Arkansas."

The dried soil is of a light umber color.

No. 407—"Same soil from an old field forty to fifty years in cultivation. Prairie. Spanish Grant. Section oo, Township 7, Range 3 west. Harold Stillwell's farm, Arkansas County." The dried soil is light buff-umber colored, lighter than the preceding.

No. 408—"Sub-soil from the same field. Harold Stillwell's farm, Arkansas County."

The dried soil is of a dirty buff color.

No. 409—"Virgin Prairie Soil, from the highest of the prairie, on Section 17, Township 7 south, Range 3 west. (This is looser and drier than the preceding.) Arkansas County, Arkansas." The dried soil is of an umber color.

No. 410—"Upland Woodland soil, adjoining the prairie, on Spanish Grant, Township 7 south, Range 3 west." (Differs from the prairie soil at Moore's and Farrely's.)

The dried soil is of a dark drab color, lighter and more yellowish than the preceding.

One thousand grains of each of these soils, thoroughly air dried, were digested for a month, at the ordinary summer temperature, in a close bottle, in water which had been charged with carbonic acid gas.

TOPOGRAPHICAL DESCRIPTION.

The infusion, after filtration, evaporated and fully dried at 212° F., gave the following dissolved materials, viz.:

	No. 406 Prairie Virgin Soil	No. 407 Old Field Soil	No. 408 Subsoil	No. 409 Prairie Virgin Soil	No. 410 Woodland Virgin Soil
Organic and Volatile Matters	0.733	0.633	0.493	1.167	0.800
Alumnia, and Oxides of Iron and Manganese and Phosphates	1.060	.703	.260	1.776	.500
Carbonate of Lime	.350	.813	.280	.747	.680
Magnesia	.153	.289	.133	.206	.172
Sulphuric Acid	.030	.039	.030	.039	.056
Potash	.048	.061	.126	.067	.084
Soda	.034	.015	.064	.051	.018
Silica	.330	.297	.280	.447	.247
Loss	.295	.017	....	....	....
Total extract, dried at 212° F. (Grains)	3.033	2.967	1.666	4.500	2.557

Submitted to chemical analysis, dried at 400° F., the composition of these soils was found to be as follows:

	No. 406 Virgin Prairie Soil	No. 407 Old Fie' Soil	No. 408 Subsoil	No. 409 Virgin Upland Prairie Soil	No. 410 Virgin Upland Woodland Soil
Organic and Volatile Matters	4.094	3.509	3.506	4.998	3.814
Alumnia	2.535	2.810	4.910	2.660	3.635
Oxide of Iron	2.740	3.415	3.965	2.140	3.015
Carbonate of Lime	.095	.195	.095	.145	.120
Magnesia	.482	.669	.526	.475	.519
Brown Oxide of Manganese	.245	.295	.345	.220	.260
Phosphoric Acid	.212	.211	.118	.163	.173
Sulphuric Acid	.071	.075	.067	.101	.067
Potash	.183	.207	.169	.103	.174
Soda	.050	10.	.044	.072	.053
Sand and Insoluble Silicates	88.465	88.790	86.460	88.865	87.965
Loss	.828	.720	....	.058	.205
Total	100.000	100.000	100.205	100.000	100.000
Moisture expelled at 400° F.	3.690	3.165	3.750	3.950	3.390

Dr. Owens gives but one analysis of well water in Arkansas county which follows:—

"The following section was taken from a well dug on Farrely's and Moore's plantation:

Soil.

Sub-soil, pale yellowish-red

Under clay, with iron gravel, made up of irregular and rounded pieces of oxide of iron about the size of a small marble, 8 feet.

Compact reddish sand, 30 feet.

Water reached in coarse white sand.

A qualitative chemical examination was made of well water at Col.

ARKANSAS COUNTY.

Farrely's & Moore's plantation. It has an alkaline reaction, turning litmus paper blue in a short time. The principal constituents are:
Chloride of sodium, (common salt),
Carbonate of soda,
Bicarbonate of lime,
Bicarbonate of magnesia,
Sulphate of magnesia,
Sulphate of lime, a trace,
Chloride of magnesium."

He also gives one analysis of Arkansas river water, and that at Dr. William's landing in Jefferson county, as follows:

"An analysis of the Arkansas river water at Dr. William's landing, the river at low-water stage, gave for the principal constituents:
Chloride of sodium, (common salt),
Carbonate of soda,
Sulphate of soda (Glauber salts),
Sulphate of magnesia (Epsom salts),
Carbonate of lime, strong,
Carbonate of magnesia,
Carbonate of potash,
Silica,
Protoxide of iron,

The river water is slightly alkaline to litmus paper, and contains more chloride of sodium than the well water."

The county is divided into twelve townships or civil districts with civil officers residing in each township. It is also divided into sixty-two school districts thus affording educational advantages to the children residing in each neighborhood in the county. In a large number of these districts, are neat and comfortable school-houses in which, as a rule, free schools are taught from three to eight months of each year.

In addition to the public school system of the county there is an academy of high character, located at Stuttgart, in which the usual branches of an academic course are taught. There are also several private schools located in the county.

The following named religious denominations have regularly organized congregations, with stated times and places for worship, dispersed over the county, there being scarcely a neighborhood without religious influence. These denominations are: Baptist, Methodist, Presbyterian, Christian, Seventh Day Baptist, Adventist and Catholic.

The mail facilities of the county are above the ordinary, as will be seen by the statement of the various mail routes through the county, with the names of post-offices and the frequency of the transportation of mails over these routes, which follows: Round trips each day (except Sunday) from Arkansas Post via Gillett, DeWitt, Olena and Almyra, to Stuttgart; from DeWitt, via Van, to Ethel; from DeWitt to St. Charles; from DeWitt, via Sassafras and Violet, to Cascoe; from Roe, on the Cotton Belt R. R., near the northern boundary of the county, via Cascoe and Mt. Adams to Crockett's Bluff; from Stuttgart to Fairmount; from Stuttgart, via Goldman, to Humphrey and from Stuttgart, via Ulm, to Roe, on the Cotton Belt R. R. The mails, on the routes

TOPOGRAPHICAL DESCRIPTION.

over the railroad, go each way daily, including Sundays. From Stuttgart, via Hagler, to Bayou Meto, and from DeWitt, via DeLuce and Tichenor, to Booty there are mails, three times a week, each way and from Humphrey to Vallier, twice a week, each way.

The principal towns of the county are Stuttgart, DeWitt, and Arkansas Post.

Stuttgart is located on Grand Prairie, in the northwest corner of the county, on the St. Louis Southwestern (Cotton Belt) R. R. It is about twenty-two miles northwest from the county capital, thirty-four miles northeast from Pine Bluff, 20 miles from Clarendon, and is the northern terminus of the Stuttgart and Arkansas River R. R. The population, according to the census of 1900 is twelve hundred and fifty-eight.

The government, under a corporation charter, granted under the statutes of the state, to cities of the second degree, is conducted by a Mayor and six Aldermen.

The citizens enjoy railroad, telegraphic and telephonic communication with the surrounding business and social world, also electric light and water privileges.

A large mercantile interest is owned and operated by energetic, enterprising men, who know the wants of the general public and are fully prepared to meet these wants in all their various demands.

There are located in the city two banks; the German-American with a capital of thirty thousand dollars, and the Citizen's Bank with a capital of twenty-five thousand dollars.

There is also a large mechanical and manufacturing interest consisting of a wheat and corn mill, saw mill, cotton gin, brick and tile factory, blacksmith, carpenter, wood, paint, shoe and harness and saddle shops.

The hotels, restaurants and livery stables are sufficient to meet the demands of the public.

A town hall and opera house are also to be found in the city.

There are eight or nine organized churches, with comfortable and well furnished houses for worship, located in the city, viz: one Methodist church, one Methodist Episcopal Church South, one Baptist, one United Presbyterian, one Christian, one German Lutheran, one German Evangelical Lutheran and one Roman Catholic. To these may be added the following named churches for the negroes, one Methodist and two Baptist.

There are two public school houses in the city—one for the white, the other for the colored children in the school district. In the white school there are about 200 pupils taught by an efficient principal with five competent assistants. In the colored school there are ——— pupils taught ——— months each year, by a principal and ——— assistants.

The principal and assistant teachers in each school are selected and employed by a local board of school directors.

In addition to the public schools, there is located here The Stuttgart Training School, a preparatory school for Hendrick's College, Arkadelphia, under the supervision of the Little Rock Conference of the

ARKANSAS COUNTY.

M. E. Church South. Classic, scientific, business, music, and art courses are taught.

Two weekly newspapers are published in the city—The Free Press, democratic and The Stuttgart Republican, republican.

Nine attorneys, four physicians and two dentists are engaged in active practice of their professions in the city.

The town is now (1903) about twenty-two years old.

DeWitt, the county capital or seat of justice in and for the county, is about one half mile from Grand Prairie, near the geographical center of the county, on the Stuttgart and Arkansas River R. R. It is about twenty-two miles, by this railroad, from Stuttgart, about twenty miles north of Arkansas Post, and fifteen miles west from St. Charles.

The population, according to the census of 1900, is three hundred and eighteen souls, but this report includes only such as reside on the one quarter section of land included in the corporate limits, when in fact the town covers more than three quarter sections, on which, not including the corporate limits there are as many, probably more souls than in the corporation, making the population of the town as a whole more than six hundred.

The corporation is governed by a mayor and 5 aldermen, under the charter granted under the statutes of the state, assuring protection to persons and property within its limits.

This town, being the seat of justice for the county, is, of course, the site of the public buildings of the county, which are a court house and jail.

The court house, built of brick, with stone trimmings and slate roof, was erected during the years 1893 and 1894 at a cost of thirty-five thousand, five hundred fifty dollars, being the second brick court house built in the town since its organization in 1855.

The main building of the jail is brick, with a frame or wooden addition to accommodate the jailer and his family.

There are three organized churches with comfortable houses for worship, in the town, viz: one M. E. Church South, one Baptist and one United Presbyterian. There are also a Methodist and Baptist church for the negroes. Their houses for worship are located near the corporate limits.

A comfortable public school building, capable of accommodating one hundred and fifty pupils, is located in the town. Under the direction of a principal, with three assistant teachers, a school is taught here from six to nine months of each year. In the suburbs of the town is located a building for the accommodation of the colored pupils, where a school is taught a like length of time each year.

There are in town one bank, with a capital of fifteen thousand dollars, seven mercantile establishments doing a general mercantile business, three family grocery stores, two drug stores, one hardware store, one furniture store, one jewelry store, one grain and feed store, one photograph gallery, one cotton gin, one corn mill, a saw mill and brick and tile factory, two blacksmith shops, one shoe shop, wood shop, two livery and sale stables, one lumber yard, and one weekly newspaper.

Two hotels meet the demands of the general public.

TOPOGRAPHICAL DESCRIPTION.

Five attorneys and four physicians are engaged in the practice of their professions here.

The citizens of the town and those within three miles of the public school building in the town are protected by a special act of the legislature against the establishment of saloons or dram shops or the sale of intoxicants of any kind.

Arkansas Post is located on the north bank of the Arkansas river, which at this point separates Arkansas from Desha county, and is about twenty miles south of DeWitt. The town has a population of about one hundred

Here are a post-office, mercantile establishments, in which a general mercantile business is conducted, blacksmith shop, cotton gin, corn mill, saw mill, etc.

At this point, in the year 1686, the first settlement, by white men in the Mississippi valley and west of that river, was made. It was the seat of civil and military authority from the organization of civil society in the territory, and the point from which such government was administered over the territory constituting the present state of Arkansas from 1721 to 1812. Here also was the first seat of justice within and for the county of Arkansas, created by an act of Missouri Territorial Legislature, December 31, 1813, and was the first seat of territorial government, established by an act of Congress, March 2, 1819. The seat of territorial government was removed in 1821 and the seat of justice of Arkansas county, in September 1855.

On the 20th of November 1819, W. E. Woodruff issued the first number of the Arkansas Gazette from a log cabin at Arkansas Post, it being the first newspaper established in the Territory of Arkansas and the second west of the Mississippi River.

In addition to the foregoing towns, there are the following villages. Located on White River with post-offices, stores, shops, etc., at each place sufficient to meet the demands of the village are, Mt. Adams, Crockett's Bluff, Cascoe and St. Charles; on the Stuttgart and Arkansas River R. R., Gillett, Olena and Almyra; and on the Cotton Belt, Goldman and Humphrey.

At a great number of the smaller post-offices in the county there are stores doing a general mercantile business.

CHAPTER I.

From Advent of De Soto in 1541 to Departure of Moscoso, 1543.

As the travels of De Soto west of the Mississippi river form an important chapter in the history of Arkansas County, a synopsis of the more notable events of these travels will be given.

The point at which De Soto crossed the river has always been one of doubt and disputation. Irving, in his "Conquest of Florida," quoting the Portugese narrative, says the crossing "was probably the lowest Chickasaw Bluff, one of the ancient crossing places between the thirty-fourth and thirty-fifth parallels of latitude." Monette, in his "Valley of the Mississippi," says: "The point where De Soto crossed the river was probably within thirty miles of Helena." Dr. Ramsay, in his "History of Tennessee," says: "It is generally conjectured that Chisca, the village near which De Soto was encamped and which bore the name of the chieftain of the province through whose territories the Spanish were passing, occupied the site of the present thriving city of Memphis, and that the point where they crossed the Mississippi was near the Chicksaw Bluff." Hempstead, in his "History of Arkansas," has given the opinion of several authors on this subject as follows: Bancroft's History of the United States—"The lowest Chickasaw Bluff (Memphis)".

Belknap—"Within the thirty-fourth degree, i. e., from the Louisiana line to a little above the mouth of White river."

Andrew Ellicott's Journal—"Thirty-four degrees and ten minutes (about the location of Sunflower Landing, Mississippi.)"

Martin's Louisiana—"A little below the lowest Chickasaw Bluff."

Nutall's Travels in Arkansas—"The lowest Chickasaw Bluff."

McCullock's Researches—"Twenty or thirty miles below the mouth of the Arkansas river;" and French, in his "Historical Collections of Louisiana," referring to an old French map, places the crossing "at what would be equal to thirty-four degrees, ten minutes."

To this must be added the opinion of Professor Shinn as given in his "School History of Arkansas": "At some point between what is now Helena and the mouth of the Arkansas."

Now it is reasonable to suppose that each author quoted drew his conclusions from the narrative of De Soto's expedition as given by one or more of the narrators of said expedition, to wit: "A Gentleman of Elvis" (Portugese Narrator), Luis Fernandez de Biedma and the Inca Garcilasso de la Vega.

To reconcile the differences of opinion or conclusion of these authors on this point and to arrive at a reasonable conclusion as to the particular place or point at which the crossing was made, is no easy matter, when it is understood that the narrators mentioned above are the only authorities on the subject.

The reader will please bear in mind that each of the narrators frequently refers to and describes notable natural or artificial objects, such as rivers, lakes, mounds, etc., and by means of the description of such objects, we are able to identify and locate many places mentioned and thus follow the route traveled by De Soto.

Irving, in his account of the approach of De Soto to the Mississippi river, says: "At length they came in sight of a village called Chisca. It was seated near a wide and rapid river and as it was the largest they had discovered, they called it Rio Grande. This was the Father of Waters, the great Mississippi."

"On a high artificial mound, on one side of the village, stood the dwelling of the cacique, which served as a fortress."

It is a fact known of all who are familiar with the topography of Memphis, that such a mound as is described by Irving is located near the bank of the river, in the southern suburb of the city, known as "Jackson Park." This is considered a potent fact to prove that the lowest Chickasaw Bluff "was the place where De Soto crossed the Mississippi river."

Another fact of equal importance to establish this proposition is the fact that after crossing the river, Garcilasso tells us, De Soto marched up the river to the town of Aquixo, situated on the bank of the river, about one and a half leagues above the point of crossing. This was a great town, evidently the headquarters or chief town of the cacique, Aquixo, "who was lord of many towns and governed many people."

Irving, in his history, tells us that when De Soto was preparing boats to cross the river, "they perceived a fleet of two hundred canoes **descending** the river. They were filled with armed Indians, showing conclusively that the village, here referred to, was a large one in which many Indians dwelt, and that its location was at what is now known as Mound City in Crittendon County, Arkansas. Here, as at Chisca, we find a large mound, as we will in several other places mentioned in the narrative of De Soto's travels as evidence of the location of Indian towns which were the headquarters or seats of the caciques or chiefs of the tribes.

"From this point," Irving tells us, they proceeded onward four days through a wilderness intersected in many places by morasses, which they were obliged to ford, and on the fifth day from the summit of a high ridge they descried a large village containing about four hundred dwellings. "It was seated on the bank of a river."

Garcilasso says they came to a small river where a bridge was made by which they passed. He also says: "This country is higher, drier and more champaign than any part bordering near the river, that, until then they had seen."

"After remaining at this place six days, they resumed their journey. They marched through a populous and champaign country where the land was more elevated, and the soil less alluvial than any they had seen on the border of the Mississippi. In two days they came to the

ARKANSAS COUNTY.

chief town where the cacique resided." It was situated on the **same side of the river,** about seven leagues above where they had crossed.

Here, or near this place, Biedma and Garcilasso both say that, by order of the Governor, a cross was planted as an emblem of their religion. The former says: "The caciques of the country make a custom of raising near their dwellings, very high hills on which they sometimes build their huts. On one of these we planted the cross." The latter, after giving an account of the appeal of the cacique to the Governor, to give sight to a blind man, says: "He commanded to make a very high cross of wood which was set up in the highest place of the town declaring that the Christians worshipped the same in resemblance and memory of that whereon Christ suffered."

Irving, in his account of the raising of the cross, says that in answer to the cacique's request that De Soto pray to his God to send rain for their parched fields, "De Soto replied that although he and all his followers were but sinners, yet they would supplicate God, the father of mercies, to show mercy unto them."

"In the presence of the cacique, he then ordered the chief carpenter—Francisco, the Genoese, to hew down the highest and largest pine tree in the vicinity and construct of it a cross. They immediately felled one of such immense size that a hundred men could not raise it from the ground. They formed of it a perfect cross, and erected it on a **high hill,** on the bank of the river, which served the Indians as a watch-tower, overlooking every eminence in the vicinity."

I have been thus minute in quoting from all the accessible authorities on this subject, that I might, with reasonable certainty, locate the point or place at which the cross was erected, and thereby add another potent fact, to prove that the lowest Chickasaw Bluff was the point at which De Soto crossed the Mississippi river.

The reader will bear in mind that after De Soto crossed the Mississippi river, he went one day's journey up the river. That, from here, he traveled four days through a wilderness intersected in many places by morasses and streams, which they crossed, and on the fifth day reached a village located on the bank of a river, the river flowing on the side of the town by which they approached it; that this village contained "about four hundred dwellings" (this fact showing conclusively that the village was not built on an artificial mound). From this place they traveled two days through a populous and champaign country where the land was more elevated and less alluvial than any they had yet seen on the borders of the Mississippi. At the end of two days' journey, they came to the chief town of the cacique, situated on the same side of the river **to** which they first crossed. On reaching it, here, they erected the cross of pine, so large that one hundred men could not lift it. Where was the cross erected? On the bank of the Mississippi, or the St. Francis river?

The writer hereof maintains that it was on the high lands on the west bank of the St. Francis river, at or near the present site of the town of Wittsburgh, in Cross county, Arkansas. His reasons for this contention are: 1st, that it was on the west bank of the first river west of the Mississippi; 2nd, that it was erected on a ridge of high land, and 3rd, that at this point pine timber was found growing; three natural monuments so plainly described by the narrators of the journey that one can not be mistaken; three such monuments to be found nowhere else within these limits west of the Mississippi river from its mouth to the mouth of the Ohio. The existence of pine timber in this vicinity has been questioned, but he knows from his personal knowledge, that on the high lands at or near Wittsburgh, pine timber was growing in the months of January and February 1845, as he was there and saw it. He also saw pine knots and the dead and seasoned limbs of the pine trees stacked on the bank of the river, for sale to the steamers as fuel.

As another fact in support of his theory, the writer would call attention to the fact that the narrative of this journey, as quoted from Irving, states, that at the point at which they first crossed the river, after leaving the Mississippi, the land was high on the side to which they crossed and that from here they journeyed to the point at which the cross was raised, showing that there was more than one point of high land on the river, and that these points were several leagues apart. This is true of the St. Francis, as all who are familiar with the topography of land bordering on the river, know that two or more points of high land from Crowley's ridge, abut on said river below Wittsburgh. Two are now recalled to the mind of the writer; one at Madison, where the railroad from Memphis to Little Rock crosses the St. Francis river; the other just above the crossing of the old military road leading from Memphis to Little Rock.

Notwithstanding the existence of these facts, it has been maintained by others that the erection of the cross was at Little Prairie on the bank of the Mississippi river, in the southeast corner of the state of Missouri. The erection of the cross and the observance of the religious ceremonies as described by Irving, could not have taken place on the bank of the Mississippi river, for the reasons following: 1st, There are no ridges of high land on the west bank of the Mississippi between the mouth of the St. Francis and the mouth of the Ohio river, a distance of more than two hundred miles; 2nd, There is no river on the west bank of the Mississippi between the St. Francis river and Little Prairie; 3d, Because De Soto's caravan could not have traveled the distance intervening between the point where they broke up their boats after crossing the Mississippi river, and Little Prairie in six days, the time they were traveling from the Mississippi to the point at which the cross was erected; for Irving tells us that while De Soto was camped on the bank of the Mississippi river he, at another time and place, despatched Juan de Anasco with eight troopers to explore the course of the river and to ascertain whether the sea was near. De Anasco returned after eight days' absence, which argues to me that he had not been able to advance above fifteen leagues on account of the windings of the river and the swamps and torrents with which it was bordered. Now, if the unencumbered horsemen were unable to travel more than fifteen leagues in four days (half the time they were gone) was it possible for the whole caravan, encumbered as it was, to travel more than three times that distance in seven days? 4th, Because Irving tells us that at the time of the erection of the cross and the observance of the religious ceremonies then engaged in, that "On the opposite shore of the river were collected fifteen or twenty thousand savages of both sexes and of all ages to witness this singular but imposing ceremony. With their arms extended and their hands raised they watched the movements of the Spaniards. Ever and anon they raised their eyes to heaven and made signs with their faces and hands as if asking God to listen to the Christian prayer. Then they would raise a low and wailing cry, like people in excessive grief, echoed by the plaintive murmurings of their children's voices."

This scene, as above described, could not have been witnessed by the parties at the cross on the opposite side of the river, had it been at Little Prairie or at any other point on the Mississippi river below the mouth of the Ohio, for Garcilasso says that "if a man stood still on the other side it could not be discovered whether he was a man or not." This fact is known to all who ever stood on its banks within the limits mentioned.

The point at which the cross was erected could not have been on the White or the Arkansas river, for the reasons that there are no high lands with pine timber on either bank of the White river below the mouth of the Cache nor on either bank of the Arkansas below Pine Bluff, and that De Soto's men could not have built a bridge across either of these rivers and crossed it in one day, as Garcilasso tells us they did at the first river they reached after leaving the Mississippi.

The name of the village where the cross was erected, as well as that of the whole province and of the cacique, was Casquin or Casqui, and the time of the erection, May, 1541. In dismissing this subject, I beg leave to quote Mr. Irving's reflections, substituting the name St. Francis for Mississippi and the four for the three centuries, and say:

"It is a reflection, replete with interest, that nearly four centuries ago, the cross, the type of our beautiful religion, was planted on the banks of the St. Francis, and its silent forests were awakened by the Christian's hymn of gratitude and praise. The effect was vivid, but transitory. The 'voice cried in the wilderness,' and reached and was answered by every heart, but it died away and was forgotten, and was not to be heard again in that savage region, for many generations. It was as if a lightning gleam had broken for a moment upon a benighted world, startling it with sudden effulgence, only to leave it in tenfold gloom. The real dawning was yet afar off from the benighted valley of the Mississippi."

It is deemed unnecessary, in the purpose of this history, to follow the route of De Soto in his travels north from the village of Casquin, at which point the cross was erected, further than to say that in his travels north or northeast, he crossed a stream or lake that required the building of bridges to enable him to approach the Mississippi river in the province of Capaha, where he remained some time and then returned to Casquin. Here he remained five days, after which he continued down the river to the province of Quiguate. From this point they proceeded north and northwest to the highlands in the northwest. Turning south, they passed south of the Arkansas river, probably to the highlands on the Ouachita, from whence they turned east, as Biedma reports, crossing the mountains and descending into an inhabited plain favorable to their designs and where was a large village built on the banks of a river which emptied into the great river they had passed. This province was called Utiangue.

Irving, in his history, says: "They reached the village of Utiangue, from which the province took its name." "It was situated in a fine plain watered by a wide, running river, the same that passed through the province of Cayas." (A foot note in Irving's history to these statements, says: "Supposed to be the Arkansas.") Here they spent the winter of 1541-1542.

"As soon as the spring was sufficiently well advanced, therefore De Soto broke up his winter cantonment at Utianque, and set out in a direction for the Rio Grande or Mississippi. He had received intelligence of a village called Anilco, situated on a great river which emptied into the Mississippi, and towards that he shaped his course."

After leaving Utiangue they passed on through the province of Ayas and stopped some days at a village in this province situated on the same river on which Cayas and Utiangue were situated, which is supposed to be the Arkansas. At this point a boat was built in which they crossed the river. Passing on down the river, they reached the province of Anilco. After passing several villages, they reached the principal one which gave its name to the province. This village of Anilco was situated on the same river that passed by Cayas and Utiangue. At Anilco, De Soto was informed that at no great distance this river emptied into the Mississippi.

If the location of the village of Anilco can, to any reasonable degree of certainty, be established, it will very materially assist in determining the point at which De Soto died and was buried. This village was situated in a champaign, that is, open, wooded country on the bank of a river, and contained about four hundred spacious houses, built around a square. The residence of the cacique, as usual, was located on a high artificial mound.

The writer maintains that this village was situated on or near the north bank of the Arkansas river and included what is now known as Menard Mound, located in the southeast corner of Arkansas County. This mound is now sixty or more feet high and is surrounded by unmistakable evidences of having been at some time the site of a large and populous settlement. It is within about eight miles of the Mississippi river and about fourteen miles of the mouth of the Arkansas, on a direct line. In support of this theory the writer would call attention to the fact that the historian of the travels of De Soto says that after passing over the highlands or mountains south of the Arkansas river, they turned east; that on reaching what is supposed to have been the Arkansas river, they traveled down that river some distance; that they crossed the same and continued down this river to Anilco, which village, they had been told, was situated on a great river which emptied into the Mississippi; and that they did find Anilco situated on the bank of the river they had crossed and down which they had traveled.

From this point, the village of Anilco, or the Menard Mound, De Soto proceeded to a large village called Guachoya, situated on the bank of the Mississippi river, as stated by Irving, quoting Garcilasso, and supposed to be the Guachoyanque referred to by Biedma in his history. After leaving Anilco they traveled four days through a hilly, uninhabited country, arriving at Guachoya, a village which contained about three hundred houses and was situated about a bow shot from the Mississippi river, on two contiguous hills with a small intervening plain which served as a public square. These hills could not have been mounds or artificial hills, as none have been found in this country large enough to hold one hundred and fifty houses; they were, of course, the product of nature and not of art.

At this village De Soto took possession of the cacique's house as his headquarters, which house was spacious and was situated on the summit of one of the hills. After remaining here some days, De Soto was induced by the cacique to return to Anilco, the cacique proposing to accompany him and aid him and his people on their return. This he did by sending a large force by water in canoes, and himself accompanying De Soto and his men, with a large force over land; the two parties to meet on a given day at Anilco. Under the agreement, those in the canoes proceeded along the Mississippi to the mouth of the river on which Anilco was situated, and up that river to the village. At the time of the departure of the canoes, De Soto, with his men, and the cacique, with his people, left, passing overland to meet the party in the canoes at the appointed time and place. The cacique of Anilco being absent at the time of their arrival, Guachoya's men at once attacked the men of Anilco, who resisted them. At the crossing of the river a portion of De Soto's men, on horseback, with Guachoya's men, routed with great slaughter, the men of Anilco, who fled back to the village, thence in wild disorder to the forests. Amid the shouts of the pursuers and the shrieks of the women and children, Guachoya now gave full sway to his thirst for vengeance, for in his whole alliance with the Spaniards and his advice to the governor to revisit this province, he was actuated by a secret desire to avenge himself upon an ancient enemy. On entering the conquered village, Guachoya's men stripped the sepulchers of their scalps and banners and carried off all their relics.

In all this they acted with such haste that the mischief was effected before De Soto was aware of it. He at once put an end to the carnage, reprimanding the cacique severely and forbidding any one to set fire to a house. His threats and precautions were ineffectual, however, for scarcely had he recrossed the river and marched a league, when, on looking back, he saw a great smoke arising from the burning village.

The reader will bear in mind that this expedition, under the joint control of De Soto and the cacique, started from the village of Guachoya, situated on two contiguous hills about a bow shot from the Mississippi river; that they met at the time appointed, at the village of Anilco, located on or near a river, supposed to be the Arkansas; that it was at the last named village, near the confluence of the two streams, (the Mississippi and the Arkansas) that De Soto was told there was situated on the bank of the Mississippi, a large village called Guachoya; that after remaining at Anilco some days, De Soto, with his army, returned to and took up his quarters in the village of Guachoya, at which place he died on the 21st day of May, 1542, after having appointed Luis de Moscoso his successor as governor of the expedition.

At what point on the Mississippi river did De Soto die and where was he buried? Was it at the mouth of Red river, near the mouth of the Arkansas, or on the highlands on the Mississippi near the present site of Helena? Each of these points has its advocates. The latter, the writer hereof maintains, is the place at which these events transpired, for the following reasons: the most important and controlling fact in the matter is that there is but one point on the west bank of the Mississippi river from its mouth to the mouth of the Ohio river, that in any wise agrees with the topographical description of the village of Guachoya, as given by Garcilasso and the Gentleman of Elvis, two historians of this expedition. All persons who are familiar with the topography of the country bordering on the Mississippi river know that there is only one point on the west bank of this river, within the limits above mentioned, at which the highlands or hills approach or abut on the river, that being at Helena, the southeastern terminus of Crowley's ridge. This ridge extends up the river to the St. Francis.

Irving, in his history of this part of the expedition, after giving an account of De Soto's arrival at Anilco, says he determined to go from that place to Guachoya; that he crossed the river opposite Anilco, "and resumed his march over a hilly, uninhabited country, and in four days arrived at the village of Guachoya."

In passing from Menard's Mound, supposed to be the site of the village of Anilco, to Helena, supposed to be the location of Guachoya, the hills over which De Soto's army passed were ridges of high land extending out in a southeast direction from Crowley's ridge, terminating, as before stated, at Helena.

The only plausible objection to the theory that De Soto passed from Anilco, or Menard's Mound, situated on the north bank of the Arkansas river, to Guachoya, or Helena, on the Mississippi, is; that Irving, in his history, says, that "De Soto crossed the river opposite the village of Anilco." Assuming that this village was on the north side of the Arkansas river, it was not necessary that De Soto cross that river to go to the highands at Helena, as that point is north of the Arkansas river; so that crossing the river at Anilco would have been traveling away from, rather than in the direction of the highlands at Helena.

There are several reasons combining to show that it was not the Arkansas river De Soto crossed, in leaving Anilco for Guachoya, but the White as this river is north and within a short distance of Menard's Mound and would have to be crossed in passing from this mound to Helena. The first and most potent reason in support of this theory is that the "hilly, uninhabited country" and the hill on which Guachoya was situated are north of the White river. Another is that there is no hilly country near the Mississippi river south of the Arkansas and no hills on the bank of the Mississippi from the mouth of the Arkansas to the mouth of the Mississippi. These facts are conclusive to the mind of the writer that it was the White and not the Arkansas river that De Soto and his army crossed upon leaving Anilco.

Another plausible argument in support of this theory, is the probability that the Arkansas and White rivers came together near this point and emptied through the same channel into the Mississippi, as they do now, at a point but a few miles below Menard's Mound, known as the "Cut-off" connecting the two rivers.

The theory that these rivers united at or near Anilco and flowed into the Mississippi through the same channel, is supported by the fact that nearly all the early maps of this section of the country fail to show White river at all, and none so far as the writer has been able to examine, shows that it empties directly into the Mississippi.

The map appended to and published with French's "Historical Collections of Louisiana" shows St. Francis and Arkansas rivers, but not the White. The map in Russell's "History of America," published in 1778, shows the Arkansas with a tributary entering it on the north side, a short distance from its mouth. Bancroft publishes a copy of map from Marquette's journal of 1681, showing a river, without name, entering the Mississippi near the thirty-third degree. This river is supposed to be the Arkansas. Winsor, in his "Cartier to Frontenac," publishes a map, copied from Joutel, printed in 1716, showing the Arkansas, but not the White. Coxe's "Carolana" tells us that the Arkansas and White rivers unite so as to form an island, and Winsor, in his "Mississippi Basin," shows a map published by James Smith in "Some Considerations on the Consequences of the French Settling Colonies on the Mississippi," in 1720. This map also shows the Arkansas and not the White river.

In addition to the foregoing is the further probability of the changing of the channels of these rivers by cut-offs and caving banks. All persons who are familiar with the history of the Mississippi and Arkansas rivers, know that their banks and channels are constantly changing, because of these cut-offs and the accretions incident thereto. In view of this, it is quite probable that the White river entered the Arkansas near the village of Anilco and was supposed, by De Soto and his men, to be the Arkansas; this, rather than the Arkansas, on which Anilco was situated, being the river they crossed in going from there to Guachoya.

The writer submits the foregoing facts, with, as he thinks, reasonable conclusions based on these facts, to establish the proposition that it was at or near the highlands at Helena, Arkansas, that Hernando De Soto died on the 21st day of May, 1542. Here, beneath the turbid waters of the Mississippi, whose perpetual ripplings are a requiem to his repose, and whose majestic flow is a fit monument to his memory, was he buried.

"He died," says Inca Garcilasso de Vega, in his chronicle, "like a Catholic Christian, imploring mercy of the most Holy Trinity; relying on the protection of the blood of Jesus Christ, our Lord; and the intercession of the Virgin, and of all the Celestial Court, and in the faith of the Roman Church."

"With these words, repeating them many times, resigned his soul to God this magnanimous and never conquered cavalier, worthy of great dignities and titles and deserving a better historian than a rude Indian."

After the death of De Soto, his successor, Luis de Moscoso, on the fourth or fifth day of June, 1542, left Guachoya and traveled west. It is not necessary to the purpose of this history, to follow Moscoso in all his wanderings south and west through the territory now included within the limits of the state of Arkansas, but from the accounts given of his travels, it is quite probable that he visited the Hot Springs, the Salt Springs and the highlands of the upper Ouachita, and after wandering further west for some time, he decided to return to Guachoya, on the Mississippi river, the point from which he started in June, 1542. On turning their faces eastward, the historian of their travels says: "Fearful of making too great a bend to the south and of striking the Mississippi below Guachoya, which was the point where they wished to arrive, they now inclined to the northeast, so as to strike the track they had made on their western course." He also says that at this point they hoped to build brigantines in which to return to their friends.

On their arrival at Anilco, they were told that at a distance of two days' journey, on the bank of the Mississippi, there were two towns, near each other in the country of Aminoya. On reaching this village and "seeing its favorable location and the abundance of the surrounding country, the governor resolved to establish his winter quarters and build his brigantines here." In a foot note to the above paragraph in Irving's history, he says: "Mr. McCullock supposes the village of Aminoya to have been situated in the neighborhood of the present town of Helena, about thirty miles above the Arkansas."

On the map published with French's "Historical Collections of Louisiana," the town or village of Aminoya is shown near the Arkansas river. The "Gentleman from Elois" calls the place Minoya, and the Portugese narrator, Aminoza.

The theory of the location of this place in the neighborhood of the highlands at Helena is strengthened by the statement of the historian of these travels that, "The old friend and ally of the Spaniards, Guachoya, hearing of their return, came with presents of provisions, and renewed his former intercourse."

It will be remembered by the reader that Guachoya, above referred to, was the chief of the province of that name, situated on the Mississippi river and that De Soto, on his first visit to the village, "took up his quarters in his house, which was situated on the summit of one of the hills overlooking the Mississippi river."

Biedma tells us, in his journal, that after wandering in the west and southwest, "We resolved to return to the village where Governor De Soto died, to build some vessels to return to our own country, but when we arrived there, we did not find the facilities we had expected and were obliged to seek another place to go into winter quarters and build our vessels." A few miles south on the river, they found a suitable place, on what is supposed to be the place now known as **Old Town Ridge.** Here, Moscoso and his men built their brigantines and supplied themselves with the necessary equipments and provisions as they were able to procure. The high water in the month of June floated the brigantines from the ways on which they were built and "the little squadron being now afloat and all ready for embarkation, the governor made his final arrangements on shore."

On the second day of July, 1543, the Spaniards, under the command of Luis de Moscoso, departed from Minoya, the village where they built their brigantines and where they had remained for six months or more, and in nineteen days reached the mouth of the Mississippi.

The time required to descend the river to the Gulf is an argument against the theory of several authors who have written on this subject, contending that Moscoso's fleet was built at and started from the mouth of Red river and that it was at that point De Soto died and was buried, for all the narrators of the travels of De Soto and Moscoso are agreed on the fact that Moscoso built his brigantines near the point on the Mississippi river at which De Soto died.

As to the distance from this point to the Gulf, as measured by the time consumed in covering the distance, the reader will remember that Moscoso went out of the river on a flood tide, for the "Gentleman of Elvis" tells us that the flood came up to the town to seek the brigantines, from whence they carried them by water to the river, and that the current was very strong and with the help of oars, went very swiftly. This being true, it would not require the number of days mentioned to float from the mouth of Red river to the Gulf, as the distance is not more than about three hundred and fifty miles, and to float this distance in nineteen days would give an average of less than twenty miles in twenty-four hours.

The "Gentleman of Elvis" in his account of this voyage, says that in their journey from Minoya to the Gulf, they "continued seventeen days in which time they made two hundred and fifty leagues." Russell, in his **"History of America,"** published in 1778, says: "We are told by Herrera, who had his information from the account of the expedition transmitted to the king, that the Spaniards sailed five hundred leagues down the Mississippi after building the boats in which they made their escape."

If the theory of the writer, supported by the testimony submitted, be correct, he thinks he has definitely located the points at which occurred four of the most notable incidents, of which any record was left, connected with the travels of the Spaniards under De Soto and Moscoso, west of the Mississippi river. First, that it was at the lowest Chickasaw Bluff that De Soto and his army crossed the Mississippi river; second, that it was on the highlands at or near Wittsburgh, on the St. Francis river in Cross county that the cross was erected and the first religious ceremonies observed; third, that it was at or near the highlands, on the Mississippi river, at Helena, in Phillips county, that De Soto died and was buried, and fourth, that it was at or near Old Town landing on Old Town Ridge, a few miles south of Helena in Phillips county, that Moscoso and his men built their brigantines in which their escape to Mexico was made.

The writer is thus particular in locating these points, to show that all four places were at one time within the geographical limits of Arkansas county as established by legislative enactment and were under her jurisdiction.

After the departure of Moscoso and his men from Minoya on July 2nd, 1543, for a period of one hundred and thirty years we have no historical information or evidence of the impress of the foot of the white man upon the soil of the great valley west of the Mississippi. Here the wild men of the forest, the beasts of hill and plain, the fowls of air, lake and river, roamed and flew and swam, undisturbed by civilized man.

From the close of the disastrous expedition of De Soto, Florida, for many years as claimed by Spain, embraced all the Atlantic Coast as far north as the Gulf of St. Lawrence, where the French had made some unsuccessful attempts to plant colonies.

No other European power pretending to claim the coast from Cape Sable on the south to the Bay of Funday on the north, nor did they attempt to establish colonies within these bounds until 1673, in which year the French government sent out an exploring party under the command of Marquette and Joliet.

CHAPTER II.

From Marquette's Visit to Mouth of Arkansas River in 1673, to Settlement of Arkansas Post, 1686.

"In 1673, M. Tolan, the French governor of Canada, took means to secure the dominion of France over all the country lying south and west of the Canadian lakes, and, anxious to discover the source, course and direction of the great river which had been mentioned to the French missionaries by the Indians of the west, to flow towards the south, he sent Marquette and Joliet to explore it to the sea." In July of this year, these pioneers and forerunners of civilization passed into the territory of what is now known as the state of Arkansas and in their account of this expedition, tell us that they descended the Mississippi river to the thirty-third degree of latitude, north, and found themselves at a village on the river side called Mitchigamea. On a map published in 1682, accompanying Bancroft's history. this village is located on the west bank of the Mississippi above the mouth of the Arkansas, and, in a foot note to French's "Historical Collections of Louisiana," in which Marquette and Joliet's account is published, he says, in reference to this village, that it was "an Indian village on the Mississippi and supposed to be the site of the present town of Helena." On the map accompanying French's "Historical Collections of Louisiana," a lake named Mitchigamea is located on the St. Francis river a few miles north of Helena.

The Indians occupying this village induced Marquette and Joliet to go ashore, which they did, but with some degree of suspicion that their signs of friendship were not genuine.

After several unsuccessful attempts to make themselves understood, they found an old man who spoke the Illinois, whom they told that they wished to go as far as the sea. He understood and told them that at the next village, called Arkansea, they could learn all about the sea.

On their arrival at Arkansea, they found a number of Indians, by whom they were kindly treated and who informed them that the sea was within ten day's journey and that they were unacquainted with the nations below, because their enemies had prevented their visiting them. These Indians were very courteous and gave freely of what they had.

To these people, Marquette tells us, he preached the Gospel to the utmost of his power, but was not sure they understood what he said to them of God. It was, however, seed sown that would in time bring forth fruit.

This was in July, 1673, and is the second account of an act of public worship left on record, the first being at or near Wittsburgh in Cross county in May, 1541, the latter at or near the mouth of the Arkansas river one hundred and thirty-two years later.

FROM 1673 TO 1686.

Marquette and his party remained here one day and then returned to Green Bay.

From the time of the departure of Marquette and Joliet from Arkansas in July, 1673, there was no return of the white man to the country till 1682.

In 1678, La Salle was commissioned by the King of France to undertake the exploration of the Mississippi, in which enterprise he very fortunately engaged the services of the Cavalier de Tonty.

1682.

In the winter of 1681-1682, La Salle, influenced by the reports of the discovery of the Mississippi river by Marquette and Joliet, and anxious to achieve the distinction of discovering its mouth, chose eighteen Abenake and Michigan Indians, to whom he added twenty-three Frenchmen, and with these, accompanied by Tonty and Membre, in canoes, on the 6th of February, 1682, "issued upon the majestic bosom of the Mississippi and on the 24th of February, 1682, landed near the third Chickasaw Bluff." This statement of the landing of La Salle at the third Chickasaw Bluff is from Farman's "Life of La Salle"; so says Winsor, in his "Cartier to Frontenac." In La Salle's account of taking possession of Louisiana, as reported in French's "Historical Collections of Louisiana," nothing is said about a bluff, but that they "went ashore on the 26th of February" and that "a Frenchman was lost in the woods."

Bancroft says: "At last in the early part of 1682, La Salle and his company descended the magnificent Mississippi to the sea." His sagacious eye discovered the great resources of the country "as he floated down the flood," and on the first Chickasaw Bluff, he framed a cabin.

Monette's account agrees with Bancroft, who, in his account of La Salle's descent of the Mississippi, says that after leaving the mouth of the Ohio, they proceeded down to the first Chickasaw Bluff.

Dr. Ramsay, in his "History of Tennessee," says of La Salle, that as he passed down the river he framed a log cabin and built a fort called "Prudhomme" on the first Chickasaw Bluff. These authors are quoted to show the confused condition in which the real facts of the expedition appear.

Notwithstanding the discrepancy in these statements, there can be no doubt as to the fact that in later years Fort Prudhomme was located at the fourth or "lowest Chickasaw Bluff."

Leaving this point, La Salle, with his men, descended the river, and, after following for several days the windings of the great river on its tortuous course, reached the village of Kappa, a band of the Arkansea, a peope dwelling near the mouth of the river which bears their name. Here they remained several days and were kindly treated by the villagers. These people, the historian of the expedition tells us, were modest and were so well formed as to be greatly admired.

Here, on the 14th of March, 1682, La Salle and Tonty, at the head of their followers, marched to the open area in the midst of the village and to the great admiration of the gazing crowd, a cross was raised bearing the arms of France. La Salle drew from the chief an acknowledgment of fealty to Louis XIV, King of France, and in his name took possession of the country, this being the first formal declaration of the sovereignty of France over this country. The reader will bear in mind that these events took place upon soil once in the geographical limits of Arkansas county.

The nation of Indians at this time dwelling on the west bank of the Mississippi near the mouth of the Arkansas was divided into four tribes, living, for the most part, in separate villages. They were Kappas or Quapaws, Tapingas or Tongingas, Toremans and Osoturag or Southons. These, according to the statement of Charlerox, who saw them in 1721, were regarded as the tallest and best formed Indians in America.

After touching at several other towns or villages of these people, the voyagers resumed their journey, guided by two of the Arkansea Indians, and continued till they reached the mouth of the Mississippi river on the 7th of April, 1682. Here, on a spot of dry ground a short distance above the mouth of the river, they raised a column bearing the arms of France and inscribed with these words: "Louis Le Grand, Roi De France Et De Navarre, Regne; Le Neuvieme Avril, 1682."

La Salle, after erecting the column, in a loud voice took possession of the country in the name of Louis XIV, King of France, giving it the name of Louisiana.

La Salle was the first Frenchman to reach the mouth of the great river, but Luis de Moscoso, the Spaniard, had passed out of its mouth into the Gulf of Mexico on July 18th, 1543, nearly one hundred and thirty-nine years before.

"The Louisiana of La Salle stretches from the Alleghanies to the Rocky Mountains, from the Rio Grande (or Mississippi) and the Gulf to the farthest springs of the Missouri."

From the mouth of the Mississippi, La Salle and his men returned, passing on their upward trip Teancos, thence to Arkansea. where they were well received. From here they went to Fort Prudhomme, where La Salle fell sick and was left, remaining here till July, at which time he resumed his journey and rejoined Tonty at Michillimacknac in September.

By letters patent granted by the King of France to the Sieur De La Salle, on the 12th of May, 1678, and by a decree of council, he was given the right and privilege of forming habitations on the lands in the territory of which he had taken possession in the name of the king; and, under this authority, La Salle, on their arrival at the Arkansas, granted to De Tonty a signory or province on the Arkansas river, hereinafter referred to.

In September, 1682, La Salle returned to France for the purpose of obtaining from the king authority and the means necessary to enable him to establish a fort on the Mississippi river, sixty leagues above its mouth, from which the French could control the country. His prayer was granted and the desired means obtained, but the object was not accomplished, as La Salle was murdered before he reached the Mississippi river.

From July, 1682, until the spring of 1686, we have no account of the return of any of La Salle's men to the Mississippi river. At the latter time, however, De Tonty, with a party, descended the Mississippi from the Illinois to its mouth in search of his lost friend, La Salle. Of this trip, De Tonty gives but a meagre account, merely stating that he went to the mouth of the river, where he found the place at which La Salle had erected the arms of the king, which having been thrown down by the flood, he took five leagues further up the river and placed them on a higher elevation. Also, he states, that on his return when at Arkansea, he granted, to some of the men who accompanied him, the privilege of making a settlement on the Arkansas river.

1684.

On the 24th of July, 1684, La Salle, with his brother and nephew, M. M. Chevalier, Jontel, soldiers, artisans and colonists, sailed from Rochelle for the new world, aiming to enter his lately discovered Louisiana through the mouth of the Mississippi river. The month of December found them in the Gulf of Mexico, but at what point, no one on board ship could tell. Finally, they landed at a point between Matagorda Island and Corpus Christi Bay, early in January, 1685.

After repeated unsuccessful efforts to find the mouth of the Mississippi, and failing to establish and maintain a colony near the point at which he landed, La Salle determined to make his way by the Mississippi and Illinois rivers to Canada. On the 12th of January, 1687, with sixteen of his men, he set out on this journey. In the course of this journey La Salle and five of his men were murdered by other members of the party, the remaining number continuing their journey, reached the Arkansas river in July, 1687, opposite a village situated on the north bank of the river.

Joutel, the historian of this journey, tells us that they "came to a river that was between us and the village, and looking over to the further side, we discovered a great cross and at a small distance from it a house built after the French fashion."

"In short, having halted for some time on the bank of that river, we spied several canoes making towards us and two men, clothed, coming out of the house we had discovered, who, the moment they saw us, fired each of them a shot to salute us."

"When we had passed the river and were all come together, we soon knew each other to be Frenchmen. Those we found were the Sieurs Contura Charpentier and De Launoy, both of them of Rouen, whom M. de Tonty, governor of Fort St. Louis, among the Illinois, had left at that post when he went down the Mississippi to look after M. de la Salle; and the nation we were then with was called Accancea."

Henry de Tonty, in his memoirs, tells us that on his return from the mouth of the Mississippi river in 1686, whither he had gone in search of La Salle, "when we were at Arkansea, ten of the Frenchmen who accompanied me asked for a settlement on the Arkansas river on a signory that M. de la Salle had granted me on our first voyage. I granted the request to some of them."

Those that accepted, remained and doubtless built the house that

ARKANSAS COUNTY.

Joutel and his companions found on their arrival at the Arkansas river in July, 1687.

John Gilmary Shea, in his "History of Catholic Missions," among the Indians, says: "Tonty, the faithful lieutenant of La Salle, had obtained of him a grant of a considerable tract on the Arkansas river. Here he built a house and fort in 1683." (This should be 1686.) Again, "By a deed dated November 26th, 1689, he gave to Father Dablon, then superior of the Canadian mission, a strip on the Arkansas river, a little east of his fort, of about eight acres, for a chapel and mission house." This mission was to begin in November, 1690. The same author tells us that the Arkansas mission was the oldest of all projected by the Jesuits, and perhaps cultivated for a time by Boucher, who was to be restored and the light hearted Du Poisson was named to it.

Du Poisson, after a voyage full of discomfort, of which he has left a most graphic account, reached the Arkansas Post on the 7th of July, 1727.

Was this settlement made by the Canadian Frenchmen in 1686 at the point now known as Arkansas Post? Was the original settlement at this point, or three leagues below, or was it on the south bank of the river? There are those who maintain that each of these questions can be answered in the affirmative.

That the original settlement or location of this post, by the Canadians, was on the north bank of the river at the present site of the town of Arkansas Post, is not doubted by the writer. The reader will remember that Joutel, in his account of the journey of the remnant of La Salle's party, from Texas to Canada, in 1687, tells us that they "came to a river that was between us and the village," that having halted for some time on the bank of the river, they saw canoes making towards them, and in these canoes the party crossed the river to the village. This party was on its way from Texas and therefore reached the Arkansas river from the south side.

In addition to this, Justin Winsor, in his "Cartier to Frontenac," at pages 318 and 319, exhibits a map to which he appends the following note: "This map by Joutel, is reduced from the upper portion of the map in MS of the narrative, which is in the Boston Public Library and is supposed to have been the copy from which the book of 1713 was printed and its map engraved." On this map, the route of Joutel and his comrades from Texas to Canada, is marked, terminating on the south bank of the Arkansas river and showing the house they saw on the north bank.

Why, or on what authority the contention is maintained that the original location was three leagues below the present site of the town, we know not. The country that distance below the Post of Arkansas is low, level and subject to overflow by water from the Mississippi, White and Arkansas rivers at an ordinary stage of high water, which occurs annually and frequently oftener, the whole region being unfit for such settlement.

The bluff or highlands upon which the village of Arkansas Post is located is the only eligible site in that vicinity for such settlement, hence the contention that at this point the first settlement made by white men west of the Mississippi and east of the Rio Grande, was made by the men to whom Tonty made the grant in 1686.

CHAPTER III.

From Settlement of Arkansas Post in 1686 to Appearance of M. Pervier as Commandant in 1726.

Prior, and up to about the year 1710, Louisiana was a vast wilderness, nominally under the government of the King of France, and the few inhabitants therein, were dependent on the authorities of Canada, from whom they were two thousand miles distant, for protection.

1711.

In 1711, the government of Louisiana was placed in the hands of Bienville, as governor-general of the province.

It will be remembered that at this time the territory forming the present state of Arkansas formed a part and was under the jurisdiction of Louisiana. Arkansas county, being a portion of the state of Arkansas, was, therefore, at one time a part of this territory.

Up to this time no settlement had been made by white men, immediately on the west bank of the Mississippi river and none in the interior, except the settlement at Arkansas Post on the north bank of the Arkansas river.

Prior to 1702, the headquarters of the governor-general and seat of the provincial government, under Bienville, had been at Dauphin's Island, and at Mobile, now in Alabama. In 1706, however, Bienville established a colony on the present site of New Orleans, to which the seat of the provincial government was later removed.

1712.

Failing in all his previous plans to colonize Louisiana, Louis XIV in 1712, granted to Anthony Crozat, a French merchant, the exclusive trade of this vast territory, hoping that this enterprising merchant, as he "had prospered in opulence to the astonishment of all the world," would induce emigration to this territory. This enterprise proved a failure, however, as it excited the jealousy of Spain, who looked upon the French occupancy of Louisiana as an enroachment on her territory.

This monoply of Crozat was terminated in 1716, by the surrender of the charter granted him by the French king, like privileges being granted to the "Western Company," better known as the "Company of Mississippi," instituted under the direction of John Law.

As the enterprise of Law is connected with the early history of Arkansas county, a short sketch of his career will not be out of place in this connection.

"John Law stands in European history as the creator of one of the most marvelous crazes ever known. This strange manifestation

ARKANSAS COUNTY.

was as much a wonder to Law's contemporaries, as it is to us." "A tract, purporting to emanate from an Englishman in the colonies and reflecting upon the consequence of the French occupation of the Great Valley, speaks of Law's success, before he reached the precipice, as 'one of the most prodigious events of any age,' and sniffs at the skeptics.

"A Scotchman, extremely nimble of mind, but destitute of sane principles, nurtured a rake and a gambler, Law had fled from London to Amsterdam to avoid arrest. Here his quick perception seized on some method he observed in the bank of Amsterdam as affording such great and possible developments as are ever attractive to those holding vagabondish notions of finance.

"Being possessed of these ideas of banking, he was anxious to, and did offer them to others, without success, until his advent in Paris. Here, in May, 1716, he opened a private bank of issue, which the government favored as a means of absorbing in its capital, seventy-five per cent of its Billets de Etat.

"Law had already attracted the attention of the Regent of France and was given the chief control of the Mississippi Company, which had been organized for the purpose of populating Louisiana, and developing its vast resources.

"About sixteen months before the new company received its charter, Law had opened his private bank in Paris. This was an opportune help, as it served to make the bank of wider interest to the kingdom.

"Meanwhile Law's projects were ripening for good, as everybody seemed to think—at least for everybody's individual good, if not for the public good. The regent then in power, placed all sorts of privileges in the extended hands of Law. The shares in his company became so buoyant in the market that nobody dreamed of a precipice.

"The one thing for Law to do, was to get all the money in France into a bank of royal prestige; then loans would no longer be necessary. Both crown and people would happily discover that true credit is what the state gains by an excess of paper over bullion. On January 1st, 1719, such a state of financial bliss came in with the new year.

"The Banque Generale of the Scotch prophet became the Banque Royale of France, with the regent for sole proprietor. A few days later, January 5th, Law was proclaimed its director. He was allowed to make an unlimited circulation of notes, and the Company of the West existed to work them off. He was permitted to put a tariff upon all things bought and sold. In this way, everything was absorbed by it.

"In July, the profits of the mint were added to the bank resources and this privilege was to run nine years. The stock gave a new bound upward, only to be temporarily depressed upon a rumor of Law's illness. By the end of the year 1719, there was half a million foreigners gesticulating in the streets of Paris, eager for something.

"The capital stock, increased to six hundred thousand shares, rose to fifteen thousand francs a share and even higher—some thousands per cent advance in the end. It came to be known that three thousand millions of livres (a livre was of the value of 19½ cents, U. S. currency) were borne on the face of its aggregated paper.

FROM 1686 TO 1726.

"In January, 1720, Law became comptroller-general of the kingdom. In February, the company absorbed the Banque Royale with all its privileges. The entire money power of the country was now at Law's disposal, and every tax came into his hands. But the fabric had begun to totter. Law was at his wits' end to keep this from being known. Shrinking hope had succeeded to buoyant exhilaration. Law worried through the summer and autumn, uncertain how to turn. By December, he was sure no one could be longer deceived. He put eight hundred livres in his pocket one day and disappeared. The end had come."

(Following is a copy of a bill of the Banque Royale—1720.)

No. 149277   Cent livres Tournois.
La Banque promet payee au Porteur a viie Cent livres Tournois en Efpeces d'Argent, valeue receiie A Paris le premier Janvier mil fept cens vingt.
Vup.r le S.r Fenellon—   Signe p.r le S.r Burgeois.
                                           Jaubion,
                                  Controlle p.r le S.r Dureveft,
                                           Renause.

Returning to the history of Arkansas county, we will proceed to show that one of the objects of the Regent of France and Law was to induce emigration to Louisiana and create an apparent prosperity therein.

To this end, concessions or grants of land were offered to those who would send settlers to and locate them in Louisiana.

One of these grants, embracing a tract of land four leagues square on the Arkansas river, was granted to John Law in 1718. The land in this grant was on both sides of the Arkansas river, a few miles above Arkansas Post.

"In March, 1719, five hundred negroes were landed, in the following October a large body of Alsatians and other Germans arrived, a portion of whom, at least, had been sent by Law as settlers upon his own grant."

As soon as the news of Law's failure and flight from France reached Louisiana, June, 1721, the Germans who had been sent by him to occupy his grant, became alarmed and abandoned the same, removing to and settling on the Mississippi river, a short distance above New Orleans, at what is now known as the "German Coast."

The point at which this settlement on Law's grant was made is a disputed question. Dumont, in his "Memoirs of Louisiana," says: "The people sent by Law settled about a league from the Arkansas Post in the depths of the woods, where they found a beautiful plain, surrounded by fertile valleys and a little stream of fine, clear, wholesome water."

Bancroft, as quoted by Prof. Shinn, in his "School History of Arkansas," says: "To Law himself, there was conceded, on the Arkansas river, one of those vast prairies, of which the wide-spreading areas of verdure are bounded only by the azure of the sky. There he designed to plant a city and villages."

ARKANSAS COUNTY.

La Harpe, who visited this country in 1723, says this settlement was north, northwest from Arkansas Post, on the right side of the river.

If this settlement was on the right bank of the river, as reported by La Harpe, it could not have been north, northwest from the village of Arkansas Post, as that direction leads almost directly from the river out into the open prairie and not into the "depths of the woods" as Dumont reports the location of the settlement.

In the opinion of the writer, this settlement was on what is now known as Lake Lenox, on the south side and near the right bank of the Arkansas river, about five miles southwest from Arkansas Post, in the "depths of the woods" surrounding the Lake from which there flows a "little stream of pure water."

The late Samuel Lenox, who was born, lived and died near this lake, which was named in honor of his father, informed the writer of the finding of an old gun, supposed to have been left by Law's colonists on their departure from this settlement The gun was plowed up near the bank of the lake about the year 1882.

At the time of the grant of the monopoly of commerce in Louisiana to Crozat in 1712, it was provided in this charter or grant, that the edicts, ordinances and customs of Paris, etc., in connection with common or civil law, were to constitute the laws of the province, with such modifications as were necessary to adapt them to a new and distant country.

The first governor under this decree was M. de la Motte, who assumed the reins of power in 1713.

"On the 5th of September, 1721, a council of administration for the affairs of the company of Louisiana, was organized and composed as follows: the governor, the lieutenant-governor, commissary director and sub director of accounts.

"By an ordinance of this council, prices were fixed, for which merchandise of the company should be sold, and the rate per cent on those sold at Arkansas was fixed at one hundred."

On the 27th of September, it was determined that negroes, on an average, be sold to the inhabitants for six hundred livres, for which their notes were to be furnished on three years credit, payable in equal installments, either in tobacco or rice.

The price of tobacco, receivable in payment for negroes, was fixed at twenty-five livres per hundred pounds, and rice at twelve livres when delivered at the company's warehouse. Wine was to be sold by the company at one hundred twenty livres per cask and brandy at the same price for a quarter cask.

Louisiana was divided into nine territorial districts, Arkansas being the eighth in number. For each district there was to be a commander or governor, and a judge from whose decisions appeals could be taken to the Supreme Council. This order, as stated by the decree, was made in order that justice might be the more easily obtained by the colonists.

In 1722, by order of the Regent of France, authority was given for a settlement at Arkansas, the chief object of which was to establish a connecting point between the Illinois and the lower part of the colony, and to facilitate the introduction of horses, mules and cattle from the Spanish provinces. In this year, the civil history of Arkansas began, as we are informed by the Hon. A. M. McVeigh, of Osceola, Arkansas, quoting La Harpe, who says: "Hitherto it had been a mere trading and military post among the Indians."

In this year, it was erected into the District of Arkansas, for the civil and military business of its inhabitants.

A judge and a commandant were appointed to reside at Arkansas Post. An officer named De La Boulaye was sent from Yazoo to command of the post in September, ostensibly to protect the Indians, but equally to protect the white settlements and the boats which stopped at this place to purchase provisions.

The religious wants of the people were supplied by the Jesuits.

La Harpe, with a detachment of sixteen men, was ordered to ascend the Arkansas river, make survey of the country, look for mines and to inform the Spanish whom he might meet, that all the territory watered by the Arkansas river, from its source to its mouth, belonged to France. On reaching Law's settlement as he passed up the river, he found only forty souls of the original colonists remaining.

Prior to this time there had been but four villages on the Arkansas river. In 1721, these villages were visited by Pierre Francis Xavier Charlevoix, a celebrated historian and traveler, who tells us that in December of that year he visited these villages. In one of them, he tells us, the Great Western Company had a magazine or warehouse. In this warehouse he met a young man who complained to him of his hard fare, and said he was weary of living in Arkansas. The village from which Charlevoix wrote his observations was on the Arkansas river. These four villages were, at that time, occupied principally by the Indians known as Ougapas or Kappas, two of the clans bore this name, Toremas, Tongenys and Southans, all known in our time as Quapaws.

These Indians, Charlevoix tells us, were the tallest and best shaped of all the savages on the continent and were called, by way of distinction, the "fire men."

Louisiana, recognizing slavery within her jurisdiction, it became necessary for the government and protection of her slaves, that ordinances or decrees be published prescribing such government. Accordingly in March, 1724, Bienville, the governor of the province, in the name of the King of France, promulgated what he called the Black Code, consisting of fifty-four articles. That the reader may know the "spirit of the times," a synopsis of this code is given.

Article I expels the Jews from the colony.

Article II compels the masters to impart religious instruction.

Article III excludes all modes of worship but the Roman Catholic.

Article IV confiscates all negroes under the supervision of any others than Catholics.

Article V requires the observance of Sunday and holiday or subjects the negroes to confiscation.

ARKANSAS COUNTY.

Article VI forbids the intermarriage of whites and blacks, of both sexes.

Articles VII, VIII, IX and X prescribe the marriage ceremony, forbid marriages among slaves without the consent of their masters, and define the relation of children to their parents, etc.

Article XI requires masters to have their Christian slaves buried in consecrated ground.

Articles XII, XIII and XIV forbid slaves carrying offensive weapons, the assembly of slaves belonging to different masters and impose penalties on masters permitting such gatherings.

Article XV forbids negroes selling commodities without permits from masters.

Articles XVI, XVII, XVIII and XIX provide at length clothing and subsistence of slaves.

Articles XX, XXI and XXII impose penalties on masters failing to provide necessary clothing, etc., and provide for the care of old and infirm slaves, declared incompetent of contracting or of owning property.

Articles XXIII, XXIV and XXV declare masters responsible for acts of slaves, slaves incapable of holding office, forbid slaves testifying and being parties to law suits.

Articles XXVI, XXVII and XXVIII permit slaves to be prosecuted criminally, and to be punished for striking master, mistress or their children.

Articles XXIX, XXX and XXXI subject slaves, guilty of theft, to corporal punishment and branding, also subject masters to damages if they do not punish them within three days after conviction.

Articles XXXII, XXXIII, XXXIV, XXXV and XXXVI prescribe the manner of punishing runaway slaves, and those harboring them.

Article XXXVII forbids judicial officers taking in suits against slaves.

Article XXXVIII forbids the use of racks in punishing slaves.

Article XXXIX commands officers of justice to enforce penalties against slaves.

Article XL declares slaves as part of the community of property between husband and wife and forbids their seizure under mortgages, etc.

Articles XLI and XLII relate to judicial forms and proceedings concerning slaves, etc.

Article XLIII forbids the sale of husband or wife separately, when belonging to the same master.

Article XLIV forbids the sale of slaves between the ages of fourteen and sixty years on plantations for any debt, except for purchase price.

Articles XLV, XLVI, XLVII, XLVIII and XLIX relate to certain formalities to be observed in judicial proceedings concerning slaves.

Article L permits masters over twenty-five years of age to manumit slaves by permission of the Supreme Council.

Article LI declares that slaves appointed by their masters as tutors to their children shall be set free.

Article LII declares all slaves, set free under this code, who were not born in Louisiana, naturalized, but incapable of receiving donations by will or otherwise.

Article LIII commands all manumitted slaves to show proper respect to their former masters, exempting them from service to these masters and from paying taxes.

Article LIV grants certain privileges to manumitted slaves, that are enjoyed by free born persons.

CHAPTER IV.

From M. Pervier's Advent in 1726 to Arrival of O'Reilly as Governor in 1769.

In the autumn of 1726 the government of Louisiana passed out of the hands of Bienville into those of M. Pervier, as commandant general of the province. The prosperity of the province continued to increase for nearly two years after M. Pervier entered upon his duties as governor general. Emigrants from France and Canada continued to swell the general population and augment the resources of the colony. The population of the province had increased from seven hundred souls in 1717 to five thousand, among whom were men of worth and enterprise. The number of slaves had increased from twenty souls to more than two thousand. The settlements were upon the alluvial soil of the Mississippi, Red, Ouachita and Arkansas rivers.

1732.

In April, 1732, the Western Company surrendered its charter to the government, as it had been unsuccessful in its operations for three years, in consequence of the failure of Law's financial schemes.

In accepting this surrender, the government purchased from the company all its effects. The property transferred to the government consisted of warehouses, goods, stock in trade, plantations with two hundred and sixty negroes, and all appendages of the plantations.

In the valuation of the company's property, negroes were valued, on an average, at seven hundred livres, or one hundred and sixty-five dollars each, horses at fifty-seven livres, or fourteen dollars and twenty-five cents. Rice was rated at three livres, or seventy-five cents per hundred pounds, nineteen hundred pounds being estimated as the value of a horse.

Gayarre, in his "History of Louisiana," informs us that "In the spring or early summer of 1736, De Grandpre, who commanded at Arkansas, sent twenty-eight Indian warriors to ascertain whether De Arlanguett was at Écorea Prudhomme, a fort or stockade built on the fourth Chickasaw Bluff, on the east bank of the Mississippi, by the French within the Chickasaw territory. These were sent by De Grandpre to find De Arlanguett and report to him. Not finding De Arlanguett, the Indians disobeyed their orders to return and report, and followed the retreating De Arlanguett, leaving De Grandpre to proceed without information.

This expedition was for the purpose of attacking the Chickasaws and English and driving them from that vicinity.

The expedition failing, De Grandpre, with his Arkansas warriors, returned to the settlement where he commanded."

Bancroft and Monette both say that the fort referred to by Gayarre

FROM 1726 TO 1769.

as Prudhomme, at the fourth Chickasaw Bluff, was called Assumption and was built near the mouth of the Margot or Wolf river, which enters the Mississippi at the upper end of the fourth Chickasaw Bluff.

The fort was built at this point as a convenient depot for the baggage and military stores necessary for the soldiers stationed there, and for the protection and care of the sick.

In 1740 this fort was dismantled and the soldiers, with their baggage and military stores, transferred to Fort St. Francis, west of the Mississippi river.

The location of Fort St. Francis is a disputed question, some claiming that Wittsburgh, in Cross county, is the point at which it was located.

Hempstead, in his History of Arkansas, says it was at Wittsburgh, and in support of this theory quotes the following, from a letter received by him from Hon. H. M. McVeigh, of Osceola, Arkansas: "An old friend of mine saw Hector, part Indian, who spent his early life among the Indians, tells me he has often picked up iron musket balls on the bluff at Wittsburgh when a boy, living among the Indians."

Bancroft, in his history, referring to this matter, says that in 1737 "To advance the colony, a royal edict permitted a ten years' freedom of commerce between the West India Islands and Louisiana; while a new expedition against the Chickasaws received aid, not from the Illinois only, but even from Montreal and Quebec, and from France, and made its rendezvous in Arkansas on the St. Francis river."

Monette, in his History of the Mississippi Valley, says: "All things being in readiness, about the last of May, the main army began to leave New Orleans for the rendezvous at the mouth of the St. Francis river, and about the last of June they reached Fort St. Francis."

The reader will bear in mind that at this time, and for years previous, England, through her American colonies, was using all means in her power to push her settlements to the west and that the "march of empire" was then on its way to the western wilds and had reached the Mississippi valley, and that in order to check this western march under the supervision and direction of England, France was exercising all her influence and using her power through her Louisiana possessions to prevent this English influence crossing the Mississippi river. To this end, forts were established from Kaskaskia, Illinois, to New Orleans, Louisiana, that French subjects from Quebec to New Orleans might be in quick communication with settlements between these points, and as their means of communication and transportation over this route was principally by water, especially from Kaskaskia to New Orleans by the Mississippi river, it is not reasonable to suppose that to protect this route France would build a fort and cause its occupancy at Wittsburgh, forty miles from the Mississippi river, the intervening distance being crossed by many swamps, lakes and bayous and filled with canebrakes. Hence the conclusion is clear to the mind of the writer that Fort St. Francis was at the mouth of the St. Francis river.

1739.

Two Frenchmen named Mallot, in exploring the upper Platte and Arkansas rivers in 1739, passed to Santa Fe in July and remained there until May, 1740, when they returned to and coursed down the Arkansas to the Mississippi.

Their report induced Bienville to suspect that the regions they had traversed were a part of China, a curious survival of the old Asiatic theory of the continent, and he, accordingly, sent an exploring party up the Canadian fork of the Arkansas, but it accomplished nothing.

The population and wealth of Louisiana had continued to increase gradually. The settlements had gradually extended and multiplied. Agricultural products adapted to the climate, were important items in the commerce with the parent country. About this time (1740) cotton was introduced as an agricultural product of Louisiana.

A large portion of the settlers at Arkansas, at this time, were Canadians, and as they had been accustomed to living among savages, they were not averse to marrying the daughters of the Arkansas and these alliances were attended with the happiest consequences.

From 1740 to 1750 we find but little of historic interest to record. In the latter year, the French government, to promote the increase of the population of Louisiana, sent to the province at its own expense, a large number of worthy but poor girls in charge of suitable agents or guardians, who were instructed to bestow them in marriage, together with a small dowry, upon the soldiers, who by their good behavior were entitled to an honorable discharge from service.

The dowry allowed to each soldier who married one of these girls, was a small tract of land, one cow and calf, one cock, five hens, a gun and ammunition, an ax and a hoe, together with a supply of garden seed.

Thus the newly married pair were enabled to begin in the world as independent heads of families. In this manner began many useful and worthy families of the French population of Louisiana, previous to the year 1751, when the last of these girls were sent.

1750.

In 1750 Captain Bossu, of the French marine, was sent by the military authorities to travel through Louisiana and report the result of his observations to his superiors.

Before leaving France, Bossu was instructed by the Marquis de l'Estrade, of the marine corps, to report to him every particular that should appear remarkable in the new country and was requested to give an account of all interesting subjects which might happen on the passage. He arrived at New Orleans on Easter day, 1751, and was received by the Marquis de Vaudreuil, governor of Louisiana, who sent him up the Mississippi river to Arkansas Post, thence to the Illinois. The impressions made on his mind by what he saw and heard were given in letters to his superiors in France, a synopsis of which, so far as they concern Arkansas, follows:

Bossu reached the Akanzas (as he called it) in October, 1751, from which point he wrote, on the 29th of this month, giving an account of his travels from New Orleans to the Akanzas. Again, on the 6th of November, he wrote, saying: "I hope the description I shall give you of this Indian nation, by drawing your attention upon their particular character, will convey a general idea of all the nations of

North America. There is indeed very little difference among them in regard to their customs and their way of thinking, and especially in regard to a Supreme Being, which in their language they call **Coyocopchill**, which signifies **the great Spirit, or the Master of life."**

"The Akanzas live on the banks of a river that bears their name; it rises in New Mexico and falls into the Mississippi. These Indians are tall, well made, brave, good swimmers, very expert in hunting and fishing, and entirely devoted to the French, of which they have given marks on several occasions.

"The country of the Akanzas is one of the finest in the world; the soil of it is so fertile that it produces, without any culture, European wheat, all kinds of food, and good fruit, unknown in France; game of all kinds is plentiful there; wild oxen, stags, roebucks, bears, tigers, leopards, foxes, wild cats, rabbits, turkeys, grouse, pheasants, partridges, quails, turtles, wood-pigeons, swans, geese, bustards, ducks of all kinds, teals, divers, snipes, water-hens, golden plovers, stares, thrushes, and other birds which are not known in Europe.

"The Akanzas have expert fellows among them, who would perhaps amaze our jugglers. I saw one of them, who, in my presence, performed a trick which will appear incredible to you; after some wry mouths, he swallowed a rib of a stag, seventeen inches long, held it with his fingers and drew it out of his stomach again.

"I must not close my letter without informing you of a singular event, which, though of very little importance, may, however, be very useful to me during my stay in America. The Akanzas have adopted me; they have acknowledged me as a warrior and a chief, and have given me the mark of it, which is the figure of a roebuck imprinted on my thigh."

Bossu tells us that at this place, he found a Mestizo Indian, who said he was the son of **Rutel**, a sailor from Britany, who lost himself when M. de La Salle came down the Mississippi river in 1682.

This Indian said that Rutel had been found by the Cenis, an Indian nation, who adopted him. He was given one of their girls as a wife, in the quality of a warrior, because of his successful use of his musket, which was, to them, unknown, against their enemies. By instructing them in navigating their canoes with oars and sails, he won their gratitude and caused them to revere him as the greatest man in the world; "and the famous Ruiter, who, from a common sailor became Lieutenant and Admiral of the United Province, was, perhaps, less revered than Rutel was among the Cenis."

Bossu, in his letter from the Natchez, mentions the fact of passing, on his route from New Orleans, the remnant of Law's colony, originally located near the Akanzas, in 1720. According to this statement the "colony was to consist of Germans and Provincials to the number of 1,500 persons; the ground for it was laid out near a wild nation called the Akancas; it was four leagues square, and the colony was erected into a dutchy. They had already transported thither the ammunition and stores for a company of dragoons, and merchandise to the value of upwards a million of livres."

On Law's failure and flight from France, the Indian company, then established in Louisiana, took possession of the goods.

ARKANSAS COUNTY.

The colonists separated, the Germans settling on the Mississippi river at the point mentioned by Bossu in his letter above referred to. Of the further history of the remaining colonists and the soldiers we have no account, except that La Harpe, who visited the place in 1723, tells us that at that time he found about forty colonists there. The population of Akanzas at this time was eighty-eight (88).

1763.

The laws and customs of Paris were in force in the French possessions in America before the ceding of that portion of her territory east of the Mississippi river to England by the treaty of Paris on the 10th of February, 1763, and remained in force in Louisiana under the secret cession of that territory to Spain in November, 1762, which was not made known till April 12th, 1764.

Many of the French residents were alarmed and dissatisfied at the transfer of this part of Louisiana. M. de Abode, the governor and director-general, **ad interim,** was furnished with instructions by which he was to be governed in surrendering the province to Spanish authority, but in consequence of the unwillingness of the French to pass from under the government of France and become citizens of Spain, the court of Madrid declined to press the formal delivery of the province. Two years having elapsed since De Abode, the director-general had received instructions to deliver the country to the Spanish authorities, the French indulged in the delusive hope of remaining under the dominion of France.

In 1766, the director-general was notified that Don Antonio de Ulloa had been appointed by the Spanish government, to take possession of the province. On his arrival at New Orleans, with two companies of Spanish infantry, he was received by the people with constrained and silent respect. Perceiving the discontent of the people, the Spanish governor-general deemed it prudent to refrain from the exercise of his authority.

In the meanwhile the governor generalship of France had passed from De Abode to M. Aubry.

On the 18th of August, 1769, the authority of France, in the person of M. Aubry, her governor or intendant, passed to Spain, in the person of O'Reilly, her representative. Thus the colony which France had established and possessed for seventy years was transferred by her to Spain. The population of all the province of Louisiana, at this time, according to the best estimates, was thirteen thousand, five hundred thirty-eight, about eighty-eight of whom resided in Arkansas.

CHAPTER V.

From O'Reilly's Arrival in 1769 to Settlement at St. Francis in 1797.

On the 17th of October, 1769, O'Reilly, the Spanish governor-general or commandant, issued certain regulations for the government of the several districts into which Louisiana was at that time divided.

All the proceedings in civil or criminal cases were to be conducted in accordance with the laws and usages of Castile and the Indies. Among these were regulations governing the Probate courts and the succession of estates.

The third article of this decree is as follows:"It shall be the care of the commandant that everything offered for sale at the Post (Arkansas), and which may be wanted for the sustenance and support of the soldiers, be sold cheap.

"There is nothing more indispensably necessary, in order that the soldiers be conscious that nothing is made out of them, than that their chief treat them with the strictest equity. When this is not the case, there never fails to be murmurs of discontent and defiance of subordination."

The "Black Code" formerly given to the King of France, was re-enacted for the protection and government of the slaves.

1765.

After the Peace of Paris in 1763, settling the boundary between the Spanish and English colonies in America, the latter government sent Lieutenant Pittman, of the Royal Engineers, to visit and report the condition of the European settlements on the Mississippi river.

In 1765, Pittman visited the settlement on the Arkansas river and published the following description of that settlement.

Post of Arkansas.

The post is situated three leagues up the river Arkansas and is built on the stockades in a quadangular form, the sides of the exterior polygon are about one hundred and eighty feet and one three pounder is mounted on the flanks and faces of each bastion.

The buildings within the fort are a barracks with three rooms for the soldiers, commanding officer's house, a powder magazine and a magazine for provisions, and an apartment for the commissary, all of which are in a ruinous condition. The fort stands about two hundred yards from the water side and is garrisoned by a captain, a lieutenant and thirty French soldiers, including sergeants and corporals. There are eight houses without the fort occupied by as many families, who have cleared the land about nine hundred yards in depth, but on account of the sandiness of the soil and the lowness of the situation, which makes it subject to be overflowed, they do not raise their necessary provisions.

ARKANSAS COUNTY.

These people subsist mostly by hunting, and every season send to New Orleans great quantities of bear oil, tallow, salted buffalo meat and a few skins.

The Arkansas or Quapas Indians live three leagues above the fort on the side of the river; they are divided into three villages, over each of which presides a chief, and a great chief over all; they amount in all to about six hundred warriors; they are reckoned among the bravest of the Southern Indians; they hunt little more than for their common subsistence and are generally at war with the nations to the westward of them as far as the river Bravo and they bring in very frequently young prisoners and horses from the Caddos, Pamine, Padoncas, etc, of which they dispose to the best advantage.

The river Arkansas is generally esteemed to be in the most moderate climate of any part of Louisiana and the lands six leagues up the river are regarded as fertile. It was here that the famous Mr. Law had his concession, which was a tract of four leagues square. When he failed the Germans whom he settled in this country left, it being too remote. They, on their petition, had lands granted them ten leagues above New Orleans and which their posterity at present possess. There are no more settlements or posts near the banks of the Mississippi until we come to Cascasques, which is three hundred and seventy leagues from the sea, but generally called four hundred; it lies in latitude 37 degrees 43 minutes north and is the first village in the country of the Illinois.

Under royal decree of the 24th of August, 1770, the civil and military governor was, alone, empowered to make concessions of land belonging to the crown. The twelfth clause of that decree was as follows: "All grants shall be made in the name of the King, by the governor-general of the province, who will, at the same time, appoint a surveyor to fix the boundaries thereof, both in front and depth, in the presence of the judge ordinary of the province and of the adjoining settlers who shall be present at the survey. The above named four persons shall sign the process verbal, which shall be made thereof and the surveyor shall make three copies of the same, one of which shall be deposited in the office of the scrivener of the government and cabildo; another shall be delivered to the governor-general and the third to the proprietor, to be annexed to the title of his grant."

In the year 1763, Pierre Laclede obtained from M. de Abode, the director-general of Louisiana, a monopoly of the fur trade with the Indians of Missouri, or upper Louisiana, and established his headquarters on the highlands where the city of St. Louis is now located. He arrived here on November 3rd, 1763, and in February, 1764, erected buildings for the protection of game and tools. Here he remained in active business pursuits, until the spring of 1778, when his business called him to New Orleans.

On his return from this city, Rozier, in his "History of the Mississippi Valley," tells us: "Pierre Liguist Laclede, the founder of St. Louis, died and was buried at the village called 'Poste des Arkansas,' on the Arkansas river, on the 20th of June, 1778. This bold, brave and indomitable adventurer has left a name as enduring as the waters of the Mississippi that now wash the shores of St. Louis."

Switzler, in his "History of Missouri," says that Laclede was buried about two hundred yards back from the west bank of the Mississippi, near the mouth of the Arkansas.

1785.

A census of the population of Louisiana was taken in 1785, showing that there were seventeen thousand, four hundred and thirty-three inhabitants in the territory and that the population had more than doubled since 1769, a period of sixteen years.

The number of free colored persons was about eleven hundred and that of the slaves and white was very nearly equal. Of the whole number, one hundred and ninety six were in Arkansas.

Don Estivan Miro succeeded to the government in 1785. The sixth regiment of the Spanish army, under the command of Don Joseph Vallier, was permanently stationed at Arkansas Post, for the defense of the district of Arkansas.

1786.

The general government of the province was placed in the hands of a governor, residing at New Orleans and lieutenant-governor at St Louis. Under these were commandants of districts. At this time Miro was governor, but the name of the commandant at Arkansas Post is not known.

The earliest records show that Captain Chalmette was in command in 1780 and that Captain Joseph Vallier was probably the commandant from 1786 to 1790. Don Carlos Villemont was his successor, serving until 1801. Governor Miro, in a dispatch dated April 15th, 1786, sent to the Spanish government, says: "The commerce in the district of Arkansas is subject to incursions and exposes the traders to no little damages on account of the Osages."

1788.

The population of Louisiana, for several years, had been gradually increasing. Spain and France and their dependencies, as well as the United States, furnishing this increase. The census taken during the year 1788 showed an aggregate population of forty-two thousand, six hundred and eleven in Louisiana and West Florida districts. This population was divided as follows: free whites, nineteen thousand, four hundred and forty-five; free persons of color, seventeen hundred and one; slaves, twenty-one thousand, four hundred and sixty-five. Of the whole number, but one hundred and nineteen were in Arkansas showing a loss of seventy-seven in three years.

1789.

Governor Miro, on the 2nd of September, 1789, issued a proclamation in which he sets forth that "his Majesty, the King of Spain, had been greatly pleased to permit the subjects and citizens of other countries to emigrate to his province of Louisiana and West Florida

ARKANSAS COUNTY.

by the Mississippi river, with their stock, household goods, furniture, etc., promising to each family, a tract of land of from two hundred and forty to eight hundred acres, free from all expense, also exempt from taxation."

Col. John Morgan, of Ohio, for some time previous to this, had attempted to establish a settlement on the Spanish side of the river. Dazzled by the splendor of this offer, he continued, with much zeal, to try to persuade the people in Eastern states to become Spanish subjects, as late as the latter part of 1789. The attempt failed, however, because of the stubborn nature of republican education, which forbids commixture with despotic habits.

In 1789, Governor Miro informed his government that he was in receipt of dispatches sent him by parties in the, then, Miro District of Tennessee, the first of these being "carried by a militia officer named Fagot, the confidential agent of the writer." Who the writer was is not stated, but in June, 1792, Fagot was again in the Miro District of Tennessee, from whence he returned to New Orleans down the Cumberland river in a boat. In the boat was a man named Derogne, a rower. This Deronge tells us that on coming near Lous le Grace (New Madrid) Fagot told him and all his men to tell the same story to the commandant, which he should. Also that the commandant at Lous le Grace gave to Fagot, a large package to be delivered to the governor, Baron de Carondelet, at New Orleans, which Fagot did.

Some private marriage records found in Arkansas county, show that in February, 1798, at or near the Post of Arkansas, Andreas Fagot was married to Catherina Pineau.

After the purchase of Louisiana by the United States, from France, in 1803, and the establishment of civil government in the District of Arkansas, we find the name of Andrea Fagot as early as the 23rd of August, 1808, in the records of the civil proceedings of the district, having been appointed and commissioned an acting justice of the peace and notary public. At this time and for several years later, he resided at or near Arkansas Post, and on his death, left a wife and several children.

The writer resided within a half mile of the widow and two of her children and was personally acquainted with them and visited them often. On one of thes visits, at the request of the widow, he examined a large number of papers she had retained in an old trunk belonging to her husband. The papers referred to various subjects, some written in English, some in French and some in Spanish. Among the latter was a commission issued by the Spanish authorities to Andreas Fagot, creating him a lieutenant in the Spanish army.

This statement is given for the purpose of showing the probable identity of the Fagot who bore the important dispatches from Miro District of Tennessee, to the governor-general at New Orleans, with the Andrea Fagot, of Arkansas Post, in 1808. It is a historical fact, known to those familiar with the history of the time, that Spain made an effort to induce the settlers west of the Alleghanies and east of the Mississippi to secede from the United States and join the Spanish colony, then controlling the commerce of the Mississippi, and it is possible that the dispatches referred to, concerned this movement.

1793.

During the governorship of Baron de Carondelet, he made many grants of land to parties in Arkansas, one of the largest of these being granted to Don Joseph Valliere, who was a captain in the sixth regiment of the Spanish army, then in service in Louisiana.

This grant was for a tract of land ten leagues square, lying on both sides of White river, near the northern limits of the state of Arkansas, and was dated June, 1793.

On June 17th, 1793, Baron de Carondelet made a concession of land to Don Carlos de Villemont, of two leagues front by one league deep, on the Mississippi river, at or near Point Chicot. Upon this tract the village of Villemont was located and upon the organization of the county of Chicot in 1823, this village was chosen as the seat of justice for the county.

The township of Villemont, now in Jefferson county, was created by the courts of Arkansas and named in honor of De Villemont.

As late as 1848, there were descendants of De Villemont residing in Arkansas county, two of whom were personally known to the writer. These are now dead, having left no descendants.

In 1795, Don Carlos De Villemont, who was then the Spanish commandant at Post of Arkansas, was granted fourteen thousand arpens of land on the Mississippi river in what is now Chicot county.

Another of these grants was made to Baron de Bastrop. This grant was twelve leagues square on the Ouachita river, principally in the state of Louisiana, but part of it in the limits of the state of Arkansas, and was dated June, 1797.

Bastrop ceded or transferred four hundred acres of this grant to Aaron Burr.

To the Marquis de Maison Rouge, in 1797, was granted a large tract on Bayou Bartholomew and Ouachita river, supposed to have included the present site of the city of Camden.

On the 27th of June, 1797, Baron de Carondelet granted to the three brothers, Elisha, William and Gabriel Winters, to William Russell, Joseph Stillwell and others, one million arpens of land near to and northwest of the Post of Arkansas.

The Winters and Stillwells, with their families, moved to and settled on their grants in the spring of 1798—the Stillwells on the west side of Grand Prairie, near the Arkansas river, about four miles west of Arkansas Post, and the Winters about two and a half miles northwest from Arkansas Post, on the east side of the prairie and west of what is now known as the "Post Bayou," a short distance from the crossing on this bayou, known as "Winter's Ford."

The Stillwells obtained grants for occupying or homesteading, which they, in due time, perfected and had confirmed.

The Winters, failing to occupy their grants within time required, finally lost the land, although one or more of them actually settled on

ARKANSAS COUNTY.

their claims and made improvements. William died and was buried on his claim.

Soon after the death of his brother, Elisha Winter brought from Lexington, Kentucky, a hewn stone or monument, three or more feet in length and of large size and caused the same to be placed, in the presence of Don Carlos de Villemont, who was at the time commandant at the Post of Arkansas. This he did for the purpose of identifying the initial point of his and his brother's grant.

Portions of this stone were on the ground near the point at which it was supposed to have been placed, originally, as late as 1850.

About 1893 or 1894, Mr. Nutter, who, at that time, owned and lived on a portion of the Winters' grant, in cultivating the ground on which the old Winter homestead stood, plowed up a one cent copper coin which purports to have been issued in 1787, named by the Numismatic Bank, of Boston, the "Mark Newby, New Jersey coin," and said to have been brought from Ireland before that date. This coin has on its obverse side, the words "Nova Caesarea" in a circle, with small bust of a horse under which is a heavy plow, and under the beam of the plow is the date. On the reverse side, the words "E Pluribus Unum" in a circle, surrounding a shield.

The writer has four other coins found in the county. The first is a sou, copper coin, having on the obverse side crossed L's (cut), with crown over them, around this in a circle being the words "Sit Nomen Domini Benedictum" and on the reverse side "Colonies Francoises" 1721 across the face with the letter H. under the date. This coin was found near the Menard Mound in the southeast corner of the county.

Previous to the issuance of this coin, a decree had been published making it a legal tender in Louisiana, and not only legal tender, but any stipulation for payment in gold or silver was made penal.

The second is silver, issued by the French government in 1792, during the reign of Louis XVI. On the obverse side is the profile of the king surrounded by the following inscription, "Louis XVI, Roi Des Francois, 1792 W," and on the reverse side a wreath surrounding a quiver and arrow. On the left of the quiver is the figure 2 and on the right, the letter S. The whole design is surrounded by the following inscription, "Vt La National Louis Le Roi La Liberta." This coin was found near Gardner's Ferry on La Grue, about six miles east of De Witt.

The third is a copper half cent issued in 1804 with profile of female in center with the word "Liberty" over her head. This coin was found on the farm of the late W. F. Ferguson, about seven miles north of De Witt.

The fourth is a two cent copper coin, issued by the Belgian government. This has, in the center of its obverse side, scroll work, upon which rests a crown and underneath is the date 1835. Surrounding the whole is the following inscription, "Leopold Premier Les Belges." On the reverse side is shown the figure of a lion sitting by a monument with his right paw resting on the monument, which bears the inscription, "Constitution Belge, 1831." Under this is "2 cents." This coin was found on the deserted place occupied by Count Beaucarme, of Belgium, who lived on the place from 1836 until his death in 1851, who will be spoken of later.

1795.

During the year 1795, the authorities of Louisiana expressed much anxiety in regard to the continued advance of the western settlements made by citizens of the United States, and at the same time apprehended hostilities on the part of the United States and an interruption of the intercourse between upper and lower Louisiana by way of the Mississippi river. Baron de Carondelet was diligent in preparing to meet the emergency. To guard against such a contingency, additional posts were established on the upper Mississippi and at several points below the mouth of the Ohio. While establishing these posts of defense against the encroachments of the Americans from the east, one at New Madrid, at Echor Morgant, at Walnut Hills and at Natchez, he he was seeking for and proving a route from lower to upper Louisiana by water west of the Mississippi. This route was by way of the Red, Ouachita and Saline rivers and Bayou Bartholomew to near the south bank of the Arkansas river, thence by the Arkansas, White, St. Francis and Tyronga rivers and White Water Creek.

By this route he had discovered that a practicable water way with short portages could be opened between the settlements in lower and upper Louisiana, as the route had been explored by experienced hunters and voyagers.

In passing from New Orleans to St. Louis, the parties went up the Mississippi river to the mouth of Red river, which they entered and continued in till the mouth of the Ouachita was reached; this they also entered and sailed to the mouth of the Saline, up that to the mouth of Bayou Bartholomew, entering that and continuing to its headwaters, near the south bank of the Arkansas river, in the vicinity of the present city of Pine Bluff; by a short portage they came to Arkansas river and sailed down it to the cut-off, through which they entered the White river, continuing up that river to the mouth of the "Old Town Bayou," which connects the Mississippi and White rivers, below the mouth of the St. Francis, thence up the Mississippi to the St. Francis, up this to the mouth of the Tyronga; entering the Tyronga and continuing therein till White Water Creek was reached, through which they again entered the Mississippi near the mouth of the Ohio.

By this route they were enabled to pass from one extremity of the Louisiana settlement west of the Mississippi, to the other, principally by water. In time of high water but one portage, from the headwaters of Bayou Bartholomew to the Arkansas river, was necessary, and their only exposure to the enemy was between "Old Town Bayou" and the St. Francis river.

"In 1795, Brigadier-General Gayoso erected a fort at the fourth Chickasaw Bluff, the Spanish being content since 1786, about which time the Chickasaw Indians had conceded the privilege, to watch their possessions, known as the Chickasaw Bluffs, from Fort Esperanza, now Hopefield, Arkansas."

On the 31st of May, 1795, Gen. Gayoso wrote his wife from

the fort on Chickasaw Bluff: "On yesterday, I passed from my post of Esperanza, over to the Chicacha Bluffs, whence I now write. I hoisted the King's flag and saluted it in the most brilliant manner from the flotilla and from the battery. It being St. Ferdinand's day (the name of my prince), I gave the post that name. It was a pleasant day, and withal my birthday, and nothing was wanting to complete my happiness but your presence." From this we see the General as a gallant and loving husband, as well as a loyal subject.

CHAPTER VI.

From Philipps' Settlement at St. Francis in 1797, to the Establishment of the Territory of Orleans in 1804.

In the year 1797, Col. Sylvanus Philipps settled at the mouth of the St. Francis river, but during the troubles between the United States and the governor-general at New Orleans, over the question of privileges claimed by the citizens of the United States on the Mississippi river, he was requested by the Spanish commandant to return to Arkansas Post.

At a later date, Col. Philipps returned to his settlement at the mouth of the St. Francis river and in 1820 the county of Philipps was established by an act of the legislature of the Territory of Arkansas, being named in honor of Col. Philipps. The land on which the city of Helena is located, was originally owned by Col. Philipps, and was named in honor of his daughter, Miss Helena Philipps.

A private record of marriages and deaths, kept by Pedro Javier, who was then the priest in charge of the Jesuit mission located at Arkansas Post, shows that from the 27th of February, 1797, to the 4th of November, 1799, he married seventeen couples and attended and made record of the death of nineteen of his parishoners. His successor, Jean Brady, from July 13th 1802, to August 22nd 1802, records but four marriages and no deaths. The names of these parties and date of marriage were as follows:

1. Francisco Himbeau to Teresa Kebed—February 27th, 1797.
2. Pedro Himbeau to Elena Jaillano—September 27th, 1797.
3. Francisco Caussot to Genorefa Nortelny—May 22nd, 1797.
4. Juan Santista Chaveley to Maria Jarb—July 24th, 1797.
5. Alberto Nardoult to Margarita Vanois—July 26th, 1797.
6. Juan Santista Himbeau to Maria Kebed—August 24th, 1797.
7. ——— to Maria Luisa Sanvais—September 26th, 1797.
8. Andreas Fagot to Catherina Pineau—February 19th, 1798.
9. Juan Santista Dagle to Susanne None (?)—19th of——1798.
10. Estevan Levasseur to Luisa Jardelas—April 16th, 1798.
11. Pedro Nuvel to Carolina Levasseur—October 25th, 1798.
12. Francisco Peltier to Barba Finet—November 5th, 1798.
13. Jan B. Greves to Maria Amable La Rue—February 3rd, 1799.
14. Joseph Soligny to Francisca Kebed—May 15th, 1799.
15. Juan Menard to Maria Calliot—June 10th, 1799.
16. Pedro Lefevre to Pelagia ——— —October 19th, 1799.
17. Francisco Barnardo de Valliere to Marianna de Torres—November 4th, 1799.
18. Carlos Vilemont to Catrina Brady—July 13th, 1802.
19. Luis Nordelot to Angelina Valliere—July 17th, 1802.

ARKANSAS COUNTY.

20. Luis Gossiot to Catalina Calliot—July 17th, 1802.
21. Estanislao Le Baisseur to Elizabeth Vigno—August 7th, 1802.
22. Josef La Riviere to Eugenia Martino—August 9th, 1802.

1798.

In 1798, General Gayoso De Lemos, Governor of the Territory, issued an address to the commandants at the different posts throughout the colonies, in which he gave instructions in relation to granting lands to settlers in the province. These instructions were as follows:

1st. "Commandants are forbidden to grant lands to a new settler coming from another spot where he had already obtained a grant. Such an one must buy land, or obtain a grant from the governor himself.

2nd. "If a settler be a foreigner, unmarried and without slaves, money or other property, no grant is to be made to him until he shall have remained five years in the post, demeaning himself well in some honest and useful occupation.

3rd. "Mechanics are to be protected, but no land is to be granted them until they shall have acquired some property and resided three years in the exercise of their occupation.

4th. "No grant of land is to be made to any unmarried emigrant who has neither trade nor property, until after a residence of four years, during which time he must have been employed in cultivating the ground.

5th. "But, if after two years, such a person shall marry the daughter of an honest farmer, with his consent, and be, by him, recommended, a grant of land may be made to him.

6th. "Liberty of conscience is not to be extended beyond the first generation. The children of the emigrants must become Catholics and emigrants not agreeing to this must not be admitted, but expelled, even when they bring property with them. This is to be explained to settlers who do not profess the Catholic faith.

7th. "In upper Louisiana, no settler is to be admitted, who is not a farmer or a mechanic.

8th. "It is especially recommended to commandants to watch that no preacher of any religion but the Catholic come into the province.

9th. "To every married emigrant of the above description, two hundred arpens may be granted, with the addition of fifty for every child he has.

10th. "If he bring negroes, twenty additional arpens are to be granted to him for each, but, in no case, are more than eight hundred arpens to be granted to an emigrant.

11th. "No land is to be granted to a trader.

12th. "Immediately on the arrival of a settler, the oath of allegiance is to be administered to him. If he has a wife, proof is to be demanded of their marriage, and if they bring property, they are to be required to disclose what part belongs to each of them and are to be informed that the discovery of any wilful falsehood in this declaration will produce the forfeiture of the land granted them and of the improvements made thereon.

13th. "Without proof of lawful marriage, no grant is to be made for any wife or negro.

14th. "The grant is to be forfeited if a settlement be not made within the year, or one-tenth part of the land put in cultivation within two years.

15th. "No grantee is to be allowed to sell his land until he has produced three crops on a tenth part of it, but in case of death, it may pass to an heir within the province, but not to one without, unless he come and settle on it.

16th. "If the grantee owes debts in the province, the proceeds of the first crop are to be applied to their discharge, in preference to that of a debt due abroad. If, before the third crop be made, it becomes necessary to evict the grantee on account of his bad conduct, the land shall be given to the young man and young woman living in one mile of it, whose good conduct may show them to be most deserving of it and the decision is to be made by an assembly of notable planters, presided over by the commandant.

17th. "Emigrants are to be settled contiguous to old establishments, without leaving any vacant lands between, in order that the people may more easily protect each other in case of an invasion by Indians, and that the administration of justice and a compliance with public regulations may be facilitated."

On the 21st day of October 1798, the king of Spain thought proper to take from the civil and military governor of the District of Louisiana, the power to grant lands to emigrants and on that day he vested this power exclusively in the Intendant of the province. In consequence of this decree, Intendant Morales, on the 17th of July, issued a new set of regulations to which the concession of lands should thereafter be subject.

In this year, a census of Louisiana was taken. This census gave the population of the District of Arkansas as three hundred and sixty-eight souls, showing an increase of one hundred and seventy-two in three years, the census of 1795 giving the district a population of one hundred and ninety-six souls.

The only taxes known or collected in the colony were a duty of six per cent on the export value, according to a very reasonable and moderate estimate made of the same and a like duty on all foreign imports.

1800.

By secret treaty made at St. Ildefonso, on October 1st, 1800, Spain ceded the province of Louisiana, according to its ancient limits, to the French Republic. The formal delivery of the province did not occur, however, till November 30th, 1803, after the French Republic had transferred the province to the United States, under the treaty, between the two countries, of April 30th, 1803.

The greater number of the settlements in the District of Arkansas up to this time had been at or near Arkansas Post.

In 1797, a settlement had been made by Col. Sylvanus Philipps, at or near the site of the present city of Helena, but because of exposure to the threatened invasion of that territory, by the citizens,

ARKANSAS COUNTY.

east of the Mississippi, he was induced to remove to Arkansas Post. In 1800, a settlement was made, by three Kentuckians, about three miles south of the mouth of the St. Francis river, at a point called Little Prairie, and during the same year William Patterson built a warehouse where the city of Helena is now located.

1802.

On October 15th, 1802, the king of Spain issued his writ from Barcelona, directing the Spanish Intendant, Marquis de Casa Calvo, then in charge of Louisiana, to deliver the province to whomsoever should be designated by the French to receive it and on June 9th, 1803, Bonaparte, as First Consul, designated citizen Pierre Clement Laussat, at New Orleans, to receive the country in the name of France. The actual delivery was not formally made till November 30th, 1803, at which time, M. Laussat, as commissioner, on the part of France, received the province. The ceremony attendant upon the formal transfer is described as follows: "On the morning of the 30th of November, 1803, the Spanish flag was displayed from a lofty flag staff in the center of the public square of New Orleans, at which time the commissioners or representatives of the two governments being present, the Spanish flag gradually descended and that of France, soon thereafter, ascended to the head of the flag staff."

Thus terminated the Spanish dominion in Louisiana, and, after a lapse of thirty-four years, the government of France was again its possessor. During the negotiations for the sale and purchase of Louisiana, its inhabitants were never contented.

The handful of settlers at Arkansas Post had been given by France to Spain, Spain gave them back to France, and France gave them to the United States.

For one hundred and seventeen years they had lived peacefully in one town and at the date of the cession numbered about six hundred.

1803.

On the 20th of December, 1803, Laussat, the representative of the French government, formally delivered the territory of Louisiana to William C. C. Claiborne, of the United States government, who, on this day, issued a proclamation in the name of the United States acknowledging her possession of the territory and declaring her authority over same.

In transferring the territory of Louisiana to the United States, the French representative, M. Laussat, said: "In conformity with the treaty, I put the United States in possession of Louisiana and its dependencies. The citizens and inhabitants who wish to remain here and obey the laws are from this moment exonerated from the oath of fidelity to the French Republic."

Governor Claiborne, in accepting, said: "This cession secures to you and your descendants, the inheritance of liberty, perpetual laws, and magistrates whom you will elect yourselves."

Thus, after occupancy of the territory with an organized form of civil government, under France and Spain, for a period of one hundred and thirteen years, it became a part of the United States, being subject to her authority. The first settlement within the borders of this territory was made at Arkansas Post, within the present limits of Arkansas county, in the year 1686.

In October, 1803, Congress had passed an act authorizing the president to take possession of the Territory of Louisiana, purchased from France, and providing for the temporary government of this territory. The second section of this act is as follows:

"And be it further enacted, that until the expiration of the present session of Congress, or unless provisions be sooner made for the temporary government of said territory, all the military, civil and judicial powers exercised by the officers of the existing government of the same shall be exercised in such manner as the president shall direct, for maintaining and protecting the inhabitants of Louisiana, in the full enjoyment of their liberty, property and religion."

Notwithstanding the peaceful acquiescence of the people of Louisiana with the transfer of the sovereignty of France to the United States, there was a suppressed excitement, however, in the minds of the French and Spanish subjects, growing out of the uncertainty of their land titles.

They feared an attempt, on the part of the citizens of the United States, to deprive them of their estates and bonds. President Jefferson soon allayed this fear by appointing a commission to inquire into the titles of the French and Spanish in the new territory.

This commission consisted of two men of French descent, J. B. C. Lucas and James Penrose, and one American, James L. Davidson. It was noted for culture and wisdom.

CHAPTER VII.

From Organization of Territory of Orleans in 1804, to the Establishment of the Territory of Missouri in 1812.

By an act of Congress of March 26th, 1804, all that portion of the Louisiana purchase lying south of the 33rd degree of north latitude was erected into the Territory of Orleans, the remaining portion of the purchase being denominated the District of Louisiana.

When the eastern portion of the Northwest Territory was organized into a separate territorial government, by an act of Congress in 1800, the remaining portion of this territory, extending west to the Mississippi river and northward to the lakes, was denominated the Indiana Territory and W. H. Harrison was appointed governor and superintendent of Indian affairs, the town of Vincennes being chosen as the capital and seat of government.

The portion of the Louisiana purchase lying north of the 33rd degree of north latitude and designated by act of Congress of March, 26th, 1804, District of Louisiana, was attached to and placed under the jurisdiction of the government of the Indiana Territory. At this time the legislative power of this territory was vested in the governor and three judges, W. H. Harrison being governor, Griffin, Vanderberg and Davis, judges.

This act of Congress empowered them to legislate for the District of Louisiana and created courts in the district in which two terms of court were to be held each year. This authority continued in force from the creation thereof till March 1805.

During the existence of this legislative authority over the District of Louisiana, which at the time included Arkansas, sixteen acts or laws for the government of its inhabitants were passed. They were designated as follows:

First, Crimes and Punishment; **second**, Justices Courts; **third**, Government of Slaves; **fourth**, Revenue; **fifth**, Militia Law; **sixth**, Office of Recorder; **seventh**, Attorneys; **eighth**, Constables; **ninth**, Boatmen; **tenth**, Defalcation; **eleventh**, Practice at Law; **twelfth**, Probate Business; **thirteenth**, Quarterly Sessions of Courts; **fourteenth**, Official Oaths; **fifteenth**, The Office and Duties of Sheriffs; and **sixteenth**, Governing Mortgages. These acts were printed and public attention called to them.

Portions of six of these laws, namely, on the subject of slaves, of records, of boatmen, of defalcation, oath of office and mortgages continued in force in the Territory of Arkansas, being digested and published as laws of the territory under an act of Congress approved June 27th, 1834. Parts of these acts were in force at the adoption of the constitution of 1836, and were digested and published in the Revised Statutes of the State.

FROM 1804 TO 1812.

Section one of the Act of 1804 and **section one** of the chapter of the Digest on the subject of conveyance of real estate; and **section one** of the Act of 1804 and **section one** of the chapter of the Digest on the subject of record, are substantially the same, as are **section three** of the Act of 1804, and **section five** of the chapter of the Digest on the subject of the record of deeds.

Sections one and **two** of the Act of 1804 and **sections eighteen** and **nineteen** of the chapter of the Digest on the subject of mortgages are practically the same.

There were seven sections of the Act of 1804, on the subject of slaves, remaining in force until 1864, at which time they were annulled by the constitution of that date.

"At this time (1804), the District of Louisiana contained the germs of two independent states, on the west side of the Mississippi, comprised in the few detached settlements upon the Arkansas river and the Mississippi south of the Missouri river. Those on the Arkansas were distributed chiefly within fifty miles of the Mississippi, at a point where a military post was established and known as the Post of Arkansas." The population of this settlement in 1804, was three hundred and sixty-eight persons, exclusive of the garrison in the post.

In the spring of 1804, Arkansas Post, Fort Esperanza and St. Louis were formally delivered to the United States. James B. Maney, Major of Artillery, was sent by General Wilkinson, to Arkansas Post. Leno, the commandant under the Spanish government, quietly gave possession of the place to the representative of the United States.

The first record of civil preceedings in the District of Arkansas, then including the territory forming the present State of Arkansas, under the jurisdiction of the United States, was at Arkansas Post, before Major James B. Maney, the civil and military governor or commandant. This was on the 5th of June, 1804, when Henry Cassady acknowledged, before Major Maney, the execution of a deed to Thomas Napier, to a tract of land adjoining the lands of Patrick Cassady, the deed being on this day recorded by Major Maney.

During the administration of civil affairs by Major Maney at Arkansas Post, a member of deeds and other instruments of writing were acknowledged before him and by him recorded.

Among these instruments was a deed from Francis Vallier to Roswell P. Johnson, dated January 12th, 1805, for eight hundred acres of land on the St. Francis river, granted to Vallier by Captain Luengo, a Spanish commandant at the Post of Arkansas, on January 26th, 1803.

The last deed recorded by Major Maney was on the 5th of March, 1805. Shortly afterward Major Maney was succeeded by Stephen Worrell, as recorder, he in turn being succeeded by R. W. Osborne, both during the year 1805.

In the fall of 1804, Jefferson commissioned Mr. Dunbar, a distinguished scientist of Natchez, to explore the Ouachita. He ascended the river as far as Hot Springs, taking its course and distances, and prepared a map of the region.

In February, 1806, President Jefferson submitted to Congress, Dunbar's observations, from which the following items touching events transpiring and observations made in what was at one time Arkansas County, are of interest. "On the morning of 22nd of November (1804), they arrived at Ecor a Fabri (Fabri's Cliffs) from eighty to one hundred feet high." This cliff or bluff is the site of the present flourishing city of Camden, Ouachita county.) On their way up the river Dunbar and party, on the 28th of November, "fell in with an old Dutch hunter and his party, consisting in all of five persons. This man had resided forty years on the Ouachita and before that period had been up the Arkansas river, the White river and the river St. Francis." Farther up the Ouachita they found that "hills frequently rise out of the level country, full of rocks and stones, hard and flinty and often resembling Turkey oil stones." Other hills were discovered of which Dunbar says: "One of them is called the glass crystal or shiny mountain, from the vast number of hexagonal prisms of very transparent and colorless crystal which are found on its surface. They are generally surmounted by pyramids at one end, rarely on both. These crystals do not produce a double refraction of the rays of light."

On their arrival at the hot springs, they found "an open log cabin and a few huts of split boards, all calculated for summer encampment, which had been erected by persons resorting to these springs for the recovery of their health."

"It is understood that the hot springs are included within a grant of some hundred acres granted by the late Spanish commandant of the Ouachita, to some of his friends, but it is not believed that a regular patent was ever issued for the place and it cannot be asserted that residence with improvements here, form a plea to claim the land upon."

On the 10th of December, Dunbar and his party visited all the hot springs. These issue on the east side of the valley.

Examination of the four principal springs, those which yield the greatest quantity of water or water of the highest temperature, showed the temperature to be as follows: No. 1, 150° F.; No. 2, 154° F.; No. 3, 136° F.; and No. 4, 132° F.

A rough estimate of the quantity of hot water delivered from all the springs at the base of the hill was one hundred and sixty-five gallons per minute, or three thousand seven hundred seventy-one and a half hogsheads in twenty-four hours.

"A series of accurate observations determined the latitude of the hot springs to be 34° 31' 4.16" N., and longitude 6 hr. 11 min. 23 sec. or 92° 50' 45" west from the meridian of Greenwich."

President Jefferson, in his message above referred to says: "In order to render the estimate as complete as may be of the Indians inhabiting the country west of the Mississippi, I add Dr. Sibley's account of those residing in and adjacent to the territory of Orleans."

Dr. Sibley, in his report says of the Indians then inhabiting the country south of the Arkansas river, and within the territory afterward included in the limits of Arkansas County: "The Arkansas live on the Arkansas river, south side, in three villages, about twelve miles above the post or station. The name of the first village is **Tawanima**, of the second **Ausota**, and of the third **Ocapa**. In all it is believed they do not exceed one hundred men and are diminishing. They are at war with the Osages, but friendly with all other peoples, white and red; are the original proprietors of the country on the river, all of which they claim for about three hundred miles above them or to the junction of the river **Cadua** with the Arkansas, above this fork the Osage claim. Their language is Osage. They generally raise corn to sell and are called honest and friendly people."

About the time of Dunbar's expedition, Don Juan Filhoil, commandant at Ouachita Post, ascended the river Ouachita to Hot Springs and wrote a description of the region, claiming the springs under a grant "said to have been issued to him by Governor Miro."

1805.

The act of Congress creating the District of Louisiana and placing it under the jurisdiction of the Territory of Indiana was repealed by act of Congress of March 3rd, 1805, organizing the Territory of Louisiana and placing the government thereof in the hands of a governor, secretary and judges.

Under this act Gen. James Wilkinson was appointed governor, Frederick Bates secretary, and John B. Lucas and Return J. Meigs, judges. The governor and judges constituted the legislature of the territory.

By an act of this legislature, the territory was divided into six judicial districts, which were named as follows: St. Charles, St. Louis, Ste. Genevieve, Cape Girardeau, New Madrid and Arkansas. This legislative body continued from March 3rd, 1805, until June 4th, 1812, at which time Congress changed the name of the territory from Louisiana to Missouri and vested the legislative power of the territory in general assembly, consisting of the governor, a legislative council and a house of representatives.

During the existence of this legislature thirty-four acts were passed for the protection of the rights and privileges of the citizens of the territory, which acts, or such part of them as were not inconsistent with the act of Congress of March 2nd, 1819, were continued and directed to be a part of the law of the land. They remained in force in Arkansas until 1835, when they were digested and published by act of Congress.

1806.

On the 27th of June, 1806, the legislature of the Territory of Louisiana passed an act establishing the District of Arkansas, and dividing the same from the New Madrid District. The line of division between the two districts began on the Mississippi river opposite the second bluff and continued west indefinitely. All the territory south of this line to the thirty-third degree of north latitude constituted the District of Arkansas.

In this district a general court was created to sit in St. Louis twice each year; in May and October.

It seems, however, that the division was not made nor the courts established until after October, 1808, at which time Governor Lewis issued his proclamation.

In 1806 President Jefferson sent Gen. Zebulon M. Pike to explore

ARKANSAS COUNTY.

the source of the Mississippi and western Louisiana. While out on this expedition Gen. Pike despatched James B. Wilkinson, with instructions to descend the Arkansas river to its mouth. Wilkinson set out on this expedition in October, 1806, reaching Arkansas Post on the 9th of January, 1807.

The territory was at this time one vast wilderness, save for the settlements at Arkansas Post, at the mouth of the St. Francis river, the site of the present city of Helena, at Esperanza or Hopefield, opposite the lowest Chickasaw Bluff, at Ecor Fabri, the present site of Camden and temporarily at Hot Springs.

In speaking of the game along the river one of Wilkinson's men said: "I believe there are, on the banks of the Arkansas river alone, sufficient buffalo, elk, and deer to feed all the savages in the United States, one century, if used without waste."

1808.

In the Missouri Gazette of the 20th of August, 1808, was reported the proclamation of Governor Lewis announcing the organization of the District of Arkansas. On the 23rd of this month he appointed and commissioned the following gentlemen to the offices named:

John W. Honey, Recorder of the District, Judge of the Probate Court, Clerk of the Common Pleas Court and Recorder of the District.

Benjamin Foy, Justice of the Peace and Judge of the Court of Common Pleas.

Joseph Stillwell, Judge of the Court of Common Pleas.

Harold Stillwell, Sheriff of the District of Arkansas.

Francis Vaugine, Judge of the Court of Common Pleas.

Andrew Fagot, Justice of the Peace, Notary Public and Coroner of the District of Arkansas.

Perley Wallis, Deputy Attorney-General for the District of Arkansas.

Each of these commissions had the official oath endorsed on it and was duly recorded by John W. Honey, recorder of the district.

The following is a copy of the commission issued to John W. Honey, as Judge of the Probate Court:

"Meriwether Lewis, Governor and Commander-in-Chief of the Territory of Louisiana,

"To all who shall see these presents, greeting: Know ye that, reposing special trust and confidence in the integrity, ability and diligence of John W. Honey, Esquire, I do appoint him Judge of Probate for the District of Arkansas, and empower him to discharge the duties of said office, according to law; to have and to hold the said office with all the powers, privileges and emoluments to the same of right appertaining, during the pleasure of the Governor of the Territory for the time being.

"In testimony whereof, I have caused the seal of the territory to be hereto affixed.

"Given under my hand at St. Louis, the twenty-third day of August

in the year of our Lord one thousand eight hundred and eight, and of the Independence of the United States, the thirty-third.
(Seal.) "MERIWETHER LEWIS.
By the Governor Signed.
"FREDERICK BATES, Secretary of the Territory of Louisiana."

Under the power and authority vested in him by virtue of this commission, Judge Honey, on the 12th of December, 1808, opened the court of Probate in and for the District of Arkansas, as will appear from the following order of the court of that date.

Territory of Louisiana } Sct.
District of Arkansas }

In the Judge of Probate's office, Monday, the twelfth day of December, in the year of our Lord, one thousand, eight hundred and eight. It being the day appointed by my notice set up in my office in pursuance of a law passed by the Legislature of the Territory, entitled "An act Authorizing the Probate of Wills and the Distribution of Interstate Real Estate and the Distribution of their Personal Estate and for other purposes therein mentioned."

I, John W. Honey, Judge of Probate for the District of Arkansas, attended in my office in the town of Arkansas in pursuance of the above mentioned notice, for the purpose of attending to all such business which might be brought before me as Judge of Probate, aforesaid.

No business appearing today, I adjourned until tomorrow morning ten o'clock.

JOHN W. HONEY.

Tuesday, December 13th, 1808.

Having adjourned to this day with an expectation of business, but it not appearing, I adjourned Sine Die.

JOHN W. HONEY, J. P. D. A.

The first application to Judge Honey for Letters of Administration was by Elizabeth Rodgers, on the 18th of December, 1808, to authorize her to administer on the estate of Adiston Rodgers. The order fails to show the grant of such letters, as it appears the applicant failed to give the necessary bond.

The will of William Patterson was probated before Judge Honey on the 7th of February, 1809, upon which he granted Letters of Executorship to Sylvanus Phillips and Daniel Mooney on the eighth of February, 1809.

On the 10th of November, 1808, a grand council of the nation of Osage, Indiana, was held at Fort Clark, on the right bank of the Missouri river, where a treaty was made by which the Osages relinquished to the United States, their claim to all lands between the Missouri and Arkansas rivers, as far west as a line drawn from Fort Clark, due south to the Arkansas. This treaty threw open to Louisiana, the said territory for settlement.

By requisition of the Secretary of War under the Act of Congress of 1808, for forming and equipping one hundred thousand militia in the United States, Governor Lewis, of the Territory of Louisiana, made a proclamation requiring the raising and equipping of three hundred and

ARKANSAS COUNTY.

seventy-seven militia in the territory. These were duly appointed in the districts of St. Charles, St. Louis, Ste. Genevieve, Cape Girardeau, New Madrid and Arkansas.

One of the strange practices of the times of which we write was the appointment of one man to a plurality of offices, as shown in the appointment of John W. Honey to the offices of Judge of the Court of Probate, Recorder of the District, Clerk of the Court of Common Pleas and Quarter Sessions, and Treasurer of the District.

All of these offices he held exercising the functions thereof, at the same time, by virtue of the commissions issued to him on the 23rd of August, 1805, all of which now appear on record in the office of the clerk of Arkansas County. Another instance of one man's being appointed to a plurality of offices was the appointment of Andrew Fagot to the offices of Justice of the Peace, Notary Public and Coroner of the District, his commissions being issued at the same time with those of John W. Honey.

At the time of the appointment of the above named parties, Governor Lewis appointed Benjamin Foy, then and for many years before and after that date, residing at old Ft. Esperanza, later known as Foy's Point, or Hopefield, opposite the city of Memphis, Tenn., one of the judges of the Court of Common Pleas Quarter Sessions, and Justice of the Peace.

In his commission as Justice of the Peace, the territorial limits of his jurisdiction are specifically stated as follows: "I do appoint him a Justice of the Peace for the several townships of the District of Arkansas, and more especially for those composing the settlements of Hopefield and the St. Francis river."

It appears from the record of marriage certificates now in the clerk's office of Arkansas County, that between the 9th of August, 1809, and the 30th of January, 1812, that Benjamin Foy solemnized the rites of matrimony in four instances; but that certificates of marriage did not reach the clerk's office for record until the 13th of April, 1812, at which time all of these certificates were filed for record.

Davis, in his "Early History of Memphis," says: "I was well acquainted with Benjamin Foy and have listened for hours to his tales of early days. At what time Judge Benjamin Foy settled on the point, I do not remember to have heard, but it certainly must have been about the commencement of the present century. Foy's Point, as it was called, held a high character, not only as a very important landing, but as the center of the most healthy, intelligent and moral community between Cape Girardeau and Natchez, which was, owing, most likely, to the example of the Judge, who, although he held his court at the Post of Arkansas, exerted his most direct influence at home, being one of those men whose very presence is a terror to evil-doers.

"He also appears to have possessed a far more extensive and correct knowledge of the country than any other man in it, and his statements were held by the government as the most reliable, which caused the point to be visited, not only by many of our most able statesmen of that day, but also by distinguished tourists from foreign countries. Among the latter, I might mention the great philosopher, historian, poet, deist, etc., Volney, who spent the winter of 1805 with the Judge, in quest of knowledge. It is said that his visit to this part of the country was to see and examine the mounds.

"Whether the great antiquarian found anything to further his purposes may be inferred from the fact that a large portion of his 'Ruins' was written in the then splendid red mansion of Judge Benjamin Foy. The old escritoire, belonging to the Judge, on which Volney wrote, remained in the family until the old man's death. Judge Overton, M. B. Winchester, John M. Lea and others made efforts to obtain it, but it seemed neither of those succeeded.

"The notorious Aaron Burr also made frequent visits to the Point about the same time, though I have not heard that the Judge, or any of the settlers, were suspected of being connected with his supposed schemes or expeditions."

1809.

Soon after the occupancy of Louisiana by the United States, people from the western states began to move slowly into this remote region, gradually augmenting the number in all the old French settlements and in the vicinity of the American posts.

The greatest immigration was to the settlements in the vicinity of Cape Girardeau, Ste. Genevieve, St. Louis and St. Charles, and those of New Madrid and the Post of Arkansas were also augmented, but in less degree, by frontier settlers.

That the reader and student of American institutions may learn some of the silent, but potent influences of the law upon citizens under our form of government, his attention is called to the following facts. By an act of Congress in 1804, the Territory of Louisiana was made subject to the jurisdiction of the Territory of Indiana with the seat of government at Vincennes. This jurisdiction then extended over the territory now embraced within the states of Illinois, Indiana, Missouri and Arkansas, the legislative authority of this vast territory being vested in a governor and judges appointed by the President. By an act of Congress on the 3rd of February, 1809, the organization of the Territory of Illinois was authorized, its government being inaugurated on the 25th of April, 1809, thus detaching it from Louisiana. A citizen of Louisiana was appointed the first secretary and acting governor. Being duly commissioned by the President, the oath of office was administered to him on the 25th of April of the same year, by one of the United States judges for the Territory of Louisiana.

All these transfers of government from the jurisdiction of one territory to that of another, under acts of Congress, were accomplished by the simple process of administering a formal oath to the person appointed to assume the duties of the office.

After the death of Governor Lewis in 1809, President Madison appointed Benjamin A. Howard, of Kentucky, governor of the Territory of Louisiana.

On the 29th of October, 1809, acting governor Bates appointed Daniel Mooney, Sheriff of the District of Arkansas, and on the 16th of November, he appointed James B. Waterman, Clerk and Recorder for the district.

ARKANSAS COUNTY.

1810.

On the 27th of September, 1810, Governor Benjamin A. Howard appointed Patrick Cassady, Judge of Probate and Clerk and Recorder of the District of Arkansas.

The population of the district at this time was **one thousand and sixty-two** persons. This population was divided as follows: Hopefield and St. Francis, **one hundred and eighty-eight**; and on the Arkansas or Arkansas Post, **eight hundred and seventy-four.**

In 1810, Governor Howard resigned and Captain William Clark, the companion of Merriwether Lewis in the celebrated trip of exploration through the Rocky Mountains and the valley of the Columbia river, was appointed by President Madison, Governor of the Territory of Louisiana.

1811.

On the 20th of February, 1811, Congress authorized the Territorial Assembly of Orleans to choose representatives to form a constitution, the election of these representatives being appointed for the third Monday in September of that year.

The delegates of this constitutional convention met on the 4th of November, 1811, in New Orleans, but adjourned until the eighteenth of the same month. After adopting a constitution, the convention adjourned, **sine die,** on the 28th of January, 1812.

By the provisions of this constitution, the name of the Territory of Orleans was changed to the State of Louisiana, which was, by an act of Congress of April 8th, 1812, admitted as one of the United States of America.

The change of the name of the Territory of Orleans to the State of Louisiana, necessitated a change in name for the Territory of Louisiana, consequently, on the 4th of June, 1812, Congress passed an act providing "that the district heretofore called Louisiana, shall hereafter be called Missouri Territory, and that the temporary government of the Territory of Missouri shall be organized and administered in the manner hereinafter prescribed."

It was in this year, 1811, that this country experienced the first of a series of earthquake shocks. On the 16th of December, the citizens of New Madrid, Missouri, and the surrounding country, felt a violent motion of the earth and for several months these shocks occurred with some frequency. New Madrid and the surrounding country seem to have been near the center of the great commotion, but a vast area of territory bears evidence of having been affected by it. Since a portion of the territory once embraced within the limits of Arkansas County was influenced by these shocks, an account of the occurrence, in the following letter, which gives the reader a full and correct description of the scenes and incidents connected with the phenomenal event, is thought to be of interest.

FROM 1804 TO 1812.

New Madrid, Territory of Miss.
March 22, 1816.

Dear Sir:
In compliance with your request, I will now give you a history, as full in detail as the limits of a letter will permit, of the late awful visitation of Providence in this vicinity. On the 16th of December, 1811, about two o'clock A. M., we were visited by a violent shock of an earthquake, accompanied by a very awful noise, resembling loud, but distant thunder, but more hoarse and vibrating, which was followed in a few moments by the complete saturation of the atmosphere with sulphurous vapor, causing total darkness.

The screams of the affrighted inhabitants, running to and fro, not knowing where to go or what to do, cries of the fowls and beasts of every species, the cracking of falling trees and the roaring of the Mississippi, the current of which was retrograde for a few moments, owing, as is supposed, to an eruption in its bed, formed a scene truly horrible.

From that time until about sunrise, a number of slight shocks occurred, at which time one, still more violent than the first, took place with the same accompaniments as the first, and the terror which had been excited in every one, and, indeed, in all animal nature, was, now, if possible, doubled. The inhabitants fled in every direction to the country, supposing, if it can be admitted that their minds were exercised at all, that there was less danger at a distance from, than near the river. In one person, a female, the alarm was so great that she fainted and could not be recovered.

There were several shocks in a day, but lighter, until the 23rd of January, 1812, when one occurred as violent as the severest of the former ones, accompanied by the same phenomena as the former. From this time until the 4th of February, the earth was in constant agitation, visibly waving as a gentle sea. On that day there was another shock, nearly as hard as the preceding ones. Next day, four shocks and on the 7th, at about four o'clock A. M., a concussion took place, so much more violent than those that had preceded it, that it was the hard shock. The awful darkness of the atmosphere, which, as formerly, was saturated with sulphurous vapor, and the violence of the tempestuous, thundering noise that accompanied it, together with all other phenomena mentioned as attending the former ones, formed a scene the description of which will require the most sublimely fanciful imagination. At first, the Mississippi seemed to recede from its banks and its waters gathered up like a mountain, leaving for a moment, many boats, which were here on their way to New Orleans, on the bare sand, in which time the poor sailors made their escape from them. It, then, rising fifteen or twenty feet perpendicularly, and expanding, as it were, at the same moment, the banks were overflowed with a retrograde current. The boats, which before had been left on the sand, were now torn from their moorings and suddenly driven up a little creek at the mouth of which they lay, to the distance in some instances, of nearly a quarter of a mile. The river, falling immediately, as rapidly as it had risen, receded within its banks again with such violence that it took whole groves of young cotton-wood trees, which hedged its borders. They were broken off with such regularity, in some instances, that persons who had not witnessed the fact, could be, with difficulty, persuaded that it had not been the work of art. A great many fish were left on the banks, living, unable to keep pace with the water. The river was literally covered with the wreck of boats and it seemed that one was wrecked, in which there were a lady and six children, all of whom were lost.

In all the hard shocks mentioned, the earth was horribly torn to pieces. The surface of hundreds of acres was, from time to time, covered over of various depths by the sand which issued from the fissures, which were made in great numbers all over the country, some of which closed up immediately after they had vomited forth their sand and water, which, it must be remembered, was the matter generally thrown up. In some places, however, there was a substance somewhat resembling coal or impure stone coal, thrown up with the sand. It is impossible to say what the depth of the fissures or irregular breaks was. We have reason to believe that some of them were very deep.

The site of this town was evidently settled down at least fifteen feet, and not more than half a mile below the town, there does not appear to be any alteration in the bank of the river, but back from the river a small distance, the numerous large ponds or lakes, as they were called, which covered a great part of the country, were nearly dried up. The beds of some of them are elevated above their former banks several feet, producing an alteration of ten, fifteen or twenty feet from their original state. And, lately, it has been discovered that a lake was formed on the opposite side of the Mississippi, in the Indian country, upwards of one hundred miles in length and from one to six miles in width, of a depth of from ten to fifty feet. It has communication with the river at both ends and it is conjectured that it will not be many years before the principal part, if not the whole of the Mississippi will pass that way.

We were constrained, by fear of our house falling, to live twelve or eighteen months after the first shock, in little light camps made of boards, but we gradually became callous and returned to our house again. Most of those who fled from the country in the time of the hard shocks, have since returned home.

We have, since their commencement in 1811, continued to feel slight shocks occasionally. It is seldom, indeed, that we are more than a week without feeling one and sometimes three or four in a day. There were two this winter past, much harder than we have felt them for two years before, but since then they appear to be lighter than they have ever been, and we begin to hope that ere long, they will entirely cease.

I have now, sir, finished my promised description of the earthquake, imperfect, it is true, but just as it occurred to my memory, many of and most of the truly awful scenes having occurred three or four years ago. They, of course, are not related with that precision which would entitle it to the character of a full and correct picture, but such as it is, it is given with pleasure, in the full confidence that it is given to a friend.

And now, sir, wishing you all good, I must bid you adieu.
ELIZA BRYAN.

The Rev. Lorenzo Dow.

P. S. There is one circumstance which I think worthy of remark. This country was formerly subject to very hard thunder, but, for more than a twelvemonth before the commencement of the earthquake, there was none at all and but very little since, a great part of which resembles subterraneous thunder. The shocks still continue, but are growing more light and less frequent.

E. B.

The effects of the earthquake referred to in the letter extended south into the District of Arkansas, evidences of which are visible at this time in the counties of Mississippi, Poinsett, Craighead, Green, Cross and Clay, and, probably in others adjoining some of these, this territory being commonly known as the "sunk lands of the St. Francis." It extends south into the state of Arkansas for a distance of about seventy miles, with a width, east and west, of about twenty miles.

Mr. Hempstead, in his excellent history of Arkansas, tells us that in the year 1811, the Rev. John P. Carnahan, a Cumberland Presbyterian preacher, "preached the first protestant sermon ever preached in Arkansas" and that "it was delivered at Arkansas Post."

CHAPTER VIII.

From the Organization of the Territory of Missouri in 1812, to the Establishment of the Territory of Arkansas in 1819.

The first notable event of the year 1812, connected with the history of the District of Arkansas, was the successful trip of the first steamer down the Mississippi along the eastern boundary of the district in the early days of January.

This was the steamer New Orleans, which was built at Pittsburgh Pennsylvania, under the direction of Mr. Roosevelt, of New York, and was on its way from Pittsburgh to New Orleans. The boat left Pittsburgh in Oct., 1811. Roosevelt, his wife and family, Mr. Baker, the engineer, Andrew Jack, the pilot and six hands with a few domestics, constituted the officers, crew and passengers. At Louisville, Ky., the boat was detained because of low water, which prevented her crossing the falls at that place, until sometime in December, 1811. This caused her to pass through the scenes of the great earthquake of 1811-1812.

Mr. Bradford, who went on board the steamer at Natchez, says: "On the morning of the 6th instant, (January, 1812), I went on board the steamer from Pittsburgh. She had passed us at the mouth of the Arkansas, three hundred and forty miles above Natchez. She was a very handsome vessel of four hundred and ten tons burden, and was impelled by a powerful engine, also made at Pittsburgh, from whence she had come in less than twenty days, although nineteen hundred miles distant." Mr. Bradford must have had reference to the running time of the boat, as the trip was begun in October, 1811.

The Territory of Orleans, in assuming the rank of an independent state, had adopted the name of the "State of Louisiana" and it was deemed expedient to change the name of the Territory of Louisiana. An act of Congress, passed June 4th, 1812, provided for the organization of a representative grade of territorial government upon the west side of the Mississippi, including all the settlements north of the western portion of the present State of Louisiana. This territory extended from latitude 33 degrees to 41 degrees north, and was known and designated as the "Missouri Territory." Its western limit was the Indian and Mexican territories in the remote west, five hundred miles beyond the Mississippi. St. Louis was made the seat of the Territorial government, and headquarters of the Governor and Superintendent of Indian Affairs.

By the provisions of this act, the General Assembly was to consist of the Governor, a Legislative Council and House of Representatives.

At the first election, there were to be thirteen representatives, the Governor dividing the territory into thirteen precincts for convenience in this election, previous to October 1st, 1812.

FROM 1812 TO 1819.

The first representatives were to meet in St. Louis the first Monday in December, 1812, and nominate eighteen persons to the President of the United States, who should appoint nine of them as members of the Legislative Council. The act also provided that the Governor should convene the first General Assembly as soon as convenient after the appointment of the Legislative Council.

On October 1st, 1812, Governor Howard issued his proclamation announcing that the Territory of Missouri would begin operations on the first day of December, 1812.

The first meeting of the House of Representatives to select a Legislative Council was held at the house of Major Peter Chouteau, Sr. This was on the 7th of December, 1812, the following being the members of the house:

St. Charles—John Pittman and Robert Spencer.

St. Louis—David Music, Bernard G. Farrar, Wm. C. Carr and Richard Caulk.

Ste. Genevieve—George Bullet, Richard S. Thomas and Isaac Mc Gready.

Cape Girardeau—George F. Bollinger and Stephen Byrd.

New Madrid—John Strader and Samuel Phillips.

The House of Representatives proceeded to nominate eighteen persons from whom the President of the United States, with the Senate, was to select nine for the council, and out of the number thus named, the following were chosen:

St. Charles—James Flaugherty and Benjamin Emmons.

St. Louis—Auguste Chouteau, Sr., and Samuel Hammond.

Ste. Genevieve—John Scott and James Maxwell.

Cape Girardeau—William Neeley and Joseph Cavenor.

New Madrid—Joseph Hunter.

The fact that these persons had been appointed and confirmed members of the temporary council was officially announced by acting Governor Bates in a proclamation dated June 3rd, 1813. This proclamation also fixed the first Monday of July, following, for the meeting of the General Assembly.

Billon, in his "Annals of St. Louis" quoting from the Missouri Gazette of December 19th, 1812, says:

"Governor Howard's proclamation of the 1st of October, dividing the Territory into five districts or counties and apportioning their representation, based upon the United States census of 1810.

First. St. Charles, north of the Missouri river, to have **two** members.

Second. St. Louis to Platin Creek, to have **four** members.

Third. Ste. Genevieve to Apple Creek to have **three** members.

Fourth. Cape Girardeau to have **two** members.

Fifth. New Madrid to the 33rd degree, to have **two** members; thirteen in all; and ordering the election on the second Monday of November (9th) next, and returns of same to be made to the Governor.

House of Representatives.

1812, Monday, December 7th, from the Journal. First Session.

The House assembled pursuant to the Governor's proclamation,

ARKANSAS COUNTY.

in a room of the house of Peter Chouteau, Sr., and were qualified by Judge J. B. C. Lucas.

Present:

From St. Charles—John Pittman and Robert Spencer, 2.

From St. Louis—David Musick, Bernard G. Farrar, Wm. C. Carr and Richard Caulk, 4.

From Ste. Genevieve—George Bullit, Richard S. Thomas and Isaac McGready, 3.

From Cape Girardeau—George F. Bollinger and Stephen Byrd, 2.

From New Madrid—John Strader and Samuel Phillips, 2. Thirteen in all.

Hon. Wm. C. Carr was elected Speaker, pro. tem., and Thos. F. Riddick, Clerk, pro. tem.; adjourned.

Tuesday, December 8th—A committee on Rules and a committee to wait on acting Gov. Bates, were appointed; adjourned.

Wednesday, December 9th—Wm. C. Carr elected permanent Speaker.

They were in session six days and adjourned on Saturday, December 12th, without day, their only business being to select eighteen persons to be submitted to the President of the United States, to select therefrom, nine to compose the legislative council of the territory. And electing Andrew Scott, clerk of the House."

It will be seen from the foregoing quotation that at the time the District of Arkansas was embraced within the representative District of New Madrid and was represented in the first House of Representatives by John Strader and Samuel Phillips.

By an act of Congress of the 6th of May, 1812, six million acres of land was directed to be surveyed and set apart for the purpose of satisfying the land bounties promised the soldiers of 1812, two million acres to be between the St. Francis and Arkansas rivers. To satisfy these claims, warrants were issued to soldiers and could only be laid on lands in the military districts of Illinois, Missouri and Arkansas.

"The great mass of warrants issued for that service has been satisfied under a lottery system, by locations in Illinois, Arkansas and Missouri."

About four hundred and seventy of these warrants, covering some seventy-five thousand, two hundred acres were located on lands in the present limits of Arkansas County.

By the treaty between France and the United States, the latter government agreed to protect each inhabitant in the ceded territory in his property, franchise and religion.

In fulfillment of this agreement, Congress, on June 13th, 1812, passed an act confirming to the inhabitants and villages or towns within the territory, their several rights to "town or village lots, out lots, common field lots and commons in, adjoining and belonging to the several villages." One of these villages was the village of Arkansas or Arkansas Post, as it is now known.

1813.

The first session of the Missouri Territorial Legislature convened in St. Louis on Monday, July 5th, 1813.

FROM 1812 TO 1819.

The Legislative Council had been chosen by the President of the United States, from the list of names presented to him by the House of Representatives of the Territorial Legislature at its December term, 1812, and was composed of the following gentlemen: James Flaugherty and Benjamin Emmons, St. Charles; Auguste Chouteau and Samuel Hammond, St. Louis; John Scott and James Maxwell, Ste. Genevieve; William Neeley and George Cavenor, Cape Girardeau; and Joseph Hunter, New Madred.

On the day appointed for the meeting of the General Assembly, "both houses united in an address to the new governor, Wm. Clark, signed by Wm. C. Carr, Speaker of the House of Representatives, and Samuel Hammond, President of the Council."

"The Governor being absent on public business, his reply to the address was not received until July 26th."

"Owing to the war, the special session soon terminated—no official journal of its acts was ever published."

Such were the first steps taken in the establishment of representative government, within the limits of the Territory of Missouri, which, at that time, included the territory constituting the present State of Arkansas.

On Monday, December 6th, 1813, the second session of the first Territorial Legislature convened in St. Louis.

"Present:

George Bullitt, George F. Bollinger, Stephen Byrd, Wm. C. Carr, Richard Caulk, Bernard G. Farrar, John Pittman, John Shrader, Robert Spencer, 9; George Bullitt was elected Speaker, Andrew Scott, Clerk, and Wm. Sullivan, Doorkeeper, and house adjourned.

Tuesday, 7th. Isaac McGready in his seat, as also Samuel Phillips, New Madrid; Messrs. Pittman and Caulk, a committee to wait on the Governor.

Wednesday, 8th. The Governor met both branches of the Legislature in the Representative Chamber and delivered his address.

9th and 10th. Richard S. Thomas, Ste. Genevieve, and Barnabas Harris, St. Louis, in their seats."

During this session of the Legislature, on January 4th, 1814, an act regulating elections was passed. This act provided that elections should be held on the first Monday in August, 1814, and every second year thereafter, the Legislature to meet on the first Monday in December.

By an act of this Legislature, dated December 31st, 1813, the county of Arkansas was created. The boundaries, as designated by this act, were as follows: "All that portion of the territory bounded north by the south line of the county of New Madrid, east, by the main channel of the Mississippi, south, by the thirty-third degree of north latitude, or north boundary of the State of Louisiana, west by the western boundary of the Osage purchase and by a line to commence upon the river Arkansas, where the boundary line of the Osage purchase intersects the same, thence in a direct line to the main source of the Ouachita, thence south to the northern boundary line of the State of Louisiana, or thirty-third degree of north latitude, shall compose a

ARKANSAS COUNTY.

county and be called and known by the name of the County of Arkansas."

The line dividing Arkansas and New Madrid counties, as referred to in the above described boundaries of Arkansas county, begins at the lower end of Island No. 19 in the Mississippi river. This island, as shown on the chart of the Mississippi river, made by Samuel Cummins from his own actual survey in 1819-1820-1821, and published in his "Western Pilot" in 1836, is about forty miles, by the course of the river, below New Madrid, and about where the line of the public survey, dividing townships seventeen and eighteen, north of the base line, passing east and west through the State of Arkansas, strikes the Mississippi river. From this point, the line dividing these counties, runs in a southwest direction to the mouth of Little Red river, on the line, at a subsequent date, dividing the counties of Jackson and White, thence up Little Red river to its source, near the line dividing the counties of Pope and Van Buren. From this point the line runs west to the Osage purchase, the western boundary of the state, thence south to the north boundary of the State of Louisiana, thence east, with this boundary to the Mississippi river and from here up the main channel of the river to the place of beginning.

Within the limits of the county as thus created, and outside the present limits of the county, at the time of its formation there were settlements at Ecore a Fabre, (the present site of the city of Camden), Arkadelphia, Hot Springs, on or near the Ouachita river, at Point Chicot, at Montgomery's Point, on the Mississippi river, above and near the mouth of White river, at Helena, at the mouth of the St. Francis river, at Hopefield or Foy's Point, opposite the present city of Memphis; at Greenoch and probably other points on the Mississippi river, at Madison and Wittsburgh on the St. Francis, at Clarendon, Des Arc and Augusta on White river, at Pine Bluff and Little Rock on the Arkansas and at Washington in Hempstead county.

There was also a settlement on Cooper's Creek in the present limits of Cross county, not far from the town of Wittsburgh. This settlement was made as early as 1798 by Samuel Fillighan, who was living there when Nicholas Righter surveyed, for William Russell, Spanish Grants Nos. 494, 495, 498, 2379, 2332, 2383, 2374, 2375 and 2387, in the year 1813. Fillighan purchased from Russell, eighty-four acres off the southwest part of Spanish Grant No. 498, the deed conveying the same bearing date of July 25th, 1820. Wittsburgh appears to be located on Spanish Grant No. 2379.

The dates and extent of the settlements referred to, the writer has no means of ascertaining, except the settlement of Fillighan, nor does he presume to say that there were no other settlements in the county at the time of its establishment.

1814.

By an act of Congress passed on the 27th of January, 1814, an additional judge was appointed for the Territory of Missouri, who should reside at or near the village of Arkansas. Under this act, the judges were required "to hold two terms in each and every year in the village of Arkansas Post."

FROM 1812 TO 1819.

In accordance with this act, George Bullit, of Missouri, was, on the 9th of February, 1814, appointed judge.

On the 23rd of June, 1814, Governor William Clark issued his proclamation, stating the number of members of the General Assembly, and ordering an election to be held on the first Monday in August.

During this year, a census was taken, showing the population of each county and the number of members of the Legislature to which each county was entitled. This census was as follows:

	Population.	No. Members.
St. Charles,	1696	3
St. Louis,	3149	6
Washington,	1010	2
Ste. Genevieve,	1741	3
Cape Girardeau,	2022	4
New Madrid,	1548	3
Arkansas,	827	1

Under this apportionment, the first session of the second Territorial Legislature met at St. Louis on Monday, the 5th of December, 1814. The journal of this session, as given by Billon in his "Annals of St. Louis" shows that all counties as above enumerated, were fully represented, except the county of Arkansas; the names of the representatives from each county being given.

Pope in his "Early Days in Arkansas" says: "Col. Alexander Walker represented Arkansas county in the Territorial Legislature of Missouri, when what is now the state of Arkansas, constituted one county of Missouri Territory."

In a foot note on page 68 of Prof. Shinn's "School History of Arkansas," he says: "One member or delegate represented Arkansas Post and Col. Alexander Walker was chosen by the people for that office."

In his statement, Pope gives no date at which Walker is supposed to have represented Arkansas county, but Prof. Shinn places his statement under date of 1812.

The reader will remember that the act creating Arkansas County was passed on December 31st, 1813, and the county was not organized until the year 1814, her citizens beig represented in the Legislature previous to this date, by a member from New Madrid county; that the first election after the organization of Arkansas county was held in August, 1814, and since elections were held biennially, the second election for representatives did not occur till 1816.

The first session of the Territorial Legislature after the creation of the county of Arkansas, convened on the 5th of December, 1814, at which time the journal fails to show the name of a representative from Arkansas county. At the next session, which convened on December 4, 1815, the name of Henry Cassady appears on the journal of the House of Representatives as the member from Arkansas county, showing conclusively that Henry Cassady was the first representative of the county. As there had been no election in the county since the one of August 1814, he must have been elected at that time, but failed to attend the session of December 1814.

The first record of judicial proceedings in the county after its organization, shows that on June 20th, 1814, the will of Louis Gocio

ARKANSAS COUNTY.

was filed and probated before Patrick Cassady, Judge of Probate, in the county, and that Letters Testamentary were granted to John Dudley and Catharine Dudley, and that on that day they filed, in said court, an inventory of the personal property belonging to the estate. A copy of this inventory follows:

"One negro woman, about forty years old.
One negro girl about fourteen years old.
One roan horse,
One gray mare,
One gray colt,
One bay mare,
One young colt,
One mule,
Seven cows,
Two calves,
Five heifers,
Four yearling steers,
One bull,
Twenty-two head of cattle,
Stock of hogs, number unknown,
Sixteen head of sheep,
Six silver spoons,
Six knives,
Two and a half dozen plates,
Four dishes,
Six bowls,
Eighteen cups and saucers,
One pitcher,
Three beds and furniture,
One cubboard, **(cupboard)**
One small cubboard,
One small trunk,
One loom and two slays,
Four plows,
Six small hoes,
Six axes,
One pair drawing chains,
Three pairs of tugs,
One drawing chain,
Sundry old burnt irons,
One drawing knife,
Three augers,
One foot-adds, **(adze)**
Three kettles,
One oven,
One frying pan,
One grid-iron,
Four smoothing irons,
One horse cart,
Three old saddles,
Four pairs bridle bitts,

FROM 1812 TO 1819.

One pair dog-irons,
One case of razors,
One pair of spurs,
One shot-gun,
Forty-one bee stands,
One demi-john,
One bottle,
One pail,
One small pail,
Two straw baskets,
One chain,
One cotton wheel,
Two pairs of cards,
   (cotton)
One grind stone,
One flax wheel,

One crop of corn standing in the field in the fall of 1813.
One crop of cotton standing in the field in the fall of 1813.
Nine hogs sent to Orleans.
Six hogs killed for the use of the family.
Three hogs sold Don Carlos de Villemont to discharge a contract by Louis Gorceaux.
One beef killed for the use of the family, of which Don Carlos de Villemont got 107 lbs. in discharge of a debt contracted by Louis Garceaux.
Three iron wedges.
Four horses, running at large on the prairie."

On June 3rd, 1814, Governor William Clark appointed Joseph Stillwell, Judge of the Court of Common Pleas, in and for the county of Arkansas, and on the 4th day of the same month, he appointed Samuel Mosley and Francis de Vaugine, judges of said court.

1815.

The second session of the second Legislature of the Missouri Territory convened at St. Louis on Monday, December 4th, 1815, at which time Henry Cassady appeared as the representative from Arkansas county. Cassady was the first representative of the county in the legislative councils of the territory, no member of the council having been appointed from Arkansas county.

"In 1815, the first surveys of the public lands by the government, was begun in Arkansas, between the Arkansas and St. Francis rivers, in the district designated by Congress to satisfy the claims of the soldiers of the war of 1812."

The Surveyor-general for the district, then composed of the territories of Illinois, Missouri and Arkansas, was William Rector, with headquarters or general land office at St. Louis.

Preliminary to surveying the lands in the Arkansas and Missouri districts, a principal meridian and base line were necessary for the purpose of describing the lands on the plats of the public surveys, by means whereof the designated tract of land could be locally identified. Consequently a meridian and base line were established.

ARKANSAS COUNTY.

The initial point of the meridian was at the mouth of the Arkansas river, and that of the base line, at the mouth of the St. Francis river, both points being, at the time of their establishment, within the limits of Arkansas county. As to the date of their establishment, I have been unable to learn the exact time, but it was between the 6th of May, 1812, and the 1st of January, 1816.

"This meridian was designated the fifth principal meridian and is coincident with 90° 58' longitude, west from Greenwich."

The common base line runs due west from the mouth of the St. Francis river, across the state.

The war existing between the United States and England from June 1812 until the 8th of January, 1815, had practically suspended the public surveying in this district, as well as retarded immigration to the same.

"About the close of the year 1815," however, "a new impulse was given to emigration west of the Mississippi."

"The American settlements began to extend rapidly, and literally overran those of the French in their course."

"The French, becoming gradually weaned from their partiality for a wilderness life, for Indian association and Indian trade, began to entertain a common feeling as American citizens, with their new neighbors, who had settled among them."

Deed Record A, dated July 15th, 1815, shows that at that time John Dodge was Clerk and Recorder of Arkansas county, but the date of his appointment is not shown.

1816.

By an act of Congress of April 29th, 1816, the sessions of the Territorial Legislature were changed from annual to biennial, the act requiring the Legislature "to meet once in every other year at St. Louis and such meetings shall be on the first Monday in December, unless they shall by law appoint a different day." This also authorized the election of one member of the Legislative Council, who should hold his office two years in addition to the number of representatives to which a county was entitled.

The third Territorial Legislature met in St. Louis on Monday, the 2nd of December, 1816, under the election held in the several counties of the territory in August, 1816.

At this session the name of Edward Hogan appears as representative in the house and the name of James Cummins as councilman, from Arkansas County.

The second section of the above mentioned act provided "that the General Assembly of said territory shall be and is hereby authorized to require the judges of the Superior Court of said territory to hold Superior and Circuit Courts, to appoint the time and places of holding the same, under such rules and regulations as the General Assembly may, in that behalf, prescribe. The Circuit Court shall be composed of one of the said judges and shall have jurisdiction in all criminal cases, and exclusive, original jurisdiction in all those which are capital and original jurisdiction in all civil cases of the value of one hundred dollars; and the Superior and Circuit Courts shall possess and exercise chancery proceedings, as well as common law jurisdiction in all civil cases, provided that there shall be an appeal in matters of law and equity, in all cases, from the Circuit Court to the Superior Court of said territory."

The Superior Court of the Territory of Missouri, at this time, consisted of the following named judges: George Bullitt, who was required to reside at or near Arkansas Post, and Silas Bent, John B. C. Lucas and Alexander Stewart. Joshua Norval was Prosecuting Attorney and John Dodge, Clerk.

That the reader of the present day may know how expeditiously justice was legally dispensed, the following judgment, copied from the docket of Peter H. Bennett, a Justice of the Peace of Chicot township, Arkansas county, is given:

"May 26th, 1816.
"Joseph Hutsel,
vs.
Henry Hopkins.

Warrant issued forthwith on an account, and tried this day. Judgment found for the plaintiff, three dollars and eighty-seven and a half cents. Execution issued the 15th of May (?), 1816, and settled by the defendant before me.

PETER H. BENNETT, J. P.

Deputy Constable, W. Peterson.

Cost, 50 cents. Justice's cost, 75 cents. Costs paid."

The population of Arkansas county at this time was **one thousand and sixty-two**, Hopefield having **one hundred and eighty-eight** and settlements on the Arkansas river **eight hundred and seventy-four**.

1817.

On the 17th of August, 1817, John Menear, John Butey and Samuel Blanchard, three flat-boatsmen, appeared before Peter H. Bennett and made oath of protest against loss of a cargo of tobacco shipped in flat-boat No. 10, belonging to Bennett and Read and consigned to Clifford and Snead of New Orleans. On the 27th of August, Peter H. Bennett, Justice of the Peace, issued a warrant to John Wilkinson, directing him to sell, as quick as possible, a hogshead of tobacco weighing one thousand, three hundred and fifteen pounds, found floating in the river, and on the 29th of this month Wilkinson made return of the sale of said tobacco, showing that it was sold for four dollars and twenty-five cents. The fees reported were as follows: Constable's fee, seventy-one and one-fourth cents; justice's fee, twenty-five cents; salvage to the taker-up, sixty-three and three-fourth cents; and an allowance for extra services, seventy-five cents.

The record of Esquire Bennett as Justice of the Peace, shows that between the 30th of May, 1816, and the 7th of January, 1819, he duly joined in marriage sixteen couples.

By a treaty entered into between the Cherokee Indians and the United States on the 8th of July, 1817, the Cherokees ceded all their territory in the states of Tennessee and Alabama to the United States, which necessitated their finding new homes. These they desired to obtain west of the Mississippi river, and, on application to the President,

ARKANSAS COUNTY.

were permitted to send an exploring party through the country between the Arkansas and White rivers, in the, then, Missouri Territory.

These Indians selected a tract of country extending from the north side of the Arkansas river, at the mouth of Point Remove Bayou, northwards, in a straight line to Chalanga Mountain, the first hill above Shield's Ferry on White river, and westward between these rivers.

All that part of said tract lying along the Arkansas river was, at the time, in the county of Arkansas.

"The first post-office established in the limits of the territory now constituting the State of Arkansas, was at Davidsonville, in the county of Lawrence, in June, 1817, the next at Arkansas Post in July, 1817. The mail furnishing these offices was carried on horseback from St. Louis, through Davidsonville and Arkansas Post to Monroe, Louisiana, and delivered at these places once in every thirty days."

The tax book for the year 1817, shows that the sum of one hundred seventy-seven dollars and twenty-two cents had been assessed for territorial purposes on the taxable property then in the county, consisting of town lots, dwelling houses, slaves, and pleasure carriages, numbered and valued as follows:

Town Lots, No. 13, Valued at $816.
Dwelling-houses, No. 109, Valued at $9,450.
Slaves, No. 206, No value given.
Pleasure Carriages, No. 2, Valued at $250.

For county purposes, the assessment on the following described property was as follows:

Cattle over three years old—No. 2,776.
Horses and mules over three years old—No. 1,034.
Stud Horses—No. 1.
Slaves between fifteen and forty-five years of age—No. 131.
Billiard Tables—None.
Single Men—No. 86.
Water, Grist and Saw Mills—No. 6.
Value, $1,000..
Tan yards—None.
Distilleries—None.
Total tax for county purposes........................$604.96
Total tax for territorial purposes..................... 177.22

Grand Total $782.18

1818.

An act of Congress of the 17th of February, 1818, provided for the establishment of land offices in the Territory of Missouri. One was directed to be established in the county of Arkansas, at such place as the President should deem most convenient for all the lands in the district, bounded as follows: beginning on the river Mississippi at the thirty-third degree of north latitude, thence up and with the Mississippi river to the mouth of the St. Francis, where the base line intersects the same; from this point, west, with the base line to where the same intersects the meridian on which the Osage boundary line is

FROM 1812 TO 1819.

run, thence due south to the thirty-third parallel of latitude and thence east, with this parallel to the place of beginning.

The office was established at Arkansas Post in 1820 and William Douglas Simms, of Alexandria, Virginia, was appointed to be Register and Henry W. Conway, Receiver of Public Moneys.

William Rector, as Surveyor-general of this district, was directed in August, 1818, by Josiah Meigs, Commissioner of the General Land Office, to begin the surveying of sixty townships for actual sale. The work was finished in 1819, but none of the land was sold until 1821.

On the 24th of August, 1818, the United States entered into a treaty with the Quapaw Indians, by which the Indians ceded to the United States, all their land, from a point ninety miles below the mouth of the Arkansas river westward to the Big Raft on Red river, and northward to the Arkansas river, except the central portion. This reserved territory was nearly a parallelogram in shape, extending from a point on the south bank of the Arkansas river opposite the Post of Arkansas, in a southwest direction to the Ouachita river; thence up that river and up the Saline river until a due north line would strike the river at Little Rock.

On the 31st of August, 1818, Governor Clark issued a proclamation calling the Legislature of the Territory of Missouri, in extra session, to meet on the 24th of October, of this year. At this session, Edward Hogan appeared as representative, and Henry Cassady, as councilman from Arkansas county. On December 23rd, 1818, the Legislature adjourned sine die, this being the last session of said Legislature to convene in the Territory of Missouri. But, before adjournment, the Legislature, on the 15th of December, passed an act creating three new counties in the territory. These were Pulaski, Clark and Hempstead. By establishing these counties, all that portion of said territory lying north and west of a line beginning at the mouth of Little Red river, now in White county, running thence to the mouth of Plum Bayou, now in Jefferson county, thence up the Arkansas river to the old Quapaw line, below Little Rock, thence south to the south fork of the Saline river, down this river to the Ouachita and down the Ouachita to the Louisiana state line, was detached from, and ceased to be a part of Arkansas county.

That the reader of the present day may know how the government provided for her soldiery in barracks or forts, at this time, the following notice from the "Raleigh Register and North Carolina Gazette" of September 25th, 1818, is inserted here.

"Office of the Commissary General of Subsistence, Washington City, August 25, 1818.

This is to give notice that separate proposals will be received at the office of the Commissary General of Subsistence, until the 20th of November next, inclusive, for the supply of rations for the use of the troops of the United States, to be delivered in bulk upon inspection as follows": (Here follows the names of twenty places or stations at which supplies are wanted. The eighteenth number of these stations is Arkansas Post, at which place the United States had a fort, for which the following military supplies were wanted).

ARKANSAS COUNTY.

    40 cwt. of bacon.
    27 bbls. of pork.
    112 bushels of peas or beans.
    91 barrels of corn meal.
    61 barrels of flour.
    25 barrels of whiskey.
    9 cwt. of soap.
    375 lbs. of candles.
    16 bushels of salt.
    250 gallons of vinegar.

One half to be delivered on the first day of June, 1819, and the remainder on the first day of December, 1819.

Signed: By order of the Secretary of War.

                                  C. VANDEVENTER,
                           Acting Commissary of Subsistence.

August 28."

In consequence of the alleged indifference of Governor Clark to the interest of the citizens of Arkansas County, the citizens thereof, in June, 1818, caused a petition to be created, praying "The Honorable The Senate and House of Representatives of the United States of America in Congress Assembled, to declare that part of the Territory of Missouri which lies north of the north boundary line of the State of Louisiana and south of a line to be run due west from the Mississippi river on the thirty-sixth parallel of north latitude to the river St. Francis, thence up the middle of the main channel of the river St. Francis to the thirty-seventh parallel of north latitude, thence due west to the western boundary of the United States west of the Mississippi river be created as a separate territory by the name of the Territory of Arkansas."

Upon this petition it is supposed that Congress granted or passed the act of March, 1819. The foregoing description of the boundaries of the Territory are copied from a duplicate copy written at the date of the original, which is now before me, to which is attached the letter of date June 25th, 1818, from Wm. Russell to the late Judge J. B. C. Lucas, of St. Louis, soliciting his assistance in the matter.

CHAPTER IX.

From the Organization of the Territory of Arkansas in 1819, to the Removal of Capital from Arkansas Post to Little Rock in 1821.

On March 2nd, 1819, Congress passed an act declaring that all that portion of the Territory of Missouri south of a line beginning on the Mississippi river at thirty-six degrees north latitude, running thence west to the St. Francis river, thence up the same to thirty-six degrees thirty minutes north latitude, thence west to the western territorial boundary line, should for the purpose of territorial government, constitute a separate territory and be called Arkansas Territory.

The second section of this act, established in said territory, a temporary government, to consist of executive, legislative and judicial branches.

The third section empowered the President to appoint the Governor, who was to reside in the territory and be commander-in-chief of the militia, with power to appoint and commission all officers required by law for said territory.

The fourth section empowered the President to appoint a secretary for the territory, who was required to reside in said territory.

The fifth section of said act was as follows:

"That the legislative power shall, until the organization of the General Assembly, hereinafter provided for, be vested in the governor and the judges of the Superior Court of the territory, who shall have power to pass any law for the administration of justice in said territory, which shall not be repugnant to this act, or inconsistent with the constitution of the United States; provided, that whenever the General Assembly shall be organized all the legislative power of the territory shall be vested in and exercised by said General Assembly."

Section thirteen enacted, "That until otherwise directed by the legislative department of said Territory of Arkansas, the seat of territorial government thereof, shall be the Post of Arkansas on the Arkansas river."

President Monroe, by virtue of the authority vested in him by this act of Congress, on March 3rd, 1819, appointed James Miller, of New Hampshire, Governor, and Robert Crittenden, of Frankfort, Kentucky, Secretary of the territory.

On the 4th of July, 1819, Arkansas began her separate existence under the name of Arkansas Territory, Congress having declared that on that day the territories with boundaries as set forth in the act of Congress of March 2, 1819, should become a separate territorial government.

ARKANSAS COUNTY.

In speaking of the territory east of the St. Francis river, between thirty-six degrees and thirty-six degrees, thirty minutes north latitude, Professor Shinn in a post note on page 81 of his excellent "School History of Arkansas" says: "This makes a break in the northern boundary" (of Arkansas). "At this time, Missouri was seeking admission to the union as a state. In the district to the extreme southeast, there were some influential men who desired to be members of a state rather than of a territory; they worked with energy and they accomplished their purpose."

Campbell, in his Gazetteer of Missouri, giving a history of Dunklin county says: "Dunklin, Pemiscot and a small portion of New Madrid, geographically belonged to Arkansas, and when Missouri was admitted, they were left south of it. But the settlers of this section, who had been among the earliest pioneers on the western bank of the Mississippi and were closely allied in many ways with the people of the district of Cape Girardeau, were so urgent in their request to be admitted within the boundaries of the state, that this portion of territory was finally added."

Mr. Crittenden reached the territory in June, 1819, and as Governor Miller did not arrive until late in the year 1819, the duty of organizing the government devolved upon Secretary Crittenden, then in the twenty-second year of his age. "With courage and ability he entered upon the duties of his office and soon had the government in good working order. He appointed sheriffs and clerks for each of the counties and convened the first Territorial Legislature."

This body consisted of the governor and the judges appointed by the President. The judges were Charles Jouett, Robert Letcher and Andrew Scott.

The first territorial legislature in the Territory of Arkansas met at Arkansas Post on July 28th, 1819, Robert Crittenden acting as governor. Charles Jouett was elected speaker and George W. Scott, clerk.

This session lasted seven days. It established two circuit courts, created the offices of territorial auditor and treasurer and made the territorial laws of Missouri, of a public nature, applicable to Arkansas. George W. Scott was appointed the first auditor and James Scull the first treasurer.

Acting Governor Crittenden appointed Eli J. Lewis, the first circuit court clerk and Hewes Scull, the first sheriff for the county of Arkansas under the territorial laws of Arkansas.

One of the acts of the territorial legislature at its first session required the clerk of the Superior Court to procure a seal "purporting to be the seal of the Superior Court of the Territory of Arkansas."

The first term of the Circuit Court of Arkansas county organized under the act of the Territorial Legislature of Arkansas, convened at Arkansas Post on the first day of November, 1819, at which time, among others, the following proceedings were had.

"At a court begun and held at the village of Arkansas, on the first Monday of November, A. D., 1819, being the first day of said month, for the county of Arkansas.

"Whereupon, James Woodson Bates, Esq., being duly commissioned by the acting Governor of the territory, a judge for the first judicial circuit for the territory of Arkansas, took his seat as judge of the court.

"Court proclaimed by the sheriff, Hewes Scull, Esq., presenting in open court, his commission from the acting Governor, appointing him Sheriff of the County of Arkansas, which commission appears, from the certificate thereon, to be duly authenticated and recorded, with the oath of office endorsed thereon.

"Eli J. Lewis produced his commission as clerk of this court, which said commission appears, from the certificate thereon, to be duly recorded, and also the oath of office endorsed thereon.

"The Sheriff returned the following panel of grand jurors, viz:

1. Joseph Stillwell,
2. Harold Stillwell,
3. Jacob Barkman,
4. James Scull,
5. Frederic Notrebe,
6. Robert Allgore,
7. Shiloh Mather,
8. Patrick Cassady,
9. James Curren,
10. John Harrington,
11. Bartley Harrington,
12. James Young,
13. John McCartney,
14. John Taylor,
15. Richmond Peeler,
16. James S. Polet,
17. John Weane,
18. Peter H. Bennett,
19. Daniel H. Baldwin,
20. J. H. Cummins,
21. Samuel H. Rutherford,
22. Samuel Lemmons.

"Whereupon the following persons, being called, appeared and took the oath of grand jurors; were charged and retired to their room, viz:

Robert McKay, Foreman.
Harold Stillwell,
Frederic Notrebe,
Robert Allgore,
Shiloh Mather,
Richmond Peeler,
James S. Petit,
Peter H. Bennett,
Daniel H. Baldwin,
John Kepler,
Patrick Cassady,
John Harrington,
James Young,

ARKANSAS COUNTY.

J. H. Cummins,
Samuel H. Rutherford,
Samuel Lemmons,
John Taylor.

"On motion of the late members of the bar of the Arkansas court, viz: Perley Wallace, Alexander S. Walker, William O. Allen, Samuel C. Roan and Henry Cassady, they and each of them, having license and having practiced law under the government of the Missouri Territory, previous to the erection of the Arkansas Territory out of the Missouri Territory.

"It is therefore considered by the court that their license be good and valid in the territory and that they be permitted to practice law in this court.

"William Trimble, Alexander Copeland and Robert C. Oden, Esq., produced their several licenses as attorneys and took the oath prescribed by law in this court.

"William Trimble, Esq., being appointed Circuit Attorney by the acting Governor, he appeared in court and took the oath prescribed by law."

At this term of court, an application was made by John H. Cummins for a divorce from his wife, Elizabeth, which was granted. At this term of court, also, John Raphael Boucrine, a subject of the king of Great Britain, made application to become a citizen of the United States by filing an application to be naturalized. This was, by the court, granted.

These orders of court, one for divorce, the other for naturalization, are given as probably the first of the kind in the territory, if not west of the Mississippi.

Acting Governor Crittenden, soon after his installation as such, issued a proclamation declaring the Territory of Arkansas to be one of the second grade of governments, and ordering an election for a delegate to Congress. This election was held on November 20th, 1819. The candidates were James Woodson Bates, Henry Cassady, Alexander S. Walker, Perley Wallace and R. F. Slaughter. Bates was the successful candidate and thus became the first delegate to Congress from the Territory of Arkansas.

On the 26th of December, Governor Miller reached the territory and at once assumed the duties of the office, relieving acting Governor Crittenden, who had, from the organization of the government until this time, so promptly and efficiently discharged the arduous duties of governor of the territory.

Judge Witter, late of Hempstead county, who was an eye witness of the occurrence, thus describes Governor Miller's arrival:

"Gen. James Miller, the hero of Lundy's Lane and Fort Erie, who had been appointed by President Monroe, governor of the territory, arrived at Arkansas Post to enter upon the discharge of the duties of said office. He came up the river in a splendidly fitted up barge with large and well furnished cabin, having most of conveniences of modern steamboats. This boat had been fitted up, manned and furnished by the U. S. Government expressly for his use. On the after part of the cabin, on both sides, her name, Arkansas, was inscribed in large gilt letters. She had a tall mast from which floated a magnificent national banner, with the word 'Arkansas,' in large letters in the center and the words, 'I'll try, sir,' the motto of the regiment he commanded at Lundy's Lane, interspersed in several places."

There were, in 1819, settlements along the Arkansas and within the limits of the county, as far west as Plum bayou. The extent of these settlements will be seen from some extracts from a journal of travels made in this year by Thomas Nutall, which follow: "Proceeding from McLane's house of entertainment at the Mississippi river, we passed up White river to the cut-off, through the cut-off to the Arkansas river, which we entered on the 16th day of February, 1819. On the 19th, we reached the house of Madame Gordon, the first that was met with on ascending the river. A mile and a half from Madame Gordon's there was a settlement consisting of four or five French families, located upon an elevated tract of public land, which is occasionally isolated by the overflow of the White and Arkansas rivers." This settlement was, at this date, probably known at "Derresseaux Hill or Surround" and was situated about one half mile east of Arkansas river on the bank of Menard's Lake and five miles below the Post of Arkansas.

Arkansas Post, the most important settlement along the river at this time, is thus described: "The town, or rather settlement, of the Post of Arkansas, was somewhat dispersed over a prairie as elevated as the Chickasaw Bluffs and contained, in all, thirty or forty houses. The merchants there, who transact nearly all the business of the Arkansas and White rivers, were Messrs. Brehan and Drake, Mr. Lewis and Monsieur Notrebe. They kept well assorted stores of merchandise, shipped from New Orleans, with the exception of some heavy articles of domestic manufacture obtained from Pittsburgh."

In speaking of the settlement of this place, Nutall says: "The first attempt at settlement on the bank of the Arkansas was begun a few miles below the bayou which communicates with White river. An extraordinary inundation occasioned the removal of the garrison to the borders of the lagoon near Madame Gordon's, and, again disturbed by the overflow, they, at length, chose the present site of Arkansas."

In the foregoing statement Mr. Nutall gives no date, nor does he state of whom the garrison consisted, whether French, Spanish or American soldiers. Neither does he give any authority for such statement.

In a preceding paragraph, he says: "On this side of the Arkansas (the White river side) the flood covers the whole intermediate space to White river, a distance of thirty miles. Within this distance cultivation can never take place, without recourse to the same industry that has reclaimed Holland from the ocean."

This being true, it is not reasonable to suppose that for military or civic purposes such places as Nutall suggests would be selected for settlement, the building of a military post, or as the site for a colony, by either the government, under whose jurisdiction the country was at that time, or those that preceded it, owning that country, eligi-

ARKANSAS COUNTY.

ble for either purpose was known to exist at the highlands of Arkansas Post.

The year 1819, was the most eventful year in the history of the Territory of Arkansas, since in that year the said territory became a separate and distinct government with all the rights, powers and privileges of such government, under the constitution and laws of the United States.

As the events connected with the organization of this government transpired in the county of Arkansas and clustered around the village of Arkansas Post, their relation is of peculiar interest to the citizens of this county. For that reason, and that they may be transmitted to coming generations, the following items relating to the Post of Arkansas, its earlier enterprises and early settlers, are given.

William E. Woodruff was born on Long Island, New York, December 24th, 1795. In 1809, he worked in a printing office in Brooklyn, serving his apprenticeship therein. From there he went to Franklin, Tennessee, where he purchased a small printing press and printer's outfit, and had it carried to the Cumberland river. It was thence transported on a keel-boat, down the Cumberland to the Ohio, down the Ohio to the Mississippi, down the Mississippi to Montgomery's Point, near the mouth of White river, from here by pirougue (dug-out) up White river to the cut-off, through the cut-off to the Arkansas river, thence up that river to the Post of Arkansas, at which place he arrived, with his printing press and material, on the 30th day of October, 1819, having been nearly three months making the journey.

Arkansas Post was a mere collection of huts and small houses and contained a population of less than one hundred persons, mostly French and Indians, with very few Americans. At the Post, no house could be found in which to set up his printing press, but Mr. Woodruff soon had a log hut in which to place his printing outfit and issue his paper. He set up the type, did his own press work and editing.

The first number of his paper was issued Saturday, November 20th, 1819. It was celled the **"Arkansas Gazette"** and is still in existence at Little Rock, being the leading journal of the state.

On the 1st of April, 1820, Mr. Woodruff was, by resolution of the General Assembly, appointed public printer. He continued to print his paper at Arkansas Post until the 24th of November, 1821, on which day he issued the last paper at that place. On the removal of the capital to Little Rock in 1821, Woodruff moved his office there.

In 1873, Judge Daniel T. Witter wrote and had published, an article concerning the Gazette while at the Post, from which the following extracts are taken: "On the evening of the 25th of December, we reached the Post of Arkansas, then the seat of government of the territory. Finding the water too low to proceed any farther till a rise in the river, we were compelled to wait there several days. Loafing about the village, I, one day, made the acquaintance of a Dr. Kay, then a resident of the Post. Among other things, he told me that a young man from New York had arrived there a few days before, with a printing press and had commenced the publication of a weekly newspaper called the 'Arkansas Gazette.' He kindly proposed that I should walk with him to the printing office and he would introduce me to the editor. I gladly accepted the proposition and went with him, and, on entering, he introduced me to his friend, Mr. Woodruff, the same little, old, white-headed gentleman you often see on the streets of Little Rock.

"He occupied a small French built house, of two rooms, the largest of which was probably eighteen or twenty feet square. In this room he had his type cases, his editor's table, his stove and his bed, with the other necessary paraphernalia of a sleeping room and printing office. In the other, a much smaller room, was his printing press fixtures and appurtenances.

"On taking leave, Mr. Woodruff politely invited me to call as often as my engagements would permit.

"Stepping in one day, I found him engaged at the press in the little room. I seated myself at his table and looked over his exchanges. I saw at my entrance that he had a young man assisting him at the press and supposed he was some printer on a tramp, who had fallen in for a job. On entering the room where I was sitting, Mr. Woodruff introduced Mr. Roane to my acquaintance. This was the late Samuel C. Roane, who, in after years, acquired fortune and fame by attending to his own business."

The Arkansas Gazette.

The issue of the "Arkansas Gazette" of November 20th, 1819, being the first newspaper published in the state, its contents, which follow, will doubtless be of interest to her citizens.

The salutatory is as follows:

"After a series of delays in transporting our material to this place and in arranging our office since our arrival, we have, at length succeeded in issuing the first number of the Gazette.

"The present size and complexion of our paper does not suit us, but this we intend to remedy as soon as our patronage will justifiy our procuring new materials and enlarge its size. We cannot omit this opportunity of expressing our thanks to those gentlemen who so generously volunteered their aid in procuring subscribers for us, and to the citizens, generally, of the village and vicinity for the liberality with which they have subscribed to the Gazette. We have, also, flattering hopes of a generous support in the distant counties of the territory, from which we have not had time for returns. It has long been the wish of many citizens of this territory, that a press should be established here. Their wish is now accomplished. We have established one, entirely at our own expense, which we intend shall be permanent, and increase with the growth of the territory. And we look, with confidence, to a liberal public for a generous reward for our labor. It is the duty of every man to be useful in whatever situation he is placed in life. We intend to keep this maxim always in view and shall be highly pleased if our exertions for the public good shall meet the approbation of an enlightened people. We deem it unnecessary at this time to make ostentatious promises, or to hold forth inducements to the public for their patronage, which we do not feel ourselves capable of realizing. It is sufficient that we declare our principles to

ARKANSAS COUNTY.

be republican and that we are strongly attached to the free and liberal constitution of our happy country.

"The Gazette is now before the public. We leave it to them to decide on its merits, while we return with pleasure, to our labors."

The following notices, extracts, etc., are copied from this issue of the Arkansas Gazette.

"The Election.

An election is held today, throughout the Territory of Arkansas, to elect one delegate to Congress, and for the election of one member of the Legislative Council and two members of the House of Representatives to represent each county in the first Legislature of the territory. The following gentlemen are candidates for delegate to Congress.

James W. Bates,
Perley Wallace,
Henry Cassady,
Robert F. Slaughter,
Alex S. Walker.

ARKANSAS COUNTY.

For Legislative Council:
Samuel C. Roane,
Sylvanus Phillips,
Frederic Notrebe.

For House of Representatives:
William Craig,
Richmond Peeler,
Bartley Harrington,
Robert McKay,
William O. Allen,
William Trimble,
Harold Stillwell,
W. B. R. Horner.

POST SCRIPT.

At a late hour, just as our paper was going to press, we received the following result of the election in this township. Congress—Bates, 84; Cassady, 10; Walker, 8; Wallace, 0.

Council—Notrebe, 60; Roane, 19; Phillips, 16.

House of Representatives—Allen, 56; Trimble, 35; Peeler, 32; McKay, 27; Harrington, 26; Stillwell, 20; Craig, 2; and Horner, 1.

List of letters remaining in the post-office at Arkansas Post on the 30th of September, 1819, which, if not taken out within three months, will be sent to the General Post-office as dead letters.

Stephen F. Austin,
William Arnett,
Joseph Barton,
E. J. S. Bell,
James Caldwell,
Wesley Copeland,
William Douglass,
Ezekial Douglass, 2,
Francis Dehauney,

John Linch,
Mrs. Morrison,
James Porter,
Stephen Martin,
Asia Mason,
His Ex., James Miller,
Samuel May,
John McClain,
John McClain or,
Joel Dillard,
Townsend Dickerson, 2,
John Emberson,
John Fulton, 2,
William Gray,
Gabriel Greathouse,
Ruth Hawkins,
John Henderson,
Nieding Hill,
John Hanks,
Dr. John Isom, 2,
John Lockeys, 2,
Chitenden Lyons, 2,
D. Waters,
John Parker,
James Porter,
John Pricket,
Nicholas Righter,
William Russell,
Richard Stites,
Andrew Scott, 2,
John Taylor, 2,
James Whitehead, 2,
Hardy Wilbanks, 2.

ELI J. LEWIS, P. M.

Married.

On Thursday evening last, by Eli J. Lewis, Esq., Monsieur Francis La Fargue to Madamoiselle Agnes Pineaus, both of this place.

On the 23rd of September, by the same, Mr. Francis Duvall to Mrs. Catherine Dudley, both of this county.

On the 14th of October, by the same, Mr. Michael Cottener to Mrs. Elizabeth Kepler, both of this county.

On the 28th of October, by the same, Mr. Brenhard Raphael to Miss Catherine Gossieaux, both of this county.

Brigadier James Miller has accepted the appointment of governor of this territory. He is now on his way and may be expected here as soon as the water rises, which is very low at present."

In this issue of the Gazette is a communication signed "A Citizen," from which the following is taken.

"The village of Arkansas stands on the north bank of the Arkansas river in N. latitude 33 degrees 58 minutes 18 seconds, about fifty-five or sixty miles by water above the confluence of said river with the

ARKANSAS COUNTY.

Mississippi, near forty miles from the Mississippi by way of the cut-off and White river and about twenty-five miles, by land, to the mouth of the latter river, which is passable at low water.

"The village of Arkansas is a French establishment, settled as early as the American Revolution. Two places on the river below, were attempted for the establishment of a Spanish garrison, but were drowned out by high water.

"The present village is entirely free from inundation as it is situated on a high tract of country that puts into the Arkansas river, say fronting the river for about two miles and running back to the prairie a distance of three miles. The prairie runs back to highlands, nearly ninety miles, dividing the waters of the Arkansas and White rivers."

The professional and business notices in this issue are as follows:

"R. C. Oden notifies the public that he will practice law in the various courts of the territory, and that his office is in Little Rock."

"Eli J. Lewis, as clerk of the Circuit Court, notifies the defendant, Nathaniel Pryor, that Samuel M. Rutherford has sued him in Tres. by Attachment."

"David E. McKenney, as clerk of the Superior Court, notifies James Latham that his wife, Susan Latham, has brought suit for divorce."

"Eli J. Lewis notifies the public that he is anxious to engage a competent person to manage a tannery."

"Stokely H. Coulter respectfully informs the citizens that he is carrying on the tailoring business on west side of Main Street, opposite Craig's Tavern."

"Daniel Mooney and Eli J. Lewis, as Executors of the will of Samuel Mosley, call upon those indebted to the Mosley estate to come forward and pay their debts, etc."

"Dr. Robert McKay respectfully calls on his debtors to come forward and make payment, 'as further indulgence cannot be given.' "

"Lewis and Thomas, Front Street, offer for sale a complete and general assortment of Dry Goods, Groceries, Hardware, Queensware, Books and Stationery—and that they have on consignment, 500 bushels of Salt, 80 barrels of good Whiskey, 1 barrel Peach Brandy, a quantity of Potter's Ware and 1 barrel of 4th proof Whiskey."

The editor gives the latest news to that date from the following points:

London, England, July 23rd; New York, N. Y., August 27th; Washington, D. C., August 24th; New Orleans, La., August 3rd; St. Louis, Mo., September 29th.

The taxes for territorial and county purposes for the year 1819 were as follows:

Territorial tax,	$1201.63
County tax,	384.47
Total—	1586.10

As a specimen of the legal proceeding in 1819, the following is copied from the record made by Esqrs. Lewis and Johnson:

"On this 16th of September, 1819, J. Norville and Samuel C.

Roane, sued William Craig for Forcible Detainer, before Eli J. Lewis and Rob Johnson, returnable October 1st at the court house. On that day court met and on its motion ordered an adjournment in consequence of a **stinking dead horse** lying under the house. After adjourning to the house of William Drope, a jury of twelve men was summoned, who, hearing the testimony, considered it two days without agreeing to a verdict. Whereupon the **parties to the suit joined in the request** that the jury be discharged, which was granted."

CHAPTER X.

From the Year 1821 to the Year 1830.

On February 7th, 1820, the first regular session of the General Assembly, with delegates elected by the people, was held at Arkansas Post. Edward McDonald, member from Lawrence county, was elected president of the Legislative Council, which corresponded to the Senate of the state Legislature, and Richard Searcy, secretary. In the House of Representatives, William Stephenson, member from Hempstead county, was elected speaker, but, after serving one day, resigned, and Joseph Hardin, of Lawrence county, was elected in his place. J. Chamberlain was elected clerk.

This session continued until the 24th of February, 1820, when a recess was taken until the first Monday in October, from which time the session continued until the 25th of October.

The members composing the Council were: Sylvanus Phillips, from Arkansas county, Jacob Barkman, from Clark county, David Clark, from Hempstead, and John McElmurray, from Pulaski. Those composing the House of Representatives, were: W. B. R. Horner and William O. Allen, from Arkansas county, Thomas Fiske, from Clark, John English and Rev. William Stephenson, from Hempstead, Joseph Hardin, Sr., and Joab Hardin, from Lawrence, and Radford Ellis and Thomas H. Tindall, from Pulaski.

The session that convened in February was held at the house of Robert Crittenden and the session of October, in a house rented from John Larkquin.

On the 18th of October, the Legislature, by an act of that date, ordered the Superior Court and General Assembly of the territory after June, 1821, to be held in Little Rock.

The time of meeting for the Legislature was changed from the first Monday in December, to the first Monday in October, commencing in 1821.

At this session of the Legislature, four new counties were created, viz: Miller, on April 1st, Phillips, on May 1st, Crawford, on October 18th and Independence, on October 23rd.

The creation of Phillips county detached all that portion of the territory, originally forming a part of Arkansas county, lying east of White river and north of Scrub-grass Creek, which connects the White with the Mississippi river.

On the first of November, 1820, Hewes Scull, then sheriff of Arkansas county, in a letter to Charles Hempstead, had this to say of the retiring Legislature: "Our Legislature has risen, after breaking down the County Court system and establishing the Common Pleas, taking the seat of government to Little Rock and taxing us the enormous price of one dollar and a half per hundred arpens of confirmed land.

FROM 1821 TO 1830.

They have made a pretty pot of fish of it from beginning to end. So much so that I do not wish to have them here again exclusive of the Lawrence members who voted with ours on some important points. The balance were determined to crush down all opposition."

The first session of the Superior Court, which had been created by an act of Congress January 27th, 1814, was held at the Post of Arkansas, in January, 1820, Judge Andrew Scott, presiding, the associate judges being Charles Jouett and Robert P. Letcher.

In 1820, President Monroe appointed Benjamin Johnson a member of the Superior Court of the territory.

The judge of the Circuit Court, failing to appear at Arkansas Post at the time appointed by law, there was no such court held in Arkansas county from November, 1819, until February, 1822. At the latter time, Richard Searcy appeared and held court four days.

A special term of the Court of Common Pleas for the county of Arkansas was held in 1820, for the purpose of appointing assessors for the several townships in the county for the year 1821. Hewes Scull, of Arkansas, —— Demoss, of Mississippi and Peter H. Bennett, of Isle of Chicot township, were appointed assessors for their respective townships. There is no date given on the record of the time of the holding of this court of which Joseph Stillwell and James Hamilton were the judges.

This is the first recorded evidence of an effort to assess and collect taxes in the county under the laws of the territory.

The tax books under the assessment of 1821 show the following description, value of taxable property, amount of taxes, etc., for county purposes:

1,533 head of cattle over 3 years of age.
324 head of horses and mules.
1 stud horse.
84 slaves between 15 and 45 years of age.
92 single white men.

Total amount of taxes on the foregoing list of taxable property and persons was $494.12.

There was nothing but land taxed for territorial purposes and no description of the land but the number of acres in each tract. The amount of taxes levied on these lands was $1,665.66.

A land office for the sale of the public lands in the Territory of Arkansas was opened at Arkansas Post in 1820. William Douglass Simms was appointed register and Henry W. Conway receiver. How long this office remained open at Arkansas Post or to what point it was removed, the writer has no information nor means of reporting.

The first steamboat to ascend the Arkansas river was the "Comet," commanded by Captain Byrne, which reached Arkansas Post on April 1st, 1820, eight days out from New Orleans. The second was the "Maid of Orleans," which reached the Post on July 20th of the same year, having been thirteen days from New Orleans.

The population of Arkansas county, according to returns of census for 1820, was twelve hundred and sixty, divided as follows:

Arkansas township, 720 souls.
Mississippi township, 82 souls.

ARKANSAS COUNTY.

Point Chicot township, 452 souls.

Total, 1,254.

Of this number, **nine** were unnaturalized foreigners, **fifty-four** slaves, **two hundred and sixty-five** engaged in agricultural pursuits, **twelve** in manufacturing, and **seventeen** in mercantile pursuits.

The territory constituting the township of Arkansas at this time included all of the present county, all of Lincoln county, and the eastern portion of Jefferson county. Mississippi township embraced the present limits of Desha county and Point Chicot, the present limits of Chicot county.

1821.

By an act of the Territorial Legislature, of October 24, 1821, it was provided that in all general and special elections for officers of government the electors should vote **"viva voce"**. The clerk of the court was required to furnish two poll books for each voting precinct, in tabular form, showing name of voter and each candidate for the various offices voted for at the head of parallel columns ruled on the book.

All elections were by **"viva voce"** vote under the constitution of 1836, but the General Assembly was empowered under the constitution to order otherwise by law.

On the 11th of May, 1821, the sheriff, who had been, at a former term of the Common Pleas Court, ordered to advertise for bids to build a jail in the county of Arkansas, reported to the court that he had been unable to obtain a bid or proposal.

The records of proceedings in both Circuit and Common Pleas Courts were kept in one book as these courts appear to have had concurrent jurisdiction in most matters, under the then existing laws of the territory. This is shown in the records of these courts from 1819 to 1834. But by an act of the Territorial Legislature of the 23rd of November, 1829, a court to be known as the County Court was created, in each county of the territory. All duties of a local nature then imposed upon the Circuit Courts were transferred to the County Courts of the respective counties.

In the Circuit Court of Arkansas county, during the concurrent jurisdiction above referred to, J. Woodson Bates, Richard Searcy, Thomas P. Eskridge, Samuel Hall, Samuel C. Roane and Alexander M. Clayton presided and in the Court of Common Pleas Joseph Stillwell presided one term and Charles Brearley, James Hamilton and Frederick Notrebe in 1820 and 1821.

Each court, as appears from the records of their proceedings, had jurisdiction over the local or internal affairs of the county, such as the establishment of townships and roads, appointment of overseers of roads, tax assessors, etc., as well as all matters connected with the administration of estates.

At the May (1821) term of the County Court, the following named persons were appointed judges of election for Arkansas county.

For the township of Richland, Bartley Harrington, O. H. Thomas and Samuel P. Green, the election to be held at the house of Bartley Harrington.

FROM 1821 TO 1830.

For Mississippi township—James S. Petty, Abraham Smalley and James Roswell, election to be held at the house of William Montgomery.

For Arkansas township—James Scull, Louis Bogy and Terence Farrelly, election to be held at the court house.

For Point Chicot township—Peter H. Bennett, James aand John Weir, election to be held at the house of Mr. James.

At the election held this year for delegate to Congress, James Woodson Bates received 135 votes and Matthew Lyon, 42, showing the total vote of the county to be 177. These votes were distributed as follows:

Arkansas township, 85 votes.
Mississippi township, 39 votes.
Richland township, 23 votes.
Point Chicot township, 30 votes.
Total, 177 votes.

1822.

At the February (1822) term of the Court of Common Pleas, Joseph Egnor was appointed constable for the township of Arkansas and at the October term of the Circuit Court, Ezekiel Black was appointed constable for Chicot township.

1823.

Judge Thomas P. Eskridge, at the July (1823) term of the Circuit Court, appointed the following persons judges of the election to be held on Monday, the 4th of August following: For Point Chicot township, Joseph Brown, James Estell, John C. Jones, election to be held at Brown's house. For Richland township, Bartley Harrington, John Deadrick, John Morrison, election to be held at the house of Mrs. Curren. For Arkansas township, Harold Stillwell, James Scull and Frederic Notrebe, election to be held in the town of Arkansas. For Mississippi township, Abram Smalley, Joseph Jacobs, Smith Brown, election to be held at the house of William Montgomery.

At the October term of this court, before Judge Eskridge, Isaac, a man of color, was convicted of the crime of stealing a gun, for which offense he was by the court "to receive on his bare back, twenty-five lashes and be sold to pay costs, amounting to the sum of $178.98½. This judgment, the record tells us, was executed and report made thereof, showing that the negro Isaac, brought at public sale, $490.

In October, 1823, the Territorial Legislature then in session, passed an act detaching "all that portion of the county of Arkansas bounded as follows: Commencing on the Mississippi, in the cypress bend at the mouth of Cypress Creek, thence with said creek to its forks; thence north or south, as the case may be, to the nearest township line; thence with said township line to the Quapaw line; thence with said boundary to the nearest range line; thence with said range line to the boundary line between Louisiana and Arkansas territory; thence with said boundary line to the Mississippi river; thence up said river to the place of beginning" to be laid off and created into a separate county to be known as Chicot county.

From a Letter Book, originally belonging to Hewes Scull, found

ARKANSAS COUNTY.

in the Clerk's Office of Arkansas county, it appears that Hewes Scull and Charles Bogy, as partners, were merchandising at Arkansas Post from December, 1823, to January, 1825, and that from the latter date until August, 1826, Scull continued the business in his own name.

From this Letter Book we learn that the leading articles of their stock consisted of sugar, coffee, salt, whiskey, powder, lead, gun flints, axes, hoes, nails and other articles of hardware, soap, cordage, etc.

On the 15th of September, 1824, they ordered the following bill of goods: "5 sets Georgets, 10 single Georgets, of large size, 5 sets brooches, 5 sets moons, 10 sets embroidered brooches, Nos. 1, 2, and 3, 10 pr. arm bands, large size, 10 prs. arm bands, No. 3 size, 100 large crosses, 200 large common bracelets, 200 fish-eye bracelets, 10 prs. wrist bands, 1½ inches, 500 large ear bobs, 20 head bands."

In exchange for these goods they received cotton, hides, peltries, furs, beeves, oil, beeswax and ox horns, which they shipped to New Orleans, sometimes on steamboats and at others on barges to the mouth of White river, thence on steamboats to New Orleans.

In the transportation of their goods from New Orleans the same plan was followed—at some times the steamers came direct to Arkansas Post, at others to the mouth of White river and from this point the goods was transported on barges to the Post.

Under a territorial statute then in force, a census of the county was taken in this year, which showed the population to be one thousand three hundred and thirty-six divided as follows:

Arkansas township, 526.
Richland township, 142.
Mississippi township, 160.
Chicot township, 508.

Of the above number one thousand one hundred and forty-three were white, one hundred seventy-seven slaves, and sixteen free persons of color. This census shows an increase of **seventy-six** souls over the census of 1820.

1824.

In 1824 the Quapaw Indians owned and occupied a district of country in Arkansas county south of the Arkansas river. By a treaty entered into at Harrington, the residence of Bartley Harrington, in Arkansas county, November 15th, 1824, this territory was ceded to the United States. The treaty was negotiated between Robert Crittenden as commissioner, on the part of the United States, and Hecaton (or Heckaton) Saracen and other chiefs and warriors of the Quapaw tribe.

In this year Ben Desha, a native of Kentucky, was appointed, by President Monroe, Receiver of Public Moneys for Little Rock Land District. Desha was a citizen of Arkansas county and died and was buried on his plantation on the south side of Arkansas river, which was later owned and occupied by the late Col. Joseph W. Clay, who also died and was buried there. This place is now in Lincoln county.

At the January term (1824) of the Circuit Court of Arkansas county, Judge Thomas P. Eskridge, by an order of his court, appointed John

FROM 1821 TO 1830.

Taylor, Jr., constable for Arkansas township, requiring bond in the sum of six hundred dollars.

At the May term of this court an order was made that a license to keep a tavern, for one year, be granted Peter Crumstack, on his paying a tax of twenty dollars to the county for this privilege. The order does not designate at what place the tavern was to be located. At the same term of the court, Joseph Drake was appointed surveyor of the county, with an order that his appointment be certified to the Governor.

On petition of sundry citizens an order was granted by the September term of the Circuit Court to open a road leading from Plum Bayou through the Post of Arkansas to the mouth of White river, which was to be divided into three road districts—the first from Plum Bayou to Bartley Harrington's, the second, from Harrington's to the Post of Arkansas, and the third from the Post to the mouth of White river.

The sheriff of Arkansas county during this year was Terence Farrelly.

During the year 1824, a Jesuit Missionary, named Odin, visited the Quapaws, on the Arkansas river within the county of Arkansas. This was the home of the aged chief Saracen, who is reported to have said, "Now will I die happy, as I have seen my father, the Black gown of France." M. Odin said mass among them and gleaned some ideas of their religious customs.

The chief, Saracen, is said to have lived on the Arkansas river, at or near the plantation long known in that vicinity as "Heckto," which, at one time belonged to the late Col. Tom Smith, of Nashville, Tennessee. It is situated on the south bank of the river and is now in Lincoln county. Near this place is the noted trading point and post-office called "Sarassa."

1825.

In August, 1825, an election for delegates and representatives, from the county to the Territorial Legislature, was held, the result of which was as follows:

For delegate to the Council, Bartley Harrington received **seventy-nine** votes, and James H. Lucas, **fifty-five.**

For representative, William Montgomery received **one hundred and twelve** votes and Wigton King, **one.**

The whole number of votes cast at this election was **one hundred and thirty-four.**

On the 13th of December, 1825, Hewes Scull, writing to his merchant in New Orleans says: "I request you to keep me informed of the rise, fall and prospects of the cotton market, as there is a large quantity yet for sale, for cash, in this county. A crop of thirty bales was purchased by Mr. Notrebe, at 16 cts. for cash, about a month back."

From this, it will be observed that even at that early day, cotton was of potent influence in the commercial affairs of the country.

That the legal fraternity of the present day, who may chance to read this, may know how technical were the courts of 1825, a reference is here made to the ruling and decree under that ruling of Chancellor Eskridge, made at the January (1825) term of his court in the case of James Hamilton vs. William Montgomery.

ARKANSAS COUNTY.

This was a bill of Discovery, filed by Hamilton against Montgomery. To this bill, a motion to dismiss for want of an affidavit as to the truth, of the allegations therein contained, was filed. On this motion the chancellor filed a written opinion, covering six pages of an eight by twelve inch page record, which, under the statute at the time, was required to be entered as the judgment or decree of court. The chancellor, in this ruling said: "Such an opinion may operate in favor of the parties, by exempting them from future cost and vexation."

As such, this decree was made for the benefit of future litigants in his courts in similar cases. In other words, the court clearly intimated that attorneys, in the future, should know the law and avoid similar mistakes.

In searching for items of historical interest among the records and files in the Clerk's office of Arkansas county, I found a small collection of original poems, in manuscript, by Hewes Scull, who was the first sheriff of the county under the territorial laws and who, for many years, resided at Arkansas Post. Believing them to possess poetic merit and that they will be of interest to the readers hereof, two of them are given. The first, whose title is "Christmas Celebration," shows the writer's appreciation of the Christian religion; the other, "La Fayette," his patriotic gratitude.

"Hark, Angels' voices rend the sky,
  Their harps sound heavenly love;
And grateful, fervent, holy joy
  Fills earth and heaven above.

Glory to God, who reigns on high!
  The Prince of Peace is born.
God's power now to man comes nigh,
  Cease sinner—cease to mourn.

Shall I be silent midst the lays
  Of heavenly melody?
Ah, Savior of a fallen race,
  My Savior deigns to be.

Inspire my heart and tune my voice
  To sing this noble theme.
Oh, let me in His birth rejoice,
  Who comes, me to redeem.

That once where saints' and angels' tongues
  God and the Lamb adore—
My voice may mingle with their songs,
  In bliss forevermore.

La Fayette.

Son of valor, heir of glory,
  Noble by the patriot's line,
Gallant warrior, chieftan hoary,
  Immortality is thine!

FROM 1821 TO 1830.

> Wreathe the laurel, Muses, with it,
>   'Tis for no ignoble name;
> Breathe the song, Inspirers, breathe it,
>   Worthy of the veteran's fame."

1826.

At the January (1826) term of the District Court of Arkansas county, Judge J. Woodson Bates appointed Nathaniel Owen, constable for the township of Arkansas for a term of two years.

At a later date (not known to the writer) Owen was appointed post-master for the office then known as Heckato, located on the south bank of the Arkansas river in Township 7 south, of Range 5 west, on the plantation of the late Col. Tom Smith, now in Lincoln county. The name of this office, tradition tells us, was changed to Nickato at the request of Owen, and was known by this name as late as 1848.

It was currently reported that during the time Owen acted as post-master at this office, for the convenience of the patrons of the office and that he might indulge his propensity to hunt and fish, he would carry the bulk of the mail matter of the office in the crown of his hat, that he might more conveniently deliver it. As the settlements, at that time, were immediately on the river, parties passing up or down the river would be likely to meet him, since the road ran near the bank of the river on which he hunted or fished; when he went up the river, such mail matter as was in his office for parties in that direction he carried with him, and when his course was down the river, mail for parties in that direction was in his hat ready for delivery.

During the time he held this position, he caused the office to be moved to two or three other points along the river, sometimes on one side and sometimes on the other, but at all times retaining the same name.

Owen was an acting justice of the peace for Old River township as late as 1848 or 1849.

About this date Owen called on the writer, who was at the time Deputy Clerk of Arkansas county, to obtain a certificate as to the official character of one of the justices of the peace in Old River township before whom Owen had made an acknowledgment of a deed from him to a party in New York, conveying his interest in certain real estate in the state of New York. On this occasion the fact developed and was by him acknowledged, that Owen was not his true name, but a part of his Christian name, which he had assumed as his surname. The reasons for this change were at the time given, but have been forgotten by the writer.

At the Januaary term of the District Court, Judge Bates granted a decree annulling the bonds of matrimony then existing between Abraham and Harriet Dardine.

During this year A. B. K. Thetford was sheriff and Eli J. Lewis clerk, for Arkansas county.

1827.

Upon a petition presented by the citizens of Richland township, before the Hon. Samuel C. Roane, Judge of the Circuit Court of Arkan-

ARKANSAS COUNTY.

sas county, an order was granted, on July 16th, 1827, for the opening of a road leading from John Jerdlas' ferry, on the south side of Arkansas river, by Antoine Barraque's, to the first Pine Bluff on the river. Enos Bogy, Bartley Harrington and John Jerdlas were appointed commissioners to view and lay out this road and report same to the court at its next term.

From this order we see that the Circuit Courts had jurisdiction over the internal affairs of the counties. Also that the location of the present city of Pine Bluff was at that time within the limits of Arkansas County.

At the November term of this court Judge Roane granted to John Palmer, Jr., the privilege of keeping a ferry across the Arkansas river in Richland township. He was ordered to pay a tax of one cent and charge at the following rates: Man and horse, 25 cts.; single man, 18¾ cts.; wagon and four horses, $1.50; wagon and two horses, $1; horned cattle, 12½ cts.

1828.

The records of the county show that two hundred tracts of **one hundred sixty** acres each of Military Bounty land were taxed for the year 1828. For territorial purposes the sum of $736 was levied and for county purposes $150.

These taxes were specific in that the annual tax on each tract of land was a specified sum per tract and not according to value. Several of these tracts appear to have been delinquent for several years, in some instances, as far back as 1825.

The first evidence of the existence of paupers in the county we find in the record of proceedings of the June (1828) term of the Circuit Court, when Judge Samuel Hall caused the following order to be entered of the record:

"August de Surville, a pauper, as set forth in his petition, is an old and infirm man so that he is unable to maintain himself. Ordered that he be allowed twenty-five dollars each three months and that William P. Hackett receipt and be trustee for the pauper aforesaid and that said trustee report and file his accounts as far as his expenditures, not exceeding the above rate."

A. B. K. Thetford was sheriff, and Eli J. Lewis clerk of the county at this date.

1829.

For the year 1829 I find but few items of historical interest and these are gleaned from the county records.

The record of the proceedings of the May term of the Circuit Court of this year contains an order granted by Judge Bates for the establishment of a new township in Arkansas county with boundaries as follows: "Commencing at the mouth of the river Augrue (now known as Lagrue Bayou) and running with said river until it strikes the boundary line of Pulaski county; thence, with this line east, until it strikes White river; thence, with White river to the mouth of the river Augrue, the place of beginning." The new township was to be known as Prairie township. This township, as established, embraced all that part of Arkansas county lying between Lagrue and White river.

On November 2nd, 1829, the Territorial Legislature, by an act of that date detached all that portion of Arkansas county lying north of the line of Township 4 south and west of line of Range 6 west, in creating the county of Jefferson.

That the reader may know how justice was officially administered at that time, the following statement is condensed from the docket of Eli J. Lewis, one of the Justices of the Peace for Arkansas County.

Eli J. Lewis, an acting Justice of the Peace in Arkansas township, issued a summons against Francis Lafargue, in favor of Samuel S. Hall, on the 1st day of December, 1829, returnable the 25th of said month.

On this summons the constable endorsed the following return: "Weather too bad to travel.—W. B. Lemmons, Constable of Arkansas Township."

On return and filing this summons, the justice marked his docket thus, "**Not served**," and that appears to be the end of the proceedings in the case.

CHAPTER XI.

From the Year 1830 to the Year 1840.

Again for the year 1830, I find no items of historical interest save in the proceedings of the County Court as given in the records of the county. Even **tradition**, that great storehouse of history, has, for this year, been barred against me.

At the April (1830) term of the County Court, Judge Terence Farrelly granted an order authorizing Rufus Mixee to keep a ferry at the mouth of White river and one authorizing the opening of a road from this ferry to Evans' wood-yard on the Mississippi river.

At this term of court A. B. K. Thetford, as sheriff of the county, reported the sale, made by him, of two runaway negro men, under the order and direction of the Circuit Court at its January term, 1830. In these reports, the incidental expenses, as well as the amount for which the negroes were sold, are set out in detail.

The closing paragraph of the order of the county court on the report of the sale of one of these negroes is as follows:

"Whereupon it was considered, and ordered by the court that the said A. B. K. Thetford pay the aforesaid expenses out of the proceeds of the sale of said negro and that the balance be retained in the hands of the sheriff, as treasurer of the county, and charged to his account, subject to the use, and to be paid over to the owner or owners of said negro should any appear and prove his title according to law; and the necessary acquittances of said owner being presented to this court, shall be considered as a quietus to said sheriff."

The foregoing paragraph discloses the fact, that at that time there was no such office as County Treasurer, the sheriff being by virtue of his office, **ex-officio** treasurer.

At this term of court the sheriff and **ex-officio** assessor of the county returned and filed his assessment list of taxable persons and real property in the county for the year 1830. "Whereupon the court ordered that the following rates of taxes be charged to the persons therein mentioned, to be levied and collected for the county tax for the year 1831:

On every **one hundred** acres of confirmed land, the sum of **twenty-five cents.**

On every slave, over **sixteen** and under **forty-five** years of age, **one dollar.**

On every head of neat cattle, over **three** years old, **six and one-quarter cents.**

On every horse, mare, mule or ass, over **three** years old, the sum of **twenty-five cents.**

On every billiard table, the sum of **thirty dollars.**

On every pleasure carriage, **ten and a half per cent of its value,** and, That clerk make out said tax list according to law and deliver the same to the sheriff, taking his receipt for the amount of said list and charging him with the same."

The record of the proceedings had at this term of court shows that there had been no final settlement with the sheriff as collector of revenue in the county, since November, 1820, at which time the Circuit Court of the county had jurisdiction over affairs of this nature, when there appears a balance of $967.43 against the sheriff. At this settlement, the sheriff filed exhibits of sums by him paid out and of fees due him, which reduced his indebtedness to $672.68 including the sum of $210.15 of Chicot county certificates.

This appears to be the first time the County Court had jurisdiction in the matter of revenue due the county.

The population of Arkansas County, as reported by the United States Marshal, for the year 1830 was **one thousand four hundred twenty-six**, an increase over the census of 1820 of only **one hundred sixty-six**. It must be remembered, however, that since 1820, all the territory constituting the county of Chicot and a large portion of that of Jefferson, with the inhabitants therein, had been, by acts of the Territorial Legislature, detached from Arkansas county.

The population of Arkansas Post at this time was **one hundred fourteen.**

1831.

On the 7th of July, 1831, the County Court of Arkansas county created two new townships in the county.

One of these, named Old River township, embraced all the territory north of the Arkansas river and west of Hannerberry Bayou and all the territory in said county south of Arkansas river and west of the line dividing Ranges 4 and 5 west, to the eastern boundary of Jefferson county. The other, named Bartholomew township, included all the territory then within the county of Arkansas, south of Cypress Creek and east of the line dividing Ranges 4 and 5 west.

1832.

On the 11th of October, 1832, John Pope, the Territorial Governor of Arkansas, in company with Wm. F. Pope, his relative and private secretary, landed at Montgomery's Point, on the Mississippi, near the mouth of White river, then in Arkansas county.

To Secretary Pope we are indebted for the following splendid description of the "Point" and its surroundings.

"Montgomery's Point, one of the oldest and most widely known landings on the Mississippi river."

"In the early settlement of Louisiana Territory, this point was the place of residence of Francis De Armond, a wealthy fur trader, and a man of considerable importance in that region of country. General William Montgomery resided at the 'Point' at this time.

A few of the old log cabins erected by Francis De Armond in 1766 were still standing, about three hundred yards back from the river.

Two large warehouses, built upon piling, stood near the water's edge and were used by the firm of Montgomery, Miller and Company,

ARKANSAS COUNTY.

for storing freight destined for points along the Arkansas and White rivers.

The hotel at the Point was owned by Gen. Montgomery, and was situated about two hundred and fifty yards from the river. The hotel building was elevated some distance above the ground on high brick pillars, and had wide verandas on all sides."

In connection with this description of Montgomery's Point, the writer begs leave to relate two incidents, reported to him by the late Jason Thetford, a younger brother of A. B. K. Thetford, who was for some years sheriff of Arkansas county, as having occurred at and near the "Point"; the first, as the personal experience of the narrator, the other as related to him by a citizen of the "Point" at the time of its occurrence.

Thetford was, at the time of the incident related from his personal knowledge, a pilot on a steamer then in the Arkansas river and New Orleans trade and on one of his trips, being detained at the "Point" for some reason, he obtained a gun and went out into the canebrake back from the river to hunt. He was out several hours, and in passing through the canebrake and open spaces in the woods, he found the skeletons of three men that, as he supposed, had been murdered and left to the ravages of the wild beasts of the wood and fowls of the air.

The other incident, as related to him, was in regard to the advent of the late Governor Yell into the Territory of Arkansas, in January, 1832, at which time, while on his way from Tennessee, he was compelled to stop over several days at Montgomery's Point, waiting for transportation to Little Rock. During this time he was asked by a stranger to obtain a gun and take a hunt with him. To this request he consented, and procuring a gun, started on the contemplated hunt, hoping to bag and bring back game of some kind. They had not been out long, till he discovered that his strange companion seemed to have great knowledge of the woods, through which they were passing, and took great pains in pointing out to Yell the direction he should go. After passing some distance from the river, they came to a dense canebrake, into which a narrow path or foot-way led and as they entered this path the stranger having Yell in his rear, requested him to enter the path first. At this, the thought flashed across Yell's mind that the stranger designed getting him into the canebrake to murder or rob him. No sooner was the thought conceived than he determined his own action. He cocked his gun, turned and presented it at the man and compelled him to return to the point at the muzzle of his gun, returning in safety to the steamer. As soon as he was where he felt safe, he permitted the stranger to go in peace, and saw no more of him.

Pope in his **Early Days in Arkansas,** says: "The Post of Arkansas was settled in 1686, by some of the followers of De Tonty, one of La Salle's lieutenants.

"Many of the French settlers left by De Tonty, at this settlement, intermarried with the Quapaw Indian women, and some of their descendants were living at Little Rock and other parts of the Territory when I came to Arkansas.

FROM 1830 TO 1840.

"The Post of Arkansas, in 1832, when I first saw it, presented a very forlorn and desolate appearance. None of the habitations of the original settlers or their immediate descendants were standing at that time.

"After the Territory passed into the hands of the French, the Post became the official residence of Don Carlos De Villemont, who had been appointed commandant of the Post, and who was holding that position at the time of the cession of the Territory to the United States by France in 1803.

"Many of the houses erected during De Villemont's administration were still standing, and were built after the French style of architecture, with high pointed roofs and gables, heavy exterior timbers and high chimneys."

To this description the writer adds that the greater number of these buildings had their floors from four to six feet from the ground, with galleries on all sides.

A number of these houses were standing at Arkansas Post and on the river a few miles below, when the Federal army captured the Confederate forces stationed at that place in January, 1863, when all the houses at the Post as well as those on the river below were destroyed.

1833.

"From the time of the organization of the Territory, in 1819, up to this time Arkansas was considered to be the extreme confines of civilization in the southwest.

"So feeble was the attraction in this remote region for the active, industrious and well disposed portion of the western pioneers, that the Arkansas Territory, in 1830, more than ten years after its organization, had acquired an aggregate population of **thirty thousand, three hundred eighty-eight souls,** including **four thousand five hundred seventy-six** slaves." Of this population, but **one thousand, four hundred twenty-six** were inhabitants of Arkansas county.

The greater portion of the small emigration or accession to the population of the territory went further west, advancing up the Arkansas river and the numerous tributaries of White river, on Little Red, Big Black, St. Francis, Saline and Ouachita river and Bayou Bartholomew.

At the general election held in 1833, Terence Farrelly was elected Councilman, and Harold Stillwell, Representative to the Territorial Legislature. For the county officers, James H. Lucas was elected Judge, John Maxwell, clerk, and A. B. K. Thetford, sheriff.

1834.

In consequence of the growth in wealth and population of the Territory, a growing desire was manifested by her citizens to doff the territorial garb and don the habiliments of statehood. This desire was manifested throughout the Territory, and was exhibited by the citizens of Arkansas county in common with the citizens of her sister counties, during the early days of the year 1834. So much so, that under the influence and efforts of Col. Sevier, the Territorial Representative in

ARKANSAS COUNTY.

Congress, a bill for the purpose was reported from the committee and presented to the House June 3rd, 1834, but did not become a law until June 1836.

Pending this question of statehood, one of its most ardent advocates and an active agent in the organization of the territory, died. This was Robert Crittenden. A history of Arkansas county, by whomsoever written, would be incomplete without reference to the name and acts of Robert Crittenden. In Hempstead's **"History of Arkansas,"** is the following tribute to Crittenden.

"By the death of Robert Crittenden, there passed away one who had, perhaps, been more prominently identified with the history of the Territory than any person then living in it, by his having served as Secretary for ten years, from 1819 to 1829, by his organization of the Territory, by his service as acting Governor, from time to time and by his prominence in politics and law matters since he had passed out of office. He was a man of fine appearance, in oratory he was elegant and impressive, and, as an advocate, was prominent and successful. His name is inseparably linked with the early history of the Territory."

1835.

On the 5th day of October, 1835, the last Territorial Legislature met at the capital. At this session, in accordance with the expressed wish of the people, the legislature passed a bill calling a convention of delegates to frame a constitution as the basis of admission of Arkansas, as a sovereign state, into the Federal Union.

"The act recited that the number of inhabitants in the Territory exceeded **forty-seven thousand seven hundred,** and directed an election to be held for delegates." In pursuance of this act, elections were held in all the counties then formed, and delegates chosen.

Arkansas county, under the provisions of this act, was entitled to one delegate and jointly with Jefferson county to one, and on the   day of   , 1835, Bushrod W. Lee was elected the delegate from Arkansas county and Terence Farrelly the delegate from Arkansas and Jefferson counties.

The convention thus provided for, met in Little Rock, January 4th, 1836, and, between that date and the 30th day of the same month, framed a constitution which was accepted by Congress on the 15th of June, 1836, at which time Arkansas became an independent sovereign state. The laws of the United States were extended over it, and one representative in Congress was allowed it, until the next census should be taken.

1836.

After the adoption of the constitution and admission of the state into the Federal Union on the 16th of June, 1836, the County Court of Arkansas county, at its July term, 1836, made provision for holding an election, under the provisions of the constitution, to elect the various officers of the state and county made elective thereby, by granting the following order: "Ordered by the court that the general election, to be holden on the first Monday of August next, for Representatives, Sena-

FROM 1830 TO 1840.

tor to the next Legislature, Clerk of the Circuit Court, Sheriff, Coroner, County Surveyor, County Treasurer, Justices of the Peace, and Constables, shall be holden at the following places in the county of Arkansas, and that the following persons be appointed judges of election, to wit: That the election in the township of Wilkinson be held at the dwelling house of Mapes Ryan and Co., and that John Wilkins, David Walters and Benjamin Cock be appointed judges of election. In Mississippi township, at the dwelling house of the late Gen. William Montgomery and that David Mefford, Rufus S. Mixter and William Mahan be appointed judges of said election. In Arkansas township, at the court house, and that John H. Lenox, Harold Stillwell and Emmanuel Pertuies be judges. In Prairie township, at the house of Solomon Garrison, and that Solomon Garrison, Severn Pepper and Benjamin Southworth be appointed judges. In Bartholomew township, at the dwelling house of Samuel H. Davis, and that Samuel H. Davis, Gary Williams and Jesse Condren be appointed judges. In Old River township, at the house of Louisa Harrington, and that William H. Dye, William Patterson and Peter C. Lindsey be appointed judges of said election. Ordered that the sheriff give notice of same according to law."

The territory mentioned in the above order included all the present limits of Arkansas and Desha counties and portions of Chicot, Jefferson, Prairie and Monroe counties.

At this election, Arkansas county was entitled to two representatives, and jointly with Jefferson county, one senator. The representatives elected were James Maxwell and James Smith, the senator, Samuel C. Roane.

The amount of taxes assessed against the persons and property in the county for the year before the adoption of the constitution was $1126.87—for the next year, after the adoption of the constitution, $761.64.

One of the immigrants to this county in the year 1836 was a Belgian count, Maria Phillippe Julian Joseph Visart, Count of Bocarme, This man settled on Little Lagrue, about twenty-five miles north of Arkansas Post, where he, with his family, remained until his death in September, 1851.

At the time of his settlement, there were not more than five or six families within as many miles of his residence; and no school, church, post-office nor trading point nearer than Arkansas Post. Here, three children, two sons and a daughter, were born to him. In 1845, the mother of these children died, and sometime between that date and 1851, when the father died, the youngest son died.

At the count's death, the son who came with him to the country, and the son and daughter who were born here, survived him.

Shortly after his arrival in the county, he purchased from the United States, two tracts of land in the vicinity of his settlement—one in his own name, the other in the name of the son who came with him to the county.

For services rendered the French government by the count, previous to his coming to this country, a pension was settled on him, which continued to the close of the year 1850, and soon after this time, he made application by filing with the Clerk of Arkansas county, his petition to become a citizen of the United States.

Occasionally during the years intervening between 1836 and 1850, the count went to France to obtain his pension.

In June, 1851, the count purchased from the state, a tract of land for his son Julian and took title to same in the name of Julian J. E. Visart.

After the death of the count, his son Julian administered upon his estate, employing the writer to assist him in this administration. Thus he was enabled to become acquainted with most of the facts related here. Before the close of this administration, Julian J. E. Visart died, leaving his minor brother and sister without home or guardian, and two infant children without a mother. Shortly after his death, the brother and sister selected the writer as their guardian, who took them into his family. After the death of the grandmother of Julian's children, at the request of their uncle and aunt, then his wards, he took these children also into his family, where all remained until they reached their majority, except the son of Julian, who after the marriage of his uncle, went to live with him.

Of these four, the two daughters were married in the writer's house, and the older son was a member of his family at the time of his marriage.

1837.

To relieve the people of the state from their financial embarrassment, incident to the great monetary crisis of 1836, the Legislature of the state resorted to the plan then current in the states, to provide such means as the times demanded, by creating Banks of Discount in the state, branches being located in the principal commercial centers of the state. Under the belief in this current theory, the Legislature, on the 6th of November, 1836, passed an act establishing the **State Bank of Arkansas.** The principal bank was located at Little Rock, with branches at Fayetteville and Batesville, and on the 15th of December of the same year, a third branch was established at Arkansas Post.

This branch was organized on December 16th. 1837, by electing Henry J. McKenzie, Frederick Notrebe, George B. Watson, Jr., John B. McClain, Harold Stillwell, James Smith, S. V. R. Ryan, Reuben Dye and Bushrod W. Lee, directors. These directors elected Terence Farrelly, President, and Eugene Notrebe, Cashier. On April 3rd, 1838, Notrebe resigned and Luther Chase was, on April 25th, appointed to succeed him.

The business of this branch was opened on January 3rd, 1839, on which date notes, to the amount of $60.950, were discounted—all having six months to run. Before the close of the month, $31,900 were added.

On January 31st, the President, in a communication to the Board of Directors, informed them that the bank circulation was but $64,000. He said, further, that could this sum be reasonably calculated upon, as being in actual circulation, passing from hand to hand as a circulating medium, he would be pleased to recommend a continuance of the liberal policy hitherto observed. "But," he said, "the daily demand at our counter leads conclusively to the opinion that not more than $15,000 or $16,000 of that sum is in transit from hand to hand." The balance, the President supposed, was withheld for the purpose of drawing specie from the bank. Notwithstanding these unfavorable conditions, the directors caused a costly banking-house to be erected.

On October 31st, 1839, this branch resolved to suspend specie payment. In April of this year they had, by a resolution, suspended discounting notes, but in December this order was rescinded and the business of discounting notes resumed.

The Legislature of 1840 authorized the Governor to appoint commissioners to examine from time to time and report the condition of the bank and its branches. One of these commissioners appointed by the Governor, was R. C. Byrd, who, in his report of the condition of the branch at Arkansas Post, says: "I find, in use, a banking-house, which, as to plan, location and workmanship, is one of the best buildings in the state." He further stated that the debts due the bank could not be collected.

At the session of the Legislature for 1842-1843, an act was passed, placing the bank of the state in liquidation, and electing a financial and executive receiver, and an attorney for the principal bank and each of its branches. Under this act, on February 3rd, 1843, Samuel Mitchell was elected executive receiver, and William A. Doherty, financial receiver. On April 5th, 1845, James M. Smith was elected financial receiver, and Mark Mitchell in March, 1847.

The following gentlemen were elected or appointed attorneys:

M. W. Dorris—February 2nd, 1843.
Isaac N. Barnett—January 3rd, 1845.
M. W. Dorris—December 18th, 1846.
M. W. Dorris—January 9th, 1849.
Thomas N. Beyers—July 14th, 1849.
F. A. James—May 26th, 1851.
M. L. Bell—October 17th, 1853.

1838.

I find but little of historic interest as having transpired in the county during the year 1838. In searching for items of interest thought to be worthy of record, I found on file in the office of the clerk of the county, the docket of James Eddington, a Justice of the Peace in Mississippi township, from which I have copied the following records, that the reader may know how justice was dispensed in those days.

"State and County,
    vs.
  William Dunn.

This 1st day of March, 1838, comes the constable, Elijah Cheatham, for the State and County of Arkansas, and brings William Dunn, the accused of the murder of William Condrel, and, after being duly tried for commitment, on the oath of George Lapsley's evidence, it being circumstantial proof of the guilt of the accused William Dunn committing said murder and the evidence of John Lanciza, Elijah Cheatham, William Baxis, Jacob Brown, James C. R. Smith, George W. Brown and Alexander Cresswell, seven other witnesses for the state. It was

ARKANSAS COUNTY.

proven by Elijah Cheatham, William Baxis, Jacob Brown and James C. R. Brown, that the accused was never absent a sufficient time to execute the crime as alleged, as he, Cheatham, proves the distance to be two miles by land and two and a half miles by water and that it would take the deceased three fourths of an hour to reach the place where he was found slain, and that said deceased left Napoleon, mouth of Arkansas river, ten minutes before three o'clock P. M.; and that the accused was never out of the company of said Cheatham more than from twenty to thirty minutes at one time, from the time said deceased left Napoleon, until about five o'clock in the evening, when said accused started for home. Also, when absent from Cheatham, it is proven said accused was in company with the other two witnesses, to wit: William Baxis and Jacob Brown, part of the time, leaving it an impossibility, beyond a doubt, for the accused William Dunn to have had time to commit the crime of murder on the body of William Condrel, the deceased. Also, from the time the deceased left Napoleon until the accused left said witness' company for home, the said William Condrel must have been far beyond the place he was found dead or slain on the 27th of February and found dead on the morning of the 28th of February, 1838. On these above grounds the accused William Dunn was acquitted.

JAMES EDDINGTON, J. P."

The other case was:
"State and County of Arkansas,
vs.
Samuel Hartley, Gilbert Rowan, John Williams and Joseph Norman.

The 11th day of May, came Elijah Cheatham and returned his warrant for the State of Arkansas, vs. Samuel Hartley, Gilbert Rowan, and others of the steamboat Mount Pleasant, and surrendered said prisoners for trial. On the evidence for the State and County of Arkansas, it was proven by John Salsbury, John Ayesman, Andrew Louther, Jonathan Church, James Baber and George W. Stare, said George W. Stare prosecuting for the state, that the said Samuel Hartley, with Gilbert Rowan, John Williams and Joseph Norman in company with the said Samuel Hartley, that the said Hartley did shoot at the grocery house of D. G. W. Leverett, in the town of Napoleon, sundry times with intent to kill persons therein; and did shoot George W. Stare in the left breast, with a ball or slug and dangerously wound the said George W. Stare, on which grounds of evidence Samuel Hartley, Gilbert Rowan, John Williams and Joseph Norman, were committed to the jail of Arkansas county for further trial in behalf of the State and County of Arkansas. Henderson Shumary and Anthony Brown were acquitted, there being no evidence against them.

John Salbury, John Ayesman, Andrew Louther, Jonathan Church, James Barber and George W. Stare, were or are recognized in behalf of the State of Arkansas to appear at the Circuit Court of said county on first day of said term, the second Monday in October, 1838.

JAMES EDDINGTON, J. P."

Dudley G. W. Leverett, whose name appears in the foregoing record, as the party owning the grocery into which the shots were fired, was clerk of Arkansas county for two years. While residing in this county he married Miss Vassar, and afterwards removed to Napoleon. After the creation of Desha county he was, in 1844, elected clerk of said county, for a term of two years.

In the fall of 1847, Leverett raised a small company of adventurous men, with whom he undertook to cross the plains and the Rocky Mountains, on their way to California. This was before the discovery of gold in that country.

After several months had passed, with no news from or of him, rumor reached his friends in this country that another party passing over the same route, found evidence of the destruction of Leverett and his entire party, by the Indians.

During the year 1838, the sheriff of Arkansas county, under provisions of law then in existence, took a census of the county. This report shows that in this year the population of the county was **two thousand five hundred, eighty-one** souls, divided as follows:

White males	926
White females	762
Free colored males	24
Free colored females	16
Slaves	851

The sheriff in his report failed to show the number of inhabitants in each township, as had been done formerly.

Arkansas county, at this time included the territory now constituting the county of Desha.

At the general election held this year James Smith was elected Senator for the counties of Arkansas and Jefferson and S. V. R. Ryan and James Maxwell, Representatives, Geo. W. Stokes, Clerk, John W. Pullen, Sheriff and Benjamin L. Haller was, by the Justices of the Peace elected County and Probate Judge.

1839.

For the year 1839, neither tradition nor record furnishes us with much of historic interest. The courts of the county disposed of such matters as were presented such as the levying of taxes, making necessary appropriations for maintaining the courts, appointing overseers of the roads, granting license, and all other orders required for the government of the internal affairs of the county.

The County Court, at its April term this year, granted an order creating a new township within the following limits: "Beginning on the bank of the Big Bayou Meto, at its mouth, thence up said bayou to the mouth of Mill or Long Bayou; thence up the same to the line between townships **four** and **five** south, thence west, along said township line to Old River township line; thence south, with said township line to the southern boundary of Arkansas county; thence east, along said boundary line, to the line between ranges **three** and **four,** west; thence along said range line north, to the Arkansas river; thence up said river, to the place of beginning; and that the same be constituted and organized a separate and distinct township, to be called and known by the name of Villemont township."

ARKANSAS COUNTY.

This name was given in honor of Don Carlos de Villemont, who, when the country was under Spanish rule, was a commandant at Arkansas Post.

The County Judge with two Justices of the Peace, the Sheriff and Clerk, constituted the County Court as the records of this time show. The record of proceedings at this term, showing the court to be composed of Benjamin Haller, presiding judge, and Nathaniel Owen and George W. Stokes, associate justices, discloses a fact not often witnessed in judicial proceedings. This is, that George W. Stokes, whose name appears as one of the Justices of the Peace composing this court, was, at the **same** time, **clerk of said court.**

CHAPTER XII.

From the Year 1840 to the Year 1845.

The internal affairs of the county, for the year 1840, as far as the writer has been able to learn, were about the same as in the previous year, with the addition of the general election for state and county officers, and the enumeration of the inhabitants of the county by the Federal authorities.

The result of the election was the choice of Benjamin L. Haller, for Representative, George W. Stokes for Clerk and John L. Jones for Sheriff.

The number of inhabitants in the county as shown by the census of 1840 was **one thousand three hundred forty-six**, a decrease of **eighty** from the census of 1830. This decrease was due to the creation of Desha county, from territory then included within Arkansas county. This territory contained a large portion of the population of Arkansas county. The population of the two counties in 1840 was **two thousand nine hundred forty-four**, an increase of **one thousand five hundred eighteen** in the same territory within the decade ending in 1840.

During this year, a female school was established at Arkansas Post, under the supervision of the Sisters of Charity of the Roman Catholic church. The school was continued about four years.

1841.

At the January term, 1841, of the County Court, David Maxwell was elected judge of said court, which office he held for one year. This is the only change found in the record of proceedings of this court for the year 1841.

1842.

Benjamin L. Haller was at the January term, 1842, of the County Court elected judge of said court. At the general election held in August this year, James Yell was elected Senator for the counties of Arkansas and Jefferson, Richmond Peeler, Representative for Arkansas county, George W. S. Cross, Clerk, and John L. Jones, Sheriff.

1843.

In 1843, there resided on what was then known as Benifield's Lake, about two miles west of Bayou Meto and one mile north of Arkansas river, a man named Benifield, engaged in farming, and cutting and rafting cypress timber. Near his residence there was a large brake of cypress in which he was engaged in cutting timber, and at the same time another man named Josiah Sharp was similarly engaged in the same brake.

Sometime in the month of December 1843, these men met in the brake, and a dispute arose between them as to the ownership of one or more of the logs or tiers of cypress prepared for floating. Out of

ARKANSAS COUNTY.

this dispute a fight arose, by agreement. Sharp, the larger and more powerful man, was armed with a hunter's ordinary butcher knife, about ten or twelve inches long, and Benifield with a cane knife about eighteen inches long; thus armed, with a cypress log between them, the fight began.

Benifield, armed with the longer knife and being the more active man, was getting the better of the fight, when Sharp, to make his short knife available contrived to get within reach of his antagonist, and, striking over Benifield's shoulder plunged his knife into the shoulder blade, breaking the knife and leaving the point in Benifield's shoulder.

Sharp, having broken his knife, was practically disarmed and unable further to defend himself and so announced to Benifield who at once ceased his attack which had been very damaging to Sharp. There they were, one or two miles from a habitation; no one to help them; Sharp, completely exhausted from loss of blood and fatigue incident to the struggle in the power of his antagonist, who was, also, suffering from fatigue and various wounds, with the point of Sharp's knife in his shoulder and unable to extract it.

In this condition, with these surroundings, Benifield helped his prostrate and helpless foe on his own horse, guiding the horse with one hand and holding Sharp on with the other till he reached his own home, where, with the help of his family, he provided for the comfort of Sharp as best he could under the circumstances.

After thus caring for Sharp, Benifield went about one mile, to the nearest landing on the Arkansas river, procured a canoe and paddled down the river another mile to the home of his nearest neighbor, who with the aid of a pair of bullet-moulds, extracted the point of Sharp's knife from his shoulder. This being accomplished he returned to his home, to look after the comfort of Sharp, who in a short time, recovered sufficiently to be removed to his own home.

The main incidents connected with this fight were elicited by the grand juries of the county, before whom the participants were summoned, Sharp in April 1844 and Benifield in October 1844. Sharp in his testimony said that Benifield made an assault on him, the said Sharp, on the 13th day of December, 1843, while Benifield's testimony was "that some time in December 1843, one Josiah Sharp did, with malice aforethought, assault him, the said Benifield, and after making several passes at him the said Benifield, with a knife did stick said knife in him, the said Benifield, to the depth of four inches and broke it off in him."

Both parties were indicted and at divers times appeared in court, but as it appears, not at the same time. This being the case, no evidence could be had of one against the other as neither seemed willing to appear and testify in the matter.

After keeping the case on the docket some time without trial they were nol prossed—Benifield's, at the April term of Circuit Court, 1846, and Sharp's at the April term 1847. Some time before 1847, however, both parties had moved from the county.

In this connection the writer reports as a fact, related to him by G. W. S. Cross, late clerk of the county, who was an uncle of the wife of Benifield, that Sharp, in referring to this difficulty in the presence of Cross, said that he could not divest himself of a strong prejudice, often degenerating into hatred, against Benifield. So powerful was this feeling that he feared that his passion would cause him to commit an assault on Benifield, and in order to avoid this he had decided to leave the county, for Benifield's acts toward him were too generous and noble to receive such a return. Under this influence he did leave the county.

1844.

One of the most memorable periods in the history of Arkansas county, is the one embracing the time of the great overflow caused by the high waters in the White and Arkansas rivers, with their tributaries, during the spring and early summer of 1844.

This overflow is particularly noticeable for its extent and duration. The water in the rivers was reported higher, and consequently more extended than any previous overflow of these rivers, known to the citizens personally or by tradition.

The water remained up and out of the banks of the rivers from April to July, a period of about ninety days which was longer than any previous overflow had lasted.

This being the case, but two farms, along the Arkansas river within the limits of this county, were cultivated, and those to but a limited extent.

From this overflow resulted great destruction of farm-houses, fencing and stock, particularly cattle and hogs, belonging to those living on or near the river. Numbers of farmers abandoned their homes, some temporarily, others permanently.

There were at this time twenty or more planters along the river, with from one hundred to five hundred acres in cultivation; some with large, others with small negro force. All these negroes were to be housed, fed and clothed and otherwise cared for by their owners, until another crop could be cultivated, gathered and marketed, for, until then, no relief could be hoped for except through the individual efforts of the owners to procure, through the influence of friends, means to tide them over to this time.

The reader will bear in mind that at this time and during the days of slavery, the paternal hand of the General Government, "full of the dollar coins on hand", was not extended to those who had been reduced to need by the overflow of the Mississippi and her tributaries. This was an instance in which the American people acted upon the advice of one of their recognized statesmen, who said, "**Let the people take care of themselves, and the government will take care of itself.**" This they did, thanks to their individual pluck and enterprise, the assistance of generous friends, fertile fields and a genial climate all under the beneficent smiles of a kind Providence.

Notwithstanding this overflow. and abundance of water it did not drown out the saloon or "dram-shop," nor quench the thirst of the "wine-bibber" and lover of strong drink, for we learn that one John McChesney kept one of these "pest-houses" in the town of Arkansas

ARKANSAS COUNTY.

Post, where a number of men, on the 24th of December, 1844, assembled to celebrate, in their peculiar way, the incoming Christmas, by indulging in a "general drunk." Among the number thus assembled were Achan Vaugine and John Notrebe, between whom a feud existed. On this occasion a fight, growing out of this feud, occurred, in which Vaugine killed Notrebe.

For this offence, Vaugine was indicted and tried at the April term, 1845, of the Circuit Court of Arkansas county, but on the grounds of self defense was acquitted.

At the general election held this year, Harris Cross was elected Representative, George W. S. Cross, Clerk and John L. Jones, Sheriff.

CHAPTER XIII.

From the Year 1845 to the Year 1850.

For historical data for the year 1845 and several succeeding years, the writer has been dependent on personal knowledge, observation and tradition or the report of events as related to him by reliable citizens of that period, with such information as he has been able to gain from the records in the office of the clerk of Arkansas county.

The county, at that time contained about twelve hundred square miles of territory, lying on both sides of the river, extending from the line dividing townships **one** and **two** south of the Base line, to the line dividing townships **eight** and **nine** south and from White river west, to the line dividing ranges **six** and **seven**, west of the principal meridian. The number of inhabitants of the county at that time is not definitely known, but is supposed to be less than three thousand, the greater number of whom resided at the Post of Arkansas or within six or eight miles east, north and west of this village on or near the Arkansas river.

Arkansas Post, the seat of justice for the county, was the only village or trading-post within the county limits. Twelve families, with a total of less than one hundred souls comprised the population of this village. An old free negro named Mary John kept here, the only hotel or public house in the county, which was, perhaps, the most celebrated in the state for the perfection of its cuisine.

There were three mercantile establishments in the town, two with a small stock of general merchandise, the other more extensive in quantity and variety; a branch of the state bank, then in liquidation, one blacksmith shop, two practising physicians and the principal post-office in the county.

There was but one other post-office in the county, that being located at or near the plantation of Col. Tom Smith on the Arkansas river, about thirty miles from Arkansas Post. This post-office was originally known as **Heckato**, but at the request of the post-master the name was changed to **Neckato**. These offices were supplied with mail once a week by carriers on horseback from Napoleon to Pine Bluff and return.

There was a tri-weekly mail by steamer from Montgomery's Point, on the Mississippi, a few miles above the mouth of White river, to Rock Roe, thence, by stage to Little Rock, but there was no post-office on White river, in the limits of this county, at that time nor for several years after. This lack of mail facilities was a source of great inconvenience to the citizens, as they had to travel from two to twenty-five miles to obtain their mail matter.

That the reader may fully understand the difference between the mail privileges of 1845 and 1901, the writer states that in 1845 there

ARKANSAS COUNTY.

were but the two offices, receiving one mail per week, in the county, while in the same territory in the year 1901 there were thirty-three post-offices and of this number, all but four or five have daily mail service. Within the present limits of the county, which is much less than in 1845, there are **twenty-three** post-offices and all but three of these have daily, except Sunday, mails.

As the only trading point in the county was at Arkansas Post, in the southeast corner of the county, persons needing supplies that could not be produced on their farms or manufactured at their homes, were forced to go to Arkansas Post or some other place at a distance, to procure such supplies. Those who lived along the Arkansas river and Bayou Meto and on Point De Luce, usually obtained their supplies from Arkansas Post, while those living on or near Lagrue and White river went to Montgomery's Point or Napoleon.

A large majority of those residing near La Grue and White river, were dependent on their stock and wild game of the forest to pay for these supplies. When supplies were needed, they would gather such quantities as were necessary of some of the following articles—beef, venison, prairie chickens, and other game, beef hides, skins and peltries —and, placing them in a canoe, go down the river or bayou to Montgomery's Point or Napoleon, where these were exchanged for the necessary supplies, which were placed in the conoe and they paddled up stream to their homes.

Parties residing on or near the prairies, and too far from these streams to take the "dug-out route", usually went to Arkansas Post in wagons, carts or on horseback. When necessity compelled these trips in "fly time" (usually from the 15th of May to the first of September) they had to go in the night or subject their teams to great suffering and themselves to annoyance from the bite of the great swarms of green heads or prairie flies. This custom of traveling over the prairies at night in "fly time" was common at this time and for many years thereafter.

At this time there were but two school-houses in the county, built by the public; one west of and near the present location of "Haller's Chapel", about four miles north of Arkansas Post, the other in what was then known as Point De Luce settlement, south of De Luce bayou and about twelve miles north of Arkansas Post. Both of these were ordinary log cabins with a log cut out of one wall to admit the light. Under this opening a writing bench, made by nailing planks on pins inserted in the wall, was placed, and the seats were split logs with wooden legs inserted in auger holes.

There was but one house dedicated to public worship, in the county and that at Arkansas Post. This was built as a chapel in connection with a female school, organized, and maintained a few years by the Roman Catholics. This school was closed early in 1845, and a few years afterwards the chapel was blown down and completely **wrecked by a windstorm.**

There were two places in the county at which large sheds were built and near them, small cabins or camps erected, for holding the annual camp meetings so common in that day. One of these camp grounds was at Lagrue Springs, about eighteen or twenty miles east of north from the Post, the other on Lenox Lake about seven miles south of the Post.

At these camp grounds, at the school houses mentioned and in private houses in other parts of the county, religious services were occasionally held. These services were often at long intervals however, because of the lack of ministers.

In the fall of 1845, a new shed and camp were built on Point De Luce where religious services were had regularly for a number of years. The building of the new shed caused the abandonment of the one at Lagrue Springs.

There were, at this date a grist and saw mill, propelled by water power, located on Little Bayou Meto, in Villemont township, and four grist mills, propelled by horse power, that were open to public use. One of these was at Harold Stillwell's, four miles west of the Post, one at Rolly Hughes, ten miles north of the Post, one at Gordon's crossing on Big Lagrue, eight or ten miles northeast from Hughes, and one at John R. Walton's, on the chute of White river, about four miles south of the present village of St. Charles. A few of the planters living on or near the Arkansas river, had grist mills attached to the machinery running their cotton gins, but these were not for public use.

A large number of the families of the county were dependent on the steel mills, then coming into use. These mills were made after the style of the coffee-mill and were fastened to a small tree or post planted in the ground near the house of the owner. They were propelled by "armstrong power".

One of the strange phases of this time was the utter indifference of a majority of the settlers as to their home holdings. It is a fact that more than two thirds of the inhabitants had squatted on government land, or land that belonged to other parties. Three fourths of the citizens living east of Big Bayou Meto and north of a line from White river to said bayou, passing four miles north of the Arkansas Post, were living on land to which they made no pretension to ownership, notwithstanding, these lands, were, and had been for years, subject to entry or purchase from the government at the price of one dollar and twenty-five cents per acre.

Two instances are here given to show the indifference of these citizens.—The first is the settlement known as Point De Luce, which in 1845 consisted of fifteen families living on or near Point De Luce bayou. Of these, but four owned the land on which they resided.

The other is that portion of the county lying on Big Lagrue and its tributaries, and between it and White river. In this region of country there was not a resident citizen who owned the land on which he lived and at that time, there were eight settlements on the bluffs abutting on White river, the lands at all these bluffs except at Crockett's Bluff and St. Charles being vacant or government lands.

The lower end of Crockett's Bluff was covered by an old soldier's warrant and the bluff at St. Charles by a Spanish grant, but neither was occupied by the owner. The title to lands on the other bluffs

ARKANSAS COUNTY.

remained with the government for several years. On November 4th, 1846, Anderson's Bluff was purchased by James Anderson, who had resided on this bluff for many years. Here he had established a ferry, which was for several years the only public ferry on White river, within the limits of Arkansas County.

These bluffs, were—St. Charles, Anderson's, Dugan's, Crockett's, Evans', Pickens' or Cascoe, Adam's or Mt. Adams and Pepper's, now known as Preston's. In addition to these, there is a bluff on the chute, known as Walton's Bluff. On this bluff a settlement had been located for more than ten years. This, too, was on government land.

The citizens of the county, outside of the village of Arkansas Post, without exception, lived in unpretentious log-cabins. Some few of these exhibited the exercise of some taste in their construction and afforded comfort to their occupants.

But, notwithstanding their limited means of accommodation, it was characteristic of all, whether neighbor or stranger, to grant shelter and rest, food and drink with hearty welcome, to all who asked. It was certainly true of these people that the "string to their door latch" always hung on the outside, and needed only to be pulled to admit the stranger to a welcome entrance.

These people could, in spirit and in truth, adopt the motto of the Highland chief and say:

"To assail a wearied man were shame
And stranger is a holy name.
Guidance and rest and food and fire
In vain he never must require."

Previous to 1845, the only public building ever erected in the county was a jail, built altogether of wood, which was at this time worthless, the officials being obliged to send prisoners to other counties for safe-keeping.

It is true that commissioners had been appointed by proper authority to select a site and build a court house thereon, but none had been built. Why, the writer knows not. The consequence was that the various courts of the county, together with the records, were, from the organization of civil authority here, till this date and for ten years after, held and kept in a hired house.

At the January term, 1845, of the county court, John M. Schultz was chosen presiding judge of said court.

1846.

At the April term, 1846, of the County Court of Arkansas county, a new township was created by order of the court, the boundaries to be as follows: "Beginning at Lacott's ferry on river Lagrue, thence with the road, to Anderson's ferry on White river; thence, up said river to the county line; thence, west, with said line to the river Lagrue; thence down the same to the beginning." This township was named Crockett township.

This court, at its July term, had under consideration a proposition to levy a tax for the purpose of building a new jail, which, on consideration of a majority of the justices of the county, was rejected.

FROM 1845 TO 1850.

In the spring of this year, a convention of the Democratic party of the county was held in the court house at Arkansas Post, at which the writer was present. The purpose of the convention was to nominate a candidate for Representative in the next legislature, at which session a United States Senator, to succeed Senator Sevier, was to be elected. As soon as organized, the convention unanimously nominated Harris Cross to succeed himself a Representative.

It was known to the leaders in this convention that Cross was a warm personal and political friend of Sevier, and if not "headed off" by the convention would vote for Sevier. As the leaders of the convention were not favorable to Sevier, supposedly from personal considerations, they endeavored to pass, in the convention, a resolution instructing their representative to use all honorable means in his power to prevent Sevier's re-election. Cross, a man of few words, but of strong will and prompt in action, was present. As soon as this resolution was read, and before the chairman could put the question of its adoption to the convention, Cross rose to his feet. Facing the chairman, extending his left arm with his hand pointing toward the chair, he said: "Gentlemen, if that is what you are after, I am not your man," and resumed his seat. This short speech postponed, indefinitely, the consideration of the resolution, and at the general election in August following, he was re-elected representative.

At this election, Richard C. Bird, of Jefferson county, was elected Senator for the counties of Jefferson, Arkansas and Desha, George W. S. Cross, Clerk, and John L. Jones, Sheriff, for Arkansas county. John M. Shultz was elected Judge of the County Court, holding over under his election in 1845.

There was little change in the internal affairs of the county during this year. But few immigrants came to the county, the greater number of whom settled in the eastern and northeastern portions of the county, between Lagrue and White river.

Some time during the summer or early fall of this year, Dr. John A. Jordan, a planter residing on the south side of Arkansas river near Thetford's ferry, lost a negro man. Whether the man ran away or was decoyed off, was not known. The general opinion, however, was that he had been influenced to leave his master, by parties then residing near Big Lagrue, as the fact was developed that one of the men suspected of being connected with the matter, had harbored and otherwise cared for the negro, for some time and another had run him off and sold him to a man in St. Louis, from which point the negro made his escape to freedom.

These facts coming to the knowledge of Jordan, he sued out warrants for the arrest of the parties implicated and placed them in the hands of John Larkey, the constable in Arkansas township, the warrants being made returnable to the office of the Justice of the Peace who issued them. The constable found but one of the accused parties—David Simcoe, the man charged with harboring and feeding the negro. At the trial of Simcoe, the proof was sufficient in the judgment of the Justice of the Peace, to commit Simcoe and order him to prison. There

ARKANSAS COUNTY.

being no jail in the county, he was sent to Pine Bluff for imprisonment, from whence he escaped and was never recaptured.

As soon as it became known that warrants were out for the arrest of the other suspected parties, they hastily left the county, to return no more. Of the accused, the following names are remembered: Joab Simcoe, a brother of the man arrested, James Gallant, a brother-in-law of Simcoe, De Armond and Thomas Watson. Watson was said to be the leader of the gang and the one who sold the negro.

One of the sad events growing out of the arrest of Simcoe, was the tragic death of John La Cotts, at Arkansas Post, in February, 1847, after the escape of Simcoe.

La Cotts resided at the crossing on Big Lagrue, on the road leading from Arkansas Post to Crockett's Bluff and St. Charles and Simcoe, on the same road, at the crossing on Caney Bayou, about two miles from La Cott's and between his place and Arkansas Post, so that in going from La Cott's to Arkansas Post, Simcoe's place must be passed. It happened that at the time of Simcoe's arrest, La Cotts was on his way to Arkansas Post and fell in with the constable, his posse and prisoner, going with them to the Post. Remaining there till after the trial, he found it too late to return home that evening, so remained in town through the night.

At the close of the trial, the greater number of those present, went from the Justice's office to the saloon or "dram-shop," some distance away, where a number of them, including the constable, imbibed freely of the intoxicants dealt out to them, so that they were bereft of charity and reason. The demon of the wine cup took possession of their passions and prevailed on the constable to arrest La Cotts because he was found in the company of Simcoe. He at once, with no authority whatever, forced La Cotts to appear before the Justice, who immediately ordered him to release La Cotts, which he did.

This treatment, on the part of the constable, caused La Cotts to declare that he would be avenged. In February following this trial, La Cotts had occasion to go again to Arkansas Post, and, on his arrival, unfortunately, found Larkey in town and near the saloon. The sight of Larkey recalled the treatment he had received and aroused his passion and desire for revenge. A meeting between them soon followed, when unpleasant threats were made, which prompted Larkey to avoid him by getting into his cart and starting for his home. As soon as La Cotts could get and mount his horse, he hastened after him. He soon overtook Larkey, stopped him in the street, and, jumping from his horse, drew a butcher knife on Larkey, yet in his cart, who, having a pistol, shot La Cotts, killing him.

The writer was present at Larkey's trial on the following day and heard the testimony establishing the facts as above related, with the further testimony that La Cotts had declared before leaving home on this occasion, that he would have satisfaction, if he had to kill Larkey. Upon this testimony Larkey was acquitted.

In closing the narrative of this unpleasant affair, the writer would say that he never heard anyone who knew La Cotts, say that suspicion rested upon him, as being, in any manner, connected with the parties accused of stealing Dr. Jordan's negro, nor that he was associated with disreputable people.

This unfortunate affair, so far as La Cotts was concerned, was, in the mind of the writer, a combination of unfortunate circumstances and **bad whiskey.**

Early in this year, John J. Higgins, from Brown county, Ohio, removed to and settled near Lagrue Springs, where he built a comfortable dwelling and store house and at once began merchandising and trading in stock. This was, possibly, the first store or trading establishment opened for business outside of Arkansas Post and north of Arkansas river in Arkansas county. This business was continued by him till the time of his death, which was rather tragic. He was driving cattle through the woods, when one attempted to escape and he pursued it on horseback, and, in urging his horse, was forced against a leaning tree or limb, knocked off his horse and so injured that he died.

1847.

On an adjourned day of the January term, 1847, of the County Court, held on the 2nd day of February, 1847, Thomas Halli Burton was elected by the Justices of this court, its presiding judge.

This court, at its October term, granted the following order on a petition to remove the seat of justice:

"It is therefore ordered that an election be held at the several places of holding elections in the several townships in said county, on the 27th day of November, A. D., 1847, (being Saturday), for the purpose of electing three commissioners to locate the seat of justice of the county of Arkansas, aforesaid; and it is further ordered that the sheriff of said county, at least fifteen days previous, give notice thereof, by posting at least three advertisements in each township in said county."

If an election was held under this order, no report of it was made to the court as no notice of such election appears on the records.

During this year there was considerable immigration to the county from Tennessee, Mississippi and Alabama, principally with some from Kentucky and Georgia, also. The greater part of these new-comers settled between Big Lagrue and White river, others on or near the Arkansas river. As a majority of these were seeking homes for permanent occupancy, they availed themselves of the great opportunity then offered of obtaining lands desirably located, at low prices, with titles to the same. This movement on the part of the new-comers prompted the old settlers, who had previously manifested great indifference as to their home holdings, to "go and do likewise."

From this time till the commencement of the war in 1861, there was a constant influx of population and wealth to the county spreading over the same, and planting settlers on the rivers and bayous and near the prairies. Few settlements, however, were made in the prairies, as the pasture privileges they afforded were preferred to the cultivation of the land. This pasturage, from the time of the earliest settlement of the county, till 1860, was so plentiful and of such advantage, that great herds of cattle and many horses were raised on the prairies

ARKANSAS COUNTY.

and in the river bottoms, with absolutely no expense to the owners, except that of marking, branding and herding them, with the payment of a small tax on all horses and cattle over three years old.

1848.

At its January term, 1848, the County Court passed an order creating a new township, to be known as Polk township, and having the following boundaries: "Beginning at the mouth of Poplar Creek, running up said creek to its head; thence direct to the head of Lynn creek; thence down said creek to Big Lagrue; thence up said Lagrue to its head and on north to the county line; thence east, with the county line to White river; thence down said river to the beginning. The place of holding the elections to be at Adam's Bluff."

During the early months of this year, a number of immigrants from the older states came to the county, the greater number of whom settled in the eastern part of the county between Big Lagrue and White river. Among these, was an old gentleman named Robinson, who had several sons and sons-in-law. Those of his family having families of their own, located on government lands near the upper end of White river prairie, and without first obtaining titles from the government, began improving the lands on which they settled. This was, unfortunately for them, the rule, as before mentioned, for no one anticipated being deprived of his home or the privilege of purchasing it when in condition to do so. Within a few months of this time, a man called Alexander Carpenter, who said he was from the state of New York, came to the county and located at Crockett's Bluff, about four miles from the Robinson settlement.

Carpenter was of commanding appearance and fine address, representing to the citizens that he was anxious to locate and remain among them, and with them, "grow up with the country." After a few months association with them, he announced his intention of going to Little Rock, where the U. S. Land Office was located, for the purpose of buying a quantity of land from the government for his own use. At the same time he offerred to purchase for any citizens of the vicinity who desired lands, if they would furnish him with the description of the desired lands and the necessary means for purchasing.

To this proposition, William Evans, an old man with large family, acceded and furnished Carpenter with a description of the land he wanted, on which he had a small farm with comfortable dwelling house, and the means to pay for same.

On reaching the Land Office, Carpenter purchased from the United States government, **five hundred sixty** acres of land, all in his own name. This embraced six or seven different tracts including Evans' homestead and nearly, or quite all the lands with their improvements upon which the Robinson family and friends had located.

Soon after Carpenter's return from Little Rock, the fact of his having purchased these lands was noised abroad and soon reached the ears of those residing on them. This, of course, created a great commotion in the community, with much indignation on the part of those who were the victims of his peculiar enterprise.

FROM 1845 TO 1850.

An effort to have an amicable settlement of the affair by the parties interested, offering to pay Carpenter the amount he had paid for the land, with a reasonable fee for his services, proving unsuccessful, the Robinsons and their friends resorted to another and more persuasive method of bringing Carpenter to terms—the **shot-gun argument.**

This argument had the desired effect, as it prompted Carpenter to accept, through a mediator, the original proposition of receiving the amount of money paid by him, with a fee for his services. On receipt of the sum agreed upon, Carpenter deeded to the respective parties, the land they occupied. This included Evans' claim.

Before closing the history of Carpenter's land operations in the county, the writer begs leave to give an account of another of his attempts at "land grabbing," which, if not so sensational as the other, will exhibit in an eminent degree, the genius of the operation.

Under the law then in force, the state donated her right to one hundred and sixty acres of land to the head of the family, with the same amount to each member of the family, on condition that the head of the family, within eighteen months from the date of his donation, build a house on this land and occupy it as his home, or clear, fence and put in state for cultivation, five acres of the tract, and that, within the same time, each member of the family, clear, fence and put in state for cultivation, a like number of acres in his tract.

In each case, the fact that the required improvements had been made within the eighteen months had to be certified under the official signature of a Justice of the Peace of the county. This certificate showed that the Justice had been on the land and knew the improvements to have been made according to law. On filing this certificate in the office of the Auditor of Public Accounts, he gave a certified copy of this certificate, which with the donation deed, was recorded in the proper record office and the donee's title to the land was complete so far as the state could make it.

Under the provisions of this law, Carpenter obtained, from the state, donation deeds to seventeen tracts of land, each containing one hundred and sixty acres, all but   in the name of Carpenters, supposed to be members of his and his relatives' families, none of whom at this time were living in the county. Within the required time, Carpenter filed the necessary certificates of improvements in the office of the Auditor, when, in fact, not a dollar's worth of improvement had been made on any one of said tracts.

How Carpenter obtained these certificates, was, at the time and yet remains, a matter of doubt. Whether he forged them, bribed the Justice of the Peace to issue them, or causd the Justice to become intoxicated and while in that condition induce him to sign previously prepared certificates is not known, though the latter opinion was the current one when the fact was discovered. All of these certificates purported to have been signed by Severn Pepper, a Justice of the Peace living on White river, on the bluff then known as Pepper's, now as Preston's Bluff.

These lands were situated between Big Lagrue and White river, and such of them as were under fradulent certificates, were, for years, called by the citizens of that vicinity, the "Peppered Lands."

Soon after these facts became public, Carpenter disposed of such interests as he had in the county and left, and rumor said that soon after leaving he met with a sad fate somewhere in north Mississippi.

The donation law, under which parties can obtain one hundred and sixty acres of land, was enacted by the Legislature of the State of Arkansas on the 23rd of December, 1840, at the suggestion of James S. Conway, the first governor of the state and believed to be the first effort by state or national government to extend its bounty in this behalf to its citizens.

This law, in a modified form, has remained in force from its first enactment to the present date. (1901)

At the general election held this year, Louis L. Refeld was elected Representative, George W. S. Cross, Clerk, and John L. Jones, Sheriff, for the county.

Up to this date there were but two post-offices in the county, and recognizing the necessity of greater mail facilities to the largely increased population, the writer caused a petition signed by the citizens along the contemplated route, to be sent to the Hon. Robert W. Johnson, then Representative in Congress, praying the establishment of a mail route from Arkansas Post via Point De Luce and Lagrue Springs, to Crockett's Bluff on White river. The request was promptly granted and post-offices established at these three points. As soon as the Postoffice Department could do so, service was established on this route by ordering a weekly mail, on horseback, from Arkansas Post to Crockett's Bluff and return. Later, the route was changed so as to go from Lagrue Springs via Captain Caleb Hewitt's, at which place a post-office called **Molino del Rey,** was established. After the removal of the seat of justice from Arkansas Post in September, 1855, another mail route was established from St. Charles via De Witt, Long Point, Belcher's and Hamilton to Brownsville, then the seat of justice of Prairie county. Over this route, mails were carried on horseback, once a week, from St. Charles to Brownsville and return.

In 1848 and 1849, post-offices were established at St. Charles, Crockett's Bluff, Cascoe and Mt. Adams on White river and at South Bend, Auburn, Cummins and Swan Lake on Arkansas river. The offices on White river were supplied with mail three times a week, by steamers from Napolean to Jacksonport, then the seat of justice of Jackson county, and those on the Arkansas received their mail from steamers running between Napolean and Pine Bluff when navigation permitted. When navigation failed, the mail was carried in stages between these points.

Tradition says that from 1820 to 1825, A. B. K. Thetford carried mail matter from Arkansas Post to Helena once a week. When the water in White river permitted, he went through from one point to the other on horseback, but when the water was too high to admit of this, he went on horseback to the bluff where the village of St. Charles is now located, where he left his horse and getting into a canoe with his mail, floated down White river to the mouth of Big

Creek east of White river, and went up that to the road leading to Helena, where he procured another horse on which he proceeded to Helena. Returning, he again took a canoe on Big Creek, floated down it to White river, went up that to the bluff and there remounted his horse and returned to Arkansas Post.

1849.

There is but little of interest to record, concerning events transpiring in the county during the year 1849.

During this year, news of the discovery of gold in California reached the county and numbers of her citizens, infected with the prevalent gold fever, went to California in quest of a fortune. Some hoped to obtain it by mining, some by trading and others by driving cattle from this country to that for market.

Of the latter class were two brothers named Murdock, who, in company with another brother, then in business in Napoleon, purchased cattle from the citizens here and drove them to California, where they obtained a profitable price for them. Returning to this county, they purchased another drove and, with it, crossed the plains and mountains a second time to California, where they remained.

The report of these men so influenced the citizens that others of them gathered herds of cattle and drove them to the same market.

Among the number thus engaged was a man named John Turner, who, by care and industry, had secured a herd of cattle with which he started across the plains, hoping to get a market for them. On the way he fell sick and died and what became of his cattle or the money he had received for them, if sold, was never known by his family.

The saddest event connected with the California cattle trade during these years, was the tragic death of George Cook, an old and respected citizen of Old River township. Cook was the owner of a large herd of cattle, which he sold to parties hailing from California, agreeing to pay for them on their safe delivery at Fort Smith, Arkansas. Cook, in company with the purchasers and their men, started with the cattle, going by way of Little Rock. Here they crossed the Arkansas river, and, after reaching the hill country west of Little Rock, the leader of the company induced Cook to leave the herd and go with him into the hills, ostensibly for the purpose of hunting deer, then plentiful in the country. Reaching an unfrequented place in the hills, this man killed Cook and pushed forward to Fort Smith. Here, it seems, he had accomplices, who, on the arrival of the cattle, took charge of them with others they had gathered at this point. The leader, with others of the party, pushed forward toward the plains without waiting for the cattle, which in charge of the remainder of the party, followed soon after.

It was some days after Cook's death before the news of it reached his friends at home, who, at once, induced William Daniels and Bazil B. Smith, two of his neighbors, to go in pursuit of the murderer. They followed him as far as Salt Lake City, where they lost all trace of him and returned home.

ARKANSAS COUNTY.

Bazil B. Smith was, for a number of years before and at the time of his death, an honored and respected citizen of De Witt.

In May of this year, the Asiatic cholera made its appearance in the county and prevailed to some extent along the Arkansas river, causing a number of deaths among the negroes living on the plantations along the river. There were no deaths from the disease among the whites within the county, but two of her oldest and most prominent citizens died of it. These were Frederick Notrebe, who died in New Orleans, and Captain Henry M. Clay, who died on the steamer upon which he was returnig from New Orleans to his home, about eight miles above Arkansas Post.

At a special election held on the 5th of February, 1849, John T. Hamilton was elected County and Probate Judge of the county, being the first person elected to that office by the people, as before that time the judges were elected by the Justices of the Peace, once a year, in their respective counties.

On the morning of the 16th day of April, this year, an unusually heavy frost appeared, killing most of the vegetation then out. The early months of the year had been favorable to the growth of farm and garden vegetables, which were, at this time, in a forward state of growth and were all more or less injured by this frost.

CHAPTER XIV.

From the Year 1850 to the Year 1855.

The greater number of immigrants to the state of Arkansas from the older states east of the Mississippi, came by water and entered the state by passing up the Arkansas and White rivers, the Arkansas passing through this county from southwest to northeast, a distance of about fifty miles, and the White forming the eastern boundary of the county, a distance of about thirty-five miles. Both streams flowing through a section of country subject to overflow, presented an uninviting appearance to those passing up or down the rivers. The consequence was that few stopped off to view or "spy out the country," but rather continued on up these rivers to the interior of the state.

After the establishment of better mail facilities through the county, the citizens, appreciating the resources of the county, began corresponding with their friends in the states from whence they came, pointing out these resources and the great advantages to be enjoyed by residents here and induced many to come and settle in the county.

This influx of emigrants to the county caused the establishment of trading posts or stores where general merchandise could be obtained. There were three such establishments on the Arkansas—one at South Bend, one at Auburn and one at Swan Lake—and three on White river—at St. Charles, Crockett's Bluff and Mount Adams.

The greater number of immigrants to the county for several years settled on the east side of the county, on Big Lagrue and between it and White river, giving this section a majority of the votes in the county, and with that majority, the political power on all local questions. This power was manifested at the general election this year, by electing one of their citizens Representative in the state Legislature, over an old and popular citizen residing at Arkansas Post.

The result of the general election of this year shows that Napoleon B. Burrow, of Jefferson county, was elected senator for the district, composed of the counties of Arkansas, Desha and Jefferson. In Arkansas county, Austin H. Ferguson was elected representative, John L. Jones, Sheriff, and William H. HalliBurton, clerk.

The report of Ashur H. Stillwell, who had been appointed Deputy Marshal of the U. S., to take a census of the county and report the material condition of the same, during this year, shows the following facts:

Whole number of inhabitants..................3245
White males 918
White females 776
   Total 1694
Free persons of color..........................13
Slaves of all kinds............................1538

ARKANSAS COUNTY.

These were distributed over the county as follows:
Arkansas township, containing Arkansas Post............584
Crockett township, containing Crockett's Bluff............230
Douglass township, (now in Lincoln county)............1095
Old River township, (now in Jefferson county)...........514
Polk township, containing Mt. Adams...................322
Prairie township, containing St. Charles.................338
Villemont township, (now in Jefferson county)...........162

The report shows that at this time there were three hundred and twenty-eight dwellings in the county occupied by as many families. The number of farms was one hundred and fifty-three. The number of acres comprising these farms was given as twelve thousand, one hundred ninety-three of improved land and thirty-eight thousand four hundred sixteen of unimproved.

The number of horses was nine hundred twenty-five, of neat cattle seven thousand four hundred sixty.

The cotton crop of the preceding year was given as three thousand seven hundred sixty-nine bales.

In the townships of Arkansas, Douglass and Old River, the greater number of the inhabitants were slaves, while in the other townships the greater number were free, thus giving to these latter, all on the east side of the county, the majority of votes, and, consequently, the control of the local affairs of the county, as that, rather than questions of politics, governed the greater number of votes on both sides of the river.

1851.

By an act of Congress, approved the 28th of September, 1850, all the swamp and overflow lands in the state were granted to the state "for the purpose of reclaiming said lands by means of levees and drains."

On the 6th of January, 1851, the Legislature of the state passed the first act on the subject of these lands. This act provided for a board of commissioners to be appointed by the governor, whose duties were to lay off levees, determine their dimensions, select and report to the Commissioner of the General Land Office at Washington, these lands and to classify and fix a price on them.

Under the provisions of this act, the "Swamp Land Commissioners" were appointed, qualified and entered upon their duties early in the year 1851.

The lands selected by the commissioners were divided into two classes, as follows: All swamp lands within six miles of a navigable stream were designated as **first class** and all others as **second class**. The price fixed on first class lands was seventy-five cents per acre and that on second class lands, fifty cents per acre.

The commissioners proceeded at once to let contracts for building levees and to receive applications to purchase lands.

The public records of the state show that as early as the 10th of October of 1851, a large number of applications to purchase such lands in Arkansas county had been made.

Large contracts were let by the commissioners to build levees along the banks of the principal rivers of the state, to be paid for in **Swamp Land Scrip**, which was receivable in payment for swamp lands.

The liberal lettings and the high price agreed to be paid for levee work, in a short time, caused a large quantity of **Swamp Land Scrip** to be given into the hands of contractors, who put it on the market for sale. The result was the depreciation of the value of the scrip then floating on the market.

This depreciation excited a spirit of speculation in swamp lands and induced residents and non-residents to purchase large quantities of these lands, which were to be found all over the county—on the rivers and bayous, on the uplands and in the prairies.

This spirit of speculation was not confined to the purchase and sale of swamp lands, but extended to the lands of the Federal Government. This speculation in lands induced immigrants to come to the county and settle, the settlements being much more generally diffused through the county than in former years. The building of levees along the banks of the Arkansas river was an assurance of practical protection against the annual overflows of that river, and large areas of land on and near its banks were occupied and improved.

Before the adoption of the levee system, there were long stretches of unoccupied lands along the Arkansas river, but as soon as levees were built, these lands were purchased and farms opened on them. Farm houses were built and other improvements made, giving an air of comfort and thrift where tangled woods and uninhabitable swamps had been in former days. At the breaking out of the civil war, nearly all lands along the river banks of the county, susceptible of cultivation, were in a high state of cultivation.

At the January term of county court, in 1851, the clerk of the court submitted a statement of the financial condition of the county on December 31st, 1850, which was as follows:

Receipts into the Treasury..................$1599.50
Amount of Appropriations....................1417.46

Leaving balance in Treasury on December 31st, 1850, of $172.04

The Legislature, at its session in 1850, enacted a law authorizing the county courts of the several counties in the state, to purchase or have built, houses for the care and comfort of the poor in their counties.

Under the provisions of this law, the county court of Arkansas county, through commissioners appointed for the purpose, purchased a small farm situated on the Southwest quarter of the Southwest fourth of Section Three in Township Seven, South of Range Three West. On this farm was a house sufficiently large to accommodate the paupers of the county and their keeper, and for several years they were cared for here. The house was about six miles north of Arkansas Post.

In 1851, Robert H. Douglass was appointed Internal Improvement Commissioner for Arkansas county, to receive and disburse the **Internal Improvement Fund** of the county. This fund arose from the sale of

ARKANSAS COUNTY.

Internal Improvement lands granted to the state of Arkansas by the Congress of the United States.

1852.

The only items sufficient for narration as having transpired in the county during the year 1852, are the results of the general election and the causes leading to these results.

Anterior to the election of 1850, all county officials were citizens of Arkansas Post or near here, and all representatives in the Legislature from the organization of the territory till this date, resided at or near this place.

At the election of 1838, Col. James Smith, a planter of large interests, who lived on his plantation about four miles above Arkansas Post, was elected to the Senate, and S. V. R. Ryan and James Maxwell to the House of Representatives. Ryan's home was near Arkansas Post, and Maxwell's about fourteen miles north of this place.

At this time the eastern boundary of the county was the Mississippi river and the southern, the northern boundary of Chicot county—some thirty miles or more south of Arkansas Post. Measuring from east to west, then, this place was near the center of the county and from north to south, rather south of the center, but practically in the center of population. Eligibly located, on a high bank on the north side of Arkansas river, Arkansas Post, then the seat of justice for the county was favorably situated for becoming a town of considerable business and population.

Notwithstanding all these advantages in favor of keeping this place near the geographical center, as well as the center of population of the county, her representatives elected in 1838—two to the House and one to the Senate—permitted the curtailment of her territory, by the creation of a new county which brought the boundaries of this new county within **four** miles of Arkansas Post on the east and **six** miles on the south. This left the county seat in the extreme southeast corner of the county—about twenty miles from the western and forty from the northern boundary of the county.

At the same session of the Legislature creating the county of Desha by which Arkansas county was dismembered of so large a portion of her territory, an act was passed to protect citizens and owners of property in the then existing county seats against loss by the removal of same. This act provided that a tax be imposed upon the property of all the citizens of the county proposing such a removal to pay the appraised value of property located in such town.

The existence of this law seems to have prevented any action on the subject of the removal of the county seat of this county to a more eligible point near the center of the county, notwithstanding the fact that a large majority of citizens who resided at points from ten to twelve miles distant from the county seat, greatly desired its removal.

At the general election of 1852, Austin H. Ferguson was re-elected representative. Residing thirty-five miles from Arkansas Post and realizing the inconveniences occasioned by being so situated, he fully appreciated the desire of a majority of his constituents for the re-

FROM 1850 TO 1855.

moval of the county seat. Prompted by these considerations, he caused the passage of an act in the Legislature of this year, repealing the law imposing taxes on property of citizens of the county to pay the appraised value of property in county seats where a removal was contemplated. He was also instrumental in the passage of another act requiring the county court of Arkansas county to order an election for the choice of three commissioners to select and determine upon a site for a new county seat.

The result of the general election of this year was as follows:
Austin H. Ferguson, representative.
William Refeld, clerk circuit court.
Jno. F. Hamilton, sheriff.
Thomas HalliBurton, county judge.

In the early days of this year, John L. Jones, who had been sheriff of the county since October, 1840, resigned his office. In April, 1852, he boarded the steamer **Pocahontas,** at his landing on the Arkansas river, for New Orleans, and was burned on this ill-fated vessel in the Mississippi river, a few miles below Napoleon, Arkansas.

The author asks the reader to pardon him in a short digression from his homely narrative, to pay a humble, but deserving tribute, to the memory of his friend, John L. Jones, the late sheriff of Arkansas county. Jones was a native of Georgia, and from that state came to Arkansas about the year 1835 and settled near Arkansas Post. In 1839, he was elected constable for Arkansas township and at the general election of 1840, was elected sheriff of the county. From that time until the election of 1852, he was, at every election, elected his own successor. Had he continued to the end of his term, October, 1852, he would have held the office twelve years. A proposed change of residence caused his resignation and he was on a business trip, preparatory to that change, when he met his sad fate.

At the April term, 1847, of the circuit court of the county, unsolicited on his part, or by his friends, the writer was appointed by Jones, his deputy. The appointment was at once reported to the court, then in session, approved and the appointee at once qualified and entered upon his duties. This relationship continued until December, 1850, at which time, contrary to the wishes of Jones, the writer resigned his appointment.

As soon as his deputy became familiar with his duties and acquainted with the citizens of the county, Jones intrusted the principal business of the office to him. The writer takes this method of perpetuating his appreciation of the friendship of his principal and saying that in all his experience through protracted life, he has had no truer, more liberal and disinterested friend than the man whose name, he is, in this manner, trying to commemorate.

On the resignation of the office of sheriff, in 1852, by John L. Jones, John T. Hamilton was appointed his successor, thereby vacating the office of county judge, to which office Thomas HalliBurton was appointed. Each of these, was, in the general election of August, 1852, elected his own successor.

The county court, at its July term, 1852, established a new town-

ARKANSAS COUNTY.

ship to be known by the name of LaGrue. Its boundaries were as follows: "Beginning at the residence of Charles Bogy, Sr., on the La Grue, running thence, to and including Roland Haller; thence, to and including Alexander Lemmon's; thence, west to the road leading from Arkansas Post to Little Rock; thence, with said road, to the north boundary line of said county; thence, with said line, to the Little La Grue; thence, down the Little La Grue to the mouth; thence, down the Big La Grue to the beginning." The voting precinct in this new township was ordered to be at the residence of John J. Higgins, at La Grue Springs. After the removal of the county seat from Arkansas Post to De Witt, the voting precinct was removed to that place.

1853.

The county court, at the January term, 1853, granted the following order:

"Election of Commissioners to locate county seat of Arkansas County.

Now, on this day, it was ordered by the court that, in obedience to an act passed at the last session of the General Assembly of the State of Arkansas and approved December 10th, 1852, requiring this court to order an election of three commissioners to locate the county seat of the county of Arkansas.

It is therefore ordered that the sheriff proceed to open and hold an election at the several precincts in Arkansas county, on Saturday, the 19th day of February, A. D., 1853, in accordance with the statute in such case made and provided."

At the election held under this order, Charles W. Belknap, Leroy Montgomery and John A. Moorman were elected commissioners, who after their qualification and organization, selected the Northeast quarter, of section four, in Township five, South of Range three West —the same being vacant and one half belonging to the state, the other to the general government. This selection, the commissioners reported to the county court at its July term, 1853.

The court then ordered an appropriation of two hundred and fifty dollars to be used in purchasing the land and defraying the expenses of the commissioners. Scrip for this purpose was issued by the clerk in sums of fifty dollars, and was given into the charge of the commissioners.

Of this appropriation the sum necessary for the purchase of the land was placed in the hands of the writer, by the commissioners, who instructed him to purchase the land they had chosen. This was done and reported to the commissioners, in whose names the purchase was made—one half in August, the other in December, 1853.

1854.

In the early months of 1854, under the direction of the county seat commissioners, Adam McCool, the county surveyor, surveyed the land selected for the new county seat, laid it off and platted it into square blocks and lots, with the proper streets and alleys.

During the progress of the survey there were but two of the commissioners present. These two, Charles W. Belknap and Leroy Montgomery, failing to agree upon a name for the new county seat, called to their help, McCool, the county surveyor, to supply the place of Dr. John A. Moorman, the absent commissioner. It was agreed that each should write the name he wished to give the new town on a ballot, placing these in a hat, the one drawn out first to be adopted. McCool, being a great admirer of De Witt Clinton, wished to express his admiration by giving the new town his name, and knowing that the county seat of another county in the state was Clinton he used De Witt as his choice. This was drawn from the hat first, and under the agreement was adopted.

This was told the writer by McCool, himself, a short time after the occurrence and is given here to correct an erroneous idea that the name was decided upon by a game of poker. The writer knows that McCool was a minister of the gospel in good standing, and that neither he nor Belknap was a poker player.

As soon as the survey was completed, the commissioners caused the proposed sale of the lots to be advertised for the month of July, 1854, at which time a number of these lots were sold. At this sale the writer was present, and, at the request of the commissioners assisted in taking notes from purchasers, preparing the necessary bond for title, etc.

The result of the general election of August, 1854 was the election of Austin H. Ferguson, Senator, for the district composed of Arkansas, Desha and Jefferson counties, Samuel Mitchell, representative, Pleasant P. Cross, sheriff and John G. Quertermous, clerk, for the county of Arkansas.

At the October term of the county court, the resignation of John A. Moorman as one of the county seat commissioners was reported and John W. Lowe was appointed in his stead.

During this year Charles W. Belknap was appointed **Internal Improvement** commissioner, to succeed Robert H. Douglass and to him the **Internal Improvement** Fund of the county was transferred.

CHAPTER XV.

From the Year 1855 to the Year 1860.

At the time of the sale of the lots in the new town, there were not more than ten families within a radius of five miles of the place, but as soon as it was known that the seat of justice was to be removed to De Witt, parties commenced purchasing lands, improving and moving on them. This inflow of population was not great, but continued until 1861, when, war being imminent, it ceased.

This immigration made it necessary for the county court to change the lines of old and establish new townships for the accommodation of citizens.

Under this influence, at its January term, 1855, the court established a new township, within the following bounds: "Commencing at the Southeast corner of Township five, South, Range four West, running thence West with the South boundary of said Township to the western boundary of Arkansas county; thence North with the western boundary of said county to the Northwest corner of the county; thence, East with the northern boundary of the county, to where said line crosses or intersects Little La Grue; thence down Little La Grue to where it croses the Range line dividing Ranges three and four West; thence South with said line to the beginning." The name given the township was **Morris** and the voting precinct was at the residence of D. S. Morris.

At the April term, 1855, of the county court, an order was given requiring the commissioners, John W. Lowe, Charles W. Belknap and Leroy Montgomery to let, to the lowest and best bidder, the contract for the erection of suitable buildings for the holding of court, at the new county seat.

Complying with this order three log buildings were erected in the new town. These were a large room for the courts, a small one for the clerk's office and another for the accommodation of jurors. This fact was reported to the county court at its July term, when it was ordered that the clerk of the court move the records of the county to the new county seat, by or before September 1st, 1855, and that all courts of the county, in future, be held in De Witt and all processes be made returnable thereto.

This was the last term of county court held in Arkansas Post and the adjourning order, on July 17th, 1855 was signed by T. P. Morrison, probate judge, and W. Duncan and Wm. McGraw, justices of the peace.

In the month of September, 1855, John G. Quertermous, clerk of the county, in compliance with the above mentioned order removed the records and files of the circuit, probate and county courts, then in his office as clerk of the circuit and **ex-officio** clerk of the probate and county courts, to the new office in De Witt.

In October, the first term of court was held here, as evidenced by an order of court made on the 15th of October, 1855. This order was signed by T. P. Morrison, judge, and Wm. McGraw and Charles J. Miller, justices of the peace.

The reader's attention is called to the fact that the log cabin in which the above mentioned order was made, was the first courthouse built within the limits of the county or the civil district preceding the organization of a county, notwithstanding the fact that civil authority had been established here for more than a century and a quarter—from 1722 to 1855.

The times for holding circuit court here in 1855, were in the months of May and November. At the November term the weather was so inclement and the accommodation for man and beast, in the new town, so meagre that, at the solicitation of the citizens Judge Sorrells, then the presiding judge, promptly consented to an adjournment for the term, so no circuit court was held in De Witt till May, 1856.

1856.

The removal of the county seat from Arkansas Post to De Witt necessitated the laying off and building of new roads throughout the county, especially from the new town. The building of bridges across the larger streams also became necessary and at the January term, 1856, of the county court, which consisted of Thomas P. Morrison, judge, with Charles J. Miller, William McGraw, E. McGuffey and H. K. Stephen justices, an order was made on this subject. This order authorized Charles W. Belknap, Internal Improvement Commissioner, to receive bids and let contracts for the building of two bridges—one across Big LaGrue and one across Little LaGrue, on the road leading from De Witt to St. Charles and Anderson's Ferry on White river. Five hundred dollars of the **Internal Improvement Fund**, not otherwise appropriated, was appropriated for this purpose.

In obedience to this order these bridges were constructed and under similar orders, granted by the court during the years from 1856 to 1860 other bridges were built. These bridges were located as follows: On the road from DeWitt to Crockett's Bluff, one was built at the crossing of Little LaGrue and one across Big LaGrue near the residence of Jesse Gravitt; one on the road leading from DeWitt to Pine Bluff via Old river and Swan Lake, one across Mill Bayou near the residence of W. D. Rodgers, one across Big Bayou Meto at the Pool crossing, one across Cross Bayou on Section 16, in Township 6 south, of Range 5 west, and one across Little Bayou Meto near the old saw mill. A bridge was built across Little LaGrue near the residence of Maj. John G. Freeman; on the road leading north from DeWitt to Sassafras Prairie and others over the smaller streams of the county.

Nearly all the bridges on the principal roads throughout the county were destroyed during the civil war, either by tearing them away or by burning.

ARKANSAS COUNTY.

At the general election of August, 1856, Samuel Mitchell was elected representative; John G. Quertermous, clerk; George W. S. Cross, sheriff; and Thomas P. Morrison, county judge.

1857.

During the year 1857 but few events of interest took place in the county. One of the most notable happenings of the year was the heavy frost of April 5th and 6th. Previous to this time the season had been unusually favorable to the growth of vegetation, so that the leaves on the trees were fully half grown and all other vegetation in field and forest was in a forward state of growth. The frost which appeared on the 5th and 6th of April was so heavy that all this growth, practically, was killed. In fact, so heavy was it, that many trees in the forest were killed, giving it, in a few days' time the appearance of December rather than of April.

At the October Term, 1857, of the county court, William H. Halli-Burton was appointed commissioner to sell to the highest and best bidder, at the court house in DeWitt, the lands and tenements belonging to the county, known as the **Poor House Place**. After notice having been given of time, place and terms, the sale took place December 10th, 1857, the property being bought by William McGraw for four hundred and twenty-five dollars. The county court being then in session, the sale was reported, approved and confirmed on this day.

After the sale of the **Poor House** property, the county court resumed the original practice of letting paupers to lowest responsible bidder, to be kept and cared for by him, wherever he desired, within the county.

1858.

The county court, on May 5th, 1858, appointed W. H. HalliBurton commissioner of public buildings, for the county of Arkansas, and by an order of that date empowered him to offer a reward of twenty-five dollars for the most acceptable plan for a court house, to be built in DeWitt, and authorized him to advertise in as many newspapers as he thought proper.

In obedience to this order, the commissioner did advertise, and in due time received several plans, with specifications, which he submitted to the court on July 20th, 1858. Of these plans, the one offered by M. D. Cheek was accepted, and the clerk was ordered to issue his warrant on the county treasurer, in favor of Cheek, for the sum of twenty-five dollars.

The commissioner was ordered to advertise in the **True Democrat** and in the **Gazette and Democrat** for proposals for building this court house, the limit of time for receiving bids being the first day of the next term of court.

In response to these advertisements, the commissioner received a number of bids which were submitted to the court at its January term, 1859, when a majority of the justices were present. Of these bids, that of W. S. Quertermous & Co., notified by David B. Quertermous, agreeing to build the house for twelve thousand dollars, was accepted by the court, and the contract for building awarded to David B. Quertermous. The commissioner was authorized to close the contract and take the necessary bond from the contractor, for the performance of the work. This was done, and the bond filed in the office of the court.

At this term of court, necessary steps were taken for levying a tax on the taxable property of the county, for the year 1859, and at the April term this tax was fixed at one-fourth of one per cent.

At the January term, 1860, W. H. HalliBurton resigned and James M. Barker was chosen by the court, his successor as commissioner of public buildings.

In April, 1860, the county court, with the consent of the contractor, made such alterations in the plan for the court house, that a further allowance of eight hundred and fifty dollars to the contractor became necessary.

The final settlement of David B. Quertermous, as contractor, was made at the July term, 1861, of the county court, when the clerk was ordered to issue in favor of D. B. Quertermous his warrant on the county treasurer for sixteen hundred nineteen dollars and eighty-nine cents, balance due him on this contract.

Early in the year 1858, George W. S. Cross, who had been elected sheriff at the election of 1856, resigned and Henry K. Stephen was appointed to succeed him.

At the general election of August, 1858, Thomas Fletcher was elected to the senate from the district composed of the counties of Arkansas, Desha and Jefferson. For Arkansas county Samuel Mitchell was elected representative; Thomas P. Morrison, county judge; John G. Quertermous, clerk; and Joseph H. Maxwell, sheriff.

One of the most remarkable records of the county court of Arkansas county was made at its July term, 1858, and that the reader may rightfully appreciate the same, it is given in full.
"Appropriation to Collector and Deputies.

"Now, on this day, the court being satisfied that, owing to the high water in the Arkansas and White rivers, the said collector has had great difficulty in collecting the county revenue of this county, it is therefore considered and ordered by the court, that the sum of one hundred dollars be and the same is, hereby, allowed to H. K. Stephen, as collector as aforesaid, and to his deputies, for an additional compensation for collecting the revenue for 1857."

1859.

At the January term, 1859, of the county court, the clerk thereof was ordered to draw from the county treasurer of Arkansas county the sum of **three hundred forty-seven dollars and fifty cents** to finish paying Stephens and Willis for building the county jail, showing that at a former term of court, this building had been ordered built.

The building was of wood and was, with other buildings in the town of DeWitt, burned by the Federal soldiers during the war between the States.

During the summer months of this year, a number of the cattle

ARKANSAS COUNTY.

men on and near the south end of Grand Prairie discovered that their cattle were mysteriously disappearing. When this discovery was made, an investigation to ascertain what became of the cattle was begun and it was found that the missing cattle were being secretly killed for beef and sold by parties living in that part of the county. Among other evidences of such killing, a number of heads and hides were found in an unused well in the yard of the suspected parties. These discoveries prompted the formation of a **"Vigilance Committee"** composed of some of the best citizens of the county, under whose direction such steps were taken that quite a number of the suspected parties left the county and have not returned.

CHAPTER XVI.

From the Year 1860 to the Year 1865.

Among the early orders of the county court at its January term, 1860, was the appointment of a county attorney, Joseph J. Poindexter being chosen for the office at a salary of **four hundred dollars** per annum payable quarterly. This is the first recorded evidence of the court's calling to its aid a legal adviser for a stated period.

In the month of September, 1860, John G. Quertermous, who had been clerk of the county of Arkansas since October, 1854, resigned, and John T. Taylor was appointed to fill his unexpired term.

The result of the election in August this year, was the re-election of Thomas Fletcher as senator from the counties of Arkansas, Desha and Jefferson, and of Jordan T. Gibson, representative from Arkansas county. Felix C. Allen was elected county and probate judge; Joseph H. Maxwell, circuit court clerk; Henry K. Stephen, sheriff; and John W. Lowe, treasurer.

The returns of the U. S. census for the year 1860 gave Arkansas county a population of **eight thousand eight hundred forty-four,** an increase of **five thousand five hundred ninety-nine** over the population of 1850, as the census for that year gave a population of **three thousand two hundred forty-five.**

1861.

The result of the presidential election of 1860 excited great apprehension in the minds of the Southern people, that sectional influence dominating congress would cause legislation unfavorable to the interests and institutions of their section of the Union. Under this apprehension, the legislature of the state of Arkansas, on the 15th of January, 1861, passed a law providing that "The governor shall issue his proclamation ordering an election in all the counties in this state to be held on the 18th day of February, 1861, which election shall be conducted as state elections are now conducted." "That, at said election, the people shall vote for a delegate or delegates to said convention, and returns of said election shall be made on the 2nd day of March, 1861; and if, on counting the votes of all the counties of this state it shall appear that a majority of all the votes cast are for a convention, then the governor shall immediately issue his proclamation, requiring the delegates, elected as aforesaid, to convene on the following Monday, and organize themselves into a state convntion."

Under the provisions of this act, an election was held on the 18th of February,1861, and on the 2nd of March, Governor Rector issued his proclamation, notifying the delegates that it appeared, upon counting the votes, that a majority of **eleven thousand five hundred and eighty-six** were for convention.

ARKANSAS COUNTY.

"At this election in Arkansas County, there were six hundred and fifty votes polled; of this number five hundred and eighteen were for convention and one hundred and thirteen against, showing a majority in favor of convention of three hundred and eighty-four. Of this number of votes polled, James L. Totten, of Prairie Township, as delegate to said convention, received five hundred and twelve, he being the only candidate voted for at said election."

Maj. Totten was a lawyer of acknowledged ability and large experience, both in his native state of Tennessee and in Mississippi. In the latter state, from whence he moved to Arkansas county, he had had some legislative experience as well.

The convention assembled at the capitol in Little Rock on Monday the 4th of March, 1861, and remained in session until the 21st of this month, when it adjourned till the 19th of August, 1861, subject to the call of the president of the convention. On the day of adjournment the following resolution was passed:

"Resolved, as the sense of this convention, that the people of Arkansas prefer a perpetuity of the Federal Union, to its dismemberment or disruption, provided it can be perpetuated upon a basis guaranteeing equal rights and privileges to all the states alike, South, as well as North."

Up to this date, there had been no effort to organize and equip military companies, hostile to the Federal government, in Arkansas county. But immediately after President Lincoln's proclamation of the 15th of April, 1861, calling for 75,000 militia "to repossess forts, places and property which have been seized from the Union," when a requisition by the Secretary of War was made on the governor of the state for 780 men, for the purpose, as Governor Rector said, "of wiping out and desolating the South," an almost unanimous disposition manifested itself in the minds of the citizen soldiery of the county to organize and equip companies to resist any and all efforts, on the part of the Federal government, to interfere with the internal affairs of the state. Between the date of the President's proclamation and the reassembling of the state convention on May 6th, 1861 (The convention having been called together by the president thereof), two large companies of militia were raised and organized. These marched to Little Rock and tendered their services to the Confederate States government.

The first company, consisting of 127 men, was raised, organized and commanded by Robert H. Crockett; the second, consisting of —— men, by David B. Quertermous, of DeWitt.

These companies formed part of the First Regiment of Arkansas Infantry, organized at Little Rock in May, 1861, to which James F. Fagan was elected colonel. The regiment was immediately sent to Virginia and participated in the battle of Manassas, July 21st, 1861, supporting Lindsay Walker's Artillery.

For want of muster rolls and other reliable data, the writer is unable to give the names of the individuals composing these companies or a detailed account of the movement of the regiment of which they formed a part. After the battle of Manassas or Bull Run, in July, 1861, this regiment was sent west of the mountains into the Tennessee valley

FROM 1860 TO 1865.

and in August, 1862, was in the battle of Shiloh. Here the regiment lost, in killed, wounded and missing, 364, but how many of these belonged to the two Arkansas county companies is not known. It was also at Perryville, Kentucky, in October, 1862; Murfreesboro, Tennessee, in December, 1862, and January, 1863; at Chickamauga, Georgia, in September, 1863; at Chattanooga, Tennessee, Missionary Ridge, Tennessee, and Ringold Gap, Georgia, in November, 1863; Resasa and Dallas, in Georgia, in May, 1864; at New Hope Church, Tullahoma, Peach Tree Creek, Atlanta and Ezra Church in July, 1864; at Jonesboro, August, 1864; Franklin, Tennessee, in November, 1864; at Nashville, Tennessee, December, 1864, and at Bentonville, in March, 1865.

There were frequent changes in these companies by promotion, resignation and death, but having obtained but little reliable information on this subject, the writer can give only a few such changes. In Company H, First Regiment, of Arkansas Infantry, Captain Crockett resigned and Jordan T. Gibson was elected his successor. Gibson was killed at Shiloh and ———Garrett succeeded him.

In Company K, of this regiment, Captain David B. Quertermous resigned and was succeeded by Martin Boswell, who on resigning, was succeeded by Felix G. Lusk.

Immediately after the issuance of President Lincoln's proclamation of April 15th, 1861, Samuel G. Smith, then residing on his father's plantation on Arkansas river, in the western part of the county, raised and organized a company of which he was elected captain. The company marched to Little Rock and joined "**Lyon's Regiment**," the **Sixth Arkansas Volunteers**, and was sent to Pocahontas, Arkansas, to North Missouri and to Columbus and Bowling Green, Kentucky. This regiment was engaged in the battle of Shiloh, Tennessee, in August, 1862, after which it was assigned to duty in Bragg's army being at Chattanooga, Tennessee, Perryville, Kentucky, Murfreesboro, Tennessee, Liberty Gap and Chickamauga, Georgia, and at Missionary Ridge and Franklin, Tennessee. Later it was assigned to service in Gen. Johnston's army, and participated in all the battles opposing Gen. Sherman in his march through Georgia. At the close of the war, the remainder of this regiment surrended with Gen. Johnston. At a re-organization of the regiment Captain Smith was elected colonel, and, rumor says, was promoted to Brigadier General, but was killed near Atlanta, before receiving his commission. After he was elected colonel, J. F. Armstrong succeeded him as captain of his company.

Charles C. Gadden, of DeWitt, organized a company in the early summer of 1861, and with it went to Little Rock, where it, with other companies, formed a regiment, but by what name or number this regiment was known the writer has been unable to learn.

At the organization of this regiment, Captain Gadden was elected Major and Wm. F. Gibson captain of his company.

The regiment of which this company was a part was present at the battle of Oak Hill in August, 1861, and participated in the actions of that eventful day.

This regiment belonged to the state troops and after the battle of Oak Hill was disbanded, but Captain Gibson, soon after re-organized his company, of which he was again elected captain, and was sent east of the Mississippi river. In what regiment this company was placed is not known to the writer.

Until the close of the war this company remained in active service. It participated in the battle of Chickamauga, where Captain Gibson, with others of his company, was serevely wounded.

At a reunion of the Confederate soldiers of Arkansas county in August, 1901, but sixty-three answered to their names at roll-call.

At the beginning of the war in 1861 there were ten practicing attorneys in Arkansas county; nine in the town of DeWitt and one at Mount Adams. Of this number eight went into active service in the army. These were Robert H. Crockett, of Mount Adams, Charles C. Gadden, Joseph J. Poindexter, Jordan T. Gibson, Justin K. Wall, ——— Wilcox, L. D. Harvey and ——— Garrett of DeWitt. Five of these were killed or died in the army. Jordan T. Gibson and L. D. Harvey were killed at Shiloh, and Justin K. Wall at Franklin, Tennessee. Where Wilcox and Garrett lost their lives is not known. Soon after the close of the war Joseph J. Poindexter removed to Texas and died, thus leaving but two of the original number—General Robert H. Crockett of Stuttgart, and Dr. C. C. Gadden, president of Galloway College at Searcy, Arkansas.

During the sitting of the state convention in 1861, two ordinances were passed providing for military expenses and the support of families of volunteers. The first of these, on May 11th, authorized "the levy of a tax for military and other purposes" and the second, on May 30th, was "to provide for the relief of families of volunteers." These ordinances provided that the county courts of the state levy a tax not exceeding one-fourth of one per cent on all taxable property in the county, for these purposes. Under such provision, the county court of Arkansas county, at its July term, 1861, levied a tax of one-fourth of one per cent, which rate was levied for the years 1862 and 1863 also.

The county court of Arkansas county, at its various terms during the years 1861-62-63-64 voted appropriations for the maintenance of indigent families of soldiers who were then in the army or had died in active service. There were two reports of the number of these families made to the court—one at the January term, 1863, and one at the July term, 1863. In the first report, it was shown that to that date, provision had been made for **one hundred and thirty-six** families, while the second report gave **two hundred and nine** families provided for.

All the courts of the county, during the year 1861, were held at the time prescribed by law.

Before passing to the events of 1862 the writer would refer once more to the acts of the state convention by quoting an ordinance passed by this body, which shows the careful interest of Arkansas county's welfare taken by her delegate to this convention. The ordinance is as follows:

"An Ordinance for the Benefit of Arkansas County:—

"Be it ordained by the people of the state of Arkansas, in convention assembled, that the present boundaries of the county of Arkansas shall never be reduced below the present limits, unless it shall be by the consent of a majority of the qualified voters of said county, expressed at a general election."

"Adopted and passed by the convention on the first day of June, A. D., 1861.

DAVID WALKER,
"President of the State Convention of Arkansas."
"Attest: ELIAS C. BOUDINOT,
"Secretary of the Arkansas State Convention.

1862.

Early in the year 1862, there were two other companies raised and organized in Arkansas county. One of these was organized by John R. Maxwell, who was elected captain, three other of its officers being Benjamin F. Quertermous, William R. Marshall and William N. Bransford. This company joined Colonel Morgan's regiment as **Company I.** Of the movements of this company or the regiment of which it formed a part, the writer has little information. It participated in the battle of Prairie Grove in Arkansas, and afterward at Shiloh, as part of the **7th Arkansas.** It was returned to the Trans-Mississippi Department in which service it remained until the close of the war. While in this service it participated in the battle of Pleasant Hill, Louisiana.

About the time of the organization of Captain Maxwell's company, Felix R. Robinson raised and organized a company of which he was elected captain, but soon after fell sick, returned home and died. As the writer remembers it, Charles J. Miller was elected to the captaincy, and the company was sent east of the Mississippi. Of what regiment it formed a part, of the battles in which it was engaged nor of the losses of the company, the writer does not know.

Early in the spring of 1862, the military authorities in the Trans-Mississippi Department ordered the erection of fortifications at St. Charles, to prevent Federal gunboats and transports ascending White river. This work and the defense of the fort were assigned to Captain Dunnington. In June of this year an attack was made on this fort by Federal authorities, an account of which, as given by Confederate authorities is as follows: "On June 16th a Federal fleet appeared in White river near St. Charles. It consisted of the ironclad gunboats St. Louis and Mound City, each mounting thirteen guns; the Lexington and Conestoga, partially ironclad, each carrying seven guns; the tug Tiger, carrying one 34 pounder howitzer; and three transports, with between 1,000 and 1,500 infantry, under Col. G. W. Fitch.

The Mauripas was at St. Charles, but would have been useless against the enemy's ironclad vessels. The obstructions being incomplete, she was sunk across the channel, together with two steamboats. Two rifle 32 pounders and four field pieces were put in battery on the bluff, manned by 79 men of the crews of the Mauripas and Pocahontas, under Captain Dunnington, of the latter vessel. Captain Williams' armed men, 35 in number, were disposed as sharpshooters, below. Those not armed were sent to the rear. Captain Fry was placed in chief command. The Federal gunboats attacked about 9 A. M. on the 17th. After an engagement of nearly three hours' duration, the Mound City was blown up by a shot from our batteries, and the rest retired out of range. The infantry then landed and carried the position; our little force spiking the guns and retiring up the river. Our loss was 6 killed, 1 wounded and 8 missing. That of the enemy was over 200. On the Mound City, alone, 180 perished. Captain Fry, the last to retreat, was severely wounded and made prisoner."

From an elaborate report made by Federal officers, of this battle, the following synopsis is given:

"St. Charles, June 17th, 1862.

"The vicinity of the enemy having been ascertained on the evening previous, a combined movement was arranged, with a view to making an attack, between Captain Kitty, senior officer of the gunboats, and —————— —————— commander of the land troops, for 6 o'clock A. M. At that hour the flotilla moved up about two and a half miles below the town. The land troops (Forty-Sixth Indiana) disembarked, and skirmishers were thrown out, who quietly drove in the enemy's pickets and pushed forwards to the foot of the bluff, upon which the village is built and their batteries were placed. Beyond the foot of the bluff, the skirmishers could not advance without being exposed to the fire of our gunboats. These boats were Mound City, St. Louis, Conestega and Lexington, four in number under command of Captain Kitty, of the Mound City, which was disabled by having steam drum burst by shot from the enemy's gun, killing by steam and otherwise, a great many. Nearly all her crew, of more than 100, were disabled, among them Captain Kitty; half or more of them were killed.

"The enemy had four guns, under command of Captain Fry, who, with 30 men, was captured, and the guns thrown into the river."

Colonel Fitch reports that 7 or 8 of the enemy were killed. These he had buried, but others killed in edge of cornfield were not buried.

The number of Federal troops engaged in this attack was not given. It was reported, at the time, that after the bursting of the steam drum of the Mound City, Captain Fry's men shot those in the water trying to escape from the steam, but Col. Fitch, in his report says that "Captain Fry denies that the men in the water were fired upon."

It will be remembered that the Confederate report of the attack on St. Charles says that the Mauripas and two steamboats in the river at St. Charles were sunk across the channel to obstruct navigation. These, however, did not effect this obstruction, as the Confederate officers desired, for the Federal fleet, after the capture of the fort, passed on up the river; afterward passing and repassing at their will.

After the capture of St. Charles Col. Fitch ordered a portion of the Federal fleet to pass up White river. As a protection against the fleets being fired upon by sharpshooters, he sent forward a regiment of infantry who should patrol the river and prevent such attacks.

On reaching a point in the open prairie near Aberdeen, on White river, this regiment was attacked by a small detachment of undisciplined Confederate cavalry under command of Capt. Patrick H. Wheat. It was a bold, but fruitless charge, the Confederates being quickly repulsed, with a loss of two killed and several wounded. The Federal loss is not known.

FROM 1860 TO 1865.

This attacking party was composed, principally, of soldiers from Arkansas county, under Capt. Marion J. Clay, with others under Capt. Wheat. One of the Confederates killed was C. C. Henderson, the other, a man from Pine Bluff, name unknown.

Soon after this little skirmish, the Federals returned to St. Charles, entered their transports and left the county.

After the evacuation of St. Charles, by the Federals, in June, 1862, the Confederates re-occupied the place under the command of Col. E. E. Portlock and remained here until January, 1863, when they were ordered, by Gen. Churchill, to his support at Arkansas Post.

At the general election held in August, 1862, the following gentlemen were elected to the offices mentioned: Dr. S. R. Richardson, representative; A. H. Almond, county and probate judge; Joseph H. Maxwell, clerk of circuit court; Duncan S. Morris, sheriff; H. G. Ramsour, county treasurer; and John A. Almond, assessor, he being the first to hold this office by election by the people, under provision of an act of the Legislature passed in 1861.

This election was the last one under Confederate authority, and all the officers of the county, elected or appointed under this election or appointed under authority of the election, continued in office, exercising such authority as was vested in them, until their successors were appointed and qualified under the authority of Gov. Murphy in the fall of 1865.

H. G. Ramsour, who had been elected county treasurer, was afterward killed by Federal soldiers, and James J. Gillcoat was appointed his successor.

By an order issued in May, 1862, by Confederate military authority, the greater part of the cotton crop then in Arkansas county, amounting to thousands of bales, was destroyed by burning. On one plantation on the Arkansas river, in this county, a crop of 2,700 bales was raised in 1861, the greater portion of which was burned in May, 1862. This crop was produced on Dr. Jordan's plantation, and the number of bales was told the writer by one of his managers.

On the 25th of October, 1862, a heavy snow fell, covering the greater portion of the state. Up to this time, there had been but little frost, and the vegetation in field and forest was quite green, with very little appearance of decay. The writer was on the road almost the entire day and "knows whereof he speaks."

In April, 1862, the clerk of the county court made his report showing the amount of county scrip issued for the maintenance of the wives and children of soldiers then on duty, from December, 1861, to date of report, to be $10,604. After this date no account of the aggregate sums of such issue appears, but up to the close of the war there was probably as great a sum issued as the records show that scrip was issued for this purpose, as late as January 10th, 1863, at which time the Federal army captured Arkansas Post.

1863.

The most important event that occurred in the county during this year was the capture of Fort Hindman, located at Arkansas Post, by the Federal forces under command of Gen. McClernand. In no available reports of this engagement is the number of the entire Federal force, consisting of a navy under Captain Porter and a land force under Gen. Sherman, given. The land force, alone, is said to have been 22,000. The fort was in command of Gen. T. J. Churchill, with a small but efficient force of Confederates. The Federal reports estimate the number of Confederate prisoners taken at 5,000, with 7 stands of colors, 17 pieces of cannon, 10 gun carriages, 11 50 Colt pistols, 40 cans of powder, 3,000 small arms, and 1,650 lbs. of shot. The Federal loss is given as 977—killed, 129, wounded 831, and missing, 17. The Confederate loss is not given.

The Confederate report of this battle says: "The Federal army entered the Arkansas river under command of Gen. McClernand with a land force of 22,000 accompanied by Admiral Porter, with eight-five transports and nine gunboats, and moved up the river to attack Fort Hindman located at Arkansas Post, under command of Brigadier-General T. J. Churchill, with an effective force of 3,000 men, with one battery of field pieces of six and twelve pounders, under command of Colonel Dunnington."

That the reader may fully understand the situation of the garrison, under Gen. Churchill, viewed from a Confederate standpoint, the official report of Gen. Churchill is given in full.

Report of the Battle of Arkansas Post.

On the morning of the 9th of January, I was informed by my pickets, stationed at the mouth of the cut-off, that the enemy with his gunboats, followed by his fleet of seventy or eighty transports, was passing into the Arkansas river. It now became evident that their object was to attack the Arkansas Post. I immediately made every arrangement to meet him and ordered out the whole force under my command, numbering about 3,000 effective men, to take position in some lower trenches, about one and a quarter miles below the fort. The **Second Brigade** under Col. Deshler, and the **Third** under Col. Dunnington, occupied the works, while the **First**, under Col. Garland, was held in reserve. Three companies of cavalry under Captains Denson, Nutt and Richardson, were sent in advance to watch the movements of the enemy. During the night, the enemy effected a landing two miles below on the north side of the river. The following day, about 9 o'clock, the gunboats commenced moving up the river and opened fire upon our position. Having but one battery of field pieces of six and twelve pounders, I did not return the fire. It was here that I expected the co-operation of the guns of the fort, but, owing to some defect in the powder, they were scarcely able to throw a shell below the trenches, much less to the fleet. About 2 o'clock P. M., discovering that I was being flanked by a large body of cavalry and artillery, I thought it advisable to fall back under cover of the guns of the fort, to an inner line of intrenchments. The enemy advanced cautiously, and, as they approached our lines, were most signally repulsed. They made no further attempt that evening to charge our works, and I employed the balance of the time until next morning in strengthening my position and completing my intrenchments. Discovering that a body of the enemy had occupied some cabins in our old encampment, I ordered Col. R. I. Mills, with his regiment, to drive them from their position, which he did most successfully, capturing several prisoners. Just before dark, Admiral Porter moved up, with several of his ironclads, to test the metal of our fort. Col. Dunnington, who commanded the fort, was ready in an instant to receive him. The fire opened and the fight lasted nearly two hours, and finally the gunboats were compelled to fall back in a crippled condition. Our loss was slight, that of the enemy much heavier. During the night, I received a telegraphic dispatch from you, ordering me "to hold out till help arrived, or until all are dead," which order was communicated to the brigade commanders, with instructions to see it carried out in spirit and letter. Next morning, I made every disposition of my forces to meet the enemy in the desperate conflict which was soon to follow. Col. Deshler, with his brigade, with the regiment of Col. Dawson attached, commanded by Lieut.-Col. Hutchinson, occupied the extreme left, Col. Garland, with his brigade, with his right resting on the fort, while Col. Dunnington commanded the river defenses. It was near twelve o'clock before the enemy got fully into position, when he commenced moving upon my lines simultaneously by land and water. Four ironclads opened upon the fort, which responded in gallant style. After a continuous fire of three hours, they succeeded in silencing every gun we had except one small six pounder Parrott gun, which was on the left side. Two boats passed up and opened a cross-fire upon the fort and our lines. Still we maintained the struggle. Their attack by land was less successful. On the right, they were repulsed twice in attempting to storm our works, and on the left, were driven back with great slaughter, in no less than eight different charges. To defend the entire line of rifle pits, I had but one battery of small field pieces, under command of Captain Hart, to whom great credit is due for the successful manner in which they were handled, contending as they did with fifty pieces in his front. The fort had now been silenced about an hour; most of the field pieces had been disabled. Still the fire raged furiously along the entire line, and that gallant band of Texans and Arkansans, having nothing now to rely upon save their muskets and bayonets, still disdained to yield to overpowering foe of 50,000 men who were pressing them from every direction. Just at this moment, to my great surprise, several white flags were displayed in the Twenty-fourth regiment Texas dismounted cavalry, First brigade, and before they could be suppressed, the enemy took advantage of them, crowded upon my lines, and, not being prevented by the brigade commander from crossing, as was his duty, I was forced to the humiliating necessity of surrendering the balance of my command.

My great hope was to keep them in check until night and then, if reinforcements did not reach me, to cut my way out. No stigma should rest upon the troops. It is no fault of theirs. They fought with a desperation and courage yet unsurpassed in this war, and I hope and trust that the traitor will yet be discovered, brought to justice and suffer the full penalty of the law. My thanks are due to Colonels An-

ARKANSAS COUNTY.

derson and Gillespie for the prompt measures taken to prevent the raising of the white flag in their regiments. In the Second Brigade, commanded by the gallant Deshler, it was never displayed.

I had ordered Col. E. E. Portlock, commanding at St. Charles, to hasten to my relief with what troops he could spare. Capt. Alf. Johnson reached the post on Saturday night, and took part in the action of the 11th. Col. Portlock, at the head of 190 men of his regiment of infantry, made the unprecedented march of 40 miles in twenty-four hours, and succeeded in entering our lines amidst a heavy fire from the enemy, on his flanks. He was just on the eve of bringing his men into action, when the surrender took place. In no battle in the war has the disparity of forces been so great. The enemy's force was full 50,000, while ours did not exceed 3,000, and yet for two days did we signally repulse and hold in check that immense body of the enemy. My loss will not exceed 60 killed, and 75 or 80 wounded. The loss of the enemy was from 1,500 to 2,000 killed and wounded.

To the members of my staff, Maj. J. K. P. Campbell, chief commissary; Dr. C. H. Smith, chief surgeon; Capt. B. L. Johnson, adjutant-general; Capt. J. J. Gaines, chief of artillery; Capt. J. M. Rose, ordinance officer; Capt. R. H. Fitzhugh, engineer corps; Capt. A. J. Little, signal corps; Lieut. A. H. Sevier, aide-de-camp; Captains Farr and Smith, volunteer aides, and J. M. McGuire, my thanks are due for many valuable services rendered me upon the battlefield. As for individual acts of gallantry, I will make more full mention hereafter.

T. J. CHURCHILL,

Brig.-Gen., commanding Lower Arkansas and White rivers.

After the surrender of the Confederate forces to Gen. McClernand, an effort was made to send a portion of his army up the Arkansas river, but in consequence of low water, the ironclads and transports could not go forward, and after having destroyed the fortifications and all the houses in the village of Arkansas Post the whole army departed down the Arkansas river.

A portion of this army, under command of Gen. Gorman, was sent up White river to St. Charles, where it captured some Confederate stores, and the small garrison left at that place by Col. Portlock.

There were but few of the Arkansas county soldiers in the army at Arkansas Post at the time of its capture. The writer can recall the names of but two—C. C. Godden, who made his escape at Memphis, Tenn., and James M. Barker, who escaped at St. Louis. Both returned to Arkansas county as soon as they had opportunity.

After the departure of Gen. McClernand's army, from Arkansas county, affairs, both public and private, continued as they had been for the two preceding years.

Nearly all the land cultivated in the county in 1863 was planted in corn and produced a large crop, particularly in Villemont and Old River Townships, which were at that time in Arkansas county. Large quantities of the crop were suffered to go to waste in the fields, because of the removal to Texas, of a large number of slave owners on and near the Arkansas river—soon after the occupancy of Pine Bluff by Federal troops.

FROM 1860 TO 1865.

A number of those moving from the county gave to their friends, remaining, the privilege of gathering such quantities of this corn as they desired, delivering in cribs or pens on the farms of the owners, one-half of all they gathered. In this way, large quantities of corn were housed on the farms where cultivated, and much carried to the homes of those gathering the crop. Yet large quantities were left to rot in the fields.

The bread used by a number of the citizens of the county during 1864 and the summer of 1865 was made from the corn cultivated and housed in 1863, the family of the writer being entirely dependent upon this crop for bread until the crop of 1865 was harvested.

The report of the clerk of the county court of the number and value of taxable property with amount of taxes assessed thereon as shown on the Resident Tax Book for 1863, is as follows:

Value of lands,	$ 171,193.00
Value of town lots	4,520.00
Value of slaves	231,150.00
Value of merchandise	500.00
Money at interest	1,000.00
Value of cattle	12,551.00
Value of horses	15,420.00
Value of mules	17,905.00
Value of gold watches	1,225.00
Value of gold and silver plate	680.00
Value of pleasure carriages	1,845.00
Total value	$457,989.00
Total state tax	$ 7,944.90
Total county tax	7,944.90
Total war tax	11,917.37
Total amount of tax	$27,807.17

It will be observed by reference to the above statement, that there was but five hundred dollars' worth of merchandise subject to taxation in the county in this year, and this item is a fair index to the condition of the citizens generally at this period.

All communication with the commercial centers of the country being cut off, the citizens were without means of obtaining supplies of any kind except such as could be produced on their farms or manufactured at home. With each succeeding year of the war, these conditions grew worse, so that to obtain the necessaries of life, the people were forced to use such means as lay in their power. They, in many instances, resorted to the old time practice of carding, spinning and weaving cloth for family use, establishing tanneries, woodshops, etc., throughout the county. This manufacture of cloth at home necessitated also the manufacture of spinning wheels and looms, but cotton and wool cards, equally necessary, could not be manufactured at home and had to be purchased elsewhere. To give the reader some idea of the prices of articles that could not be produced at home, but were indispensable to the wants of the people, the writer recalls the fact that early in 1862 he paid $25,

ARKANSAS COUNTY.

in Confederate currency, for a pair of cotton cards and in the winter of 1864, $75 in Greenbacks, for three bushels of salt manufactured at a salt well in Louisiana.

At the July term of the county court, this year, a tabulated statement of the number and names of indigent families of soldiers then in the army or who had died in the service, that had been provided for by the county to that date, showed the number of such families to be 209. The number of deaths of heads of these families while in the service was shown to be 72.

The last term of the Circuit Court, held in the county under Confederate authority, was on the 11th of May, 1863, with Hon. John C. Murry as judge, and David W. Carroll as prosecuting attorney. Joseph H. Maxwell was clerk and Duncan S. Morriss sheriff.

The Courts of Probate were regularly held during the war, under Confederate authority until the 13th of October, 1863. During the years 1860 and 1861 they were presided over by Hon. F. C. Allen and in 1862 and 1863 by Hon. A. H. Almond.

1864.

On the 8th of December, 1863, President Lincoln issued his proclamation to the citizens of the Southern states then in rebellion, as he termed it, declaring that on their compliance with such conditions as were made known in this proclamation, they should be restored to citizenship, etc., etc. The proclamation also contained the following: "And I do further proclaim, declare and make known, that whenever, in any of the states of Arkansas, Texas, Louisiana, Mississippi, Tennessee, Alabama, Georgia, Florida, South Carolina and North Carolina, a number of persons, not less than one-tenth in number, of the votes cast in such state at the presidential election in the year 1860—shall re-establish a government which shall be republican in form—such shall be recognized as the true government of the state."

Influenced by this proclamation, such citizens as were in the lines and under the protection of the Federal army called meetings and took steps to hold elections to choose delegates to a Constitutional Convention. This movement was inaugurated by the citizens of Sebastion and Crawford counties, and between the issuance of the President's proclamation on the 8th of December, 1863 and the 4th of January, 1864, elections were held in several counties of the state, choosing these delegates. On the 4th of January, 1864, parties claiming to be delegates from **thirty-three** of the **sixty** counties of the state assembled at the capitol—Arkansas county, however, was not represented. The convention proceeded to formulate a constitution which was to be submitted to the people on the 14th of March, 1864 for ratification or rejection. On this and the two succeeding days, elections were held and reports from such places as held elections showed the following result: A vote of **12,177** for and **266** against the constitution. At the same time elections for state and county officers were had.

It will be remembered that Arkansas county was not represented in the so-called Constitutional Convention, yet on the days designated by an ordinance of the convention, an election was held at the court

FROM 1860 TO 1865.

house in DeWitt at which votes were cast for all the offices made elective under this constitution. At this election the following persons were returned as elected to the offices named: G. C. Crosson, representative in the state legislature; ——— ———, county and probate judge; Robert P. Ware, sheriff; Joseph H. Maxwell, clerk of the circuit court; John J. Gillcoat, treasurer, and ——— ———, assessor.

At this election ——— votes were cast. Of this number ——— were for and ——— against the constitution.

Soon after the result of this election became known, a squad of Confederate soldiers raided the county, capturing some and frightening others of the officers elected, out of the county. Among the latter was G. C. Crosson, who fled to DeVall's Bluff, where he sought the protection of the military authorities. His family, after a short time, followed, and he spent the remainder of his life there. Notwithstanding this he claimed to be and was recognized as the representative from Arkansas county.

Crosson came to Arkansas county from Illinois in the summer or fall of 1860. He stopped first at Arkansas Post, from which place he moved to DeWitt, where he was elected justice of the peace, holding the office until his hasty departure from the county in March, 1864. He frequently assisted, as associate justice, in holding the county court, and was one of the court at its January term, 1864, when on the 18th of this month an appropriation was made for the support of 173 families of Confederate soldiers, who were then in the army or had died in the service. This was the last term of the county court held under Confederate authority.

After the organization of the Murphy government in Arkansas and the occupancy of the greater portion of the state north and east of Little Rock, by Federal forces, a detachment of Federal soldiers under command of ——— ———, was sent to St. Charles, which they fortified and where they remained until the fall of 1865. A portion of this garrison was composed of negroes. These, or some of them, brutally murdered Mesdames Rosson and Toombs, who lived about one mile from this post, their husbands being, at the time, in the Confederate army. Both were women of high character and were great friends. For several years previous to the war, their husbands had been partners in a mercantile business at St. Charles. Whether the murderers were punished by the military authorities for their crime, is not known to the writer.

Soon after the occupancy of St. Charles by the Federals, a telegraph line was established by them, from DeVall's Bluff via St. Charles, to the mouth of White river, and an active and vigilant scouting party was necessary for its protection. These constant and active movements of Federal soldiers through the county with garrisons at Pine Bluff, DeVall's Bluff and St. Charles, caused the withdrawal of nearly all Confederate forces from the county, thus leaving the citizens subject to the will of the Federals. In some instances, the citizens received much ill treatment at the hands of these soldiers and in others kindly consideration—due mainly to the manner in which they received and treated the Federals.

ARKANSAS COUNTY.

During the occupancy of these points, squads of soldiers were sent out through the county from time to time. One of these, passing through DeWitt, burned the county jail and a number of store houses and residences. Another set fire to the court house just before leaving town, but the fire was discovered in time to save the house from serious damage. Martin B. Billingsley, a lad fourteen years of age, discovered and extinguished the fire and for this service the county court, at its January term, 1866, made an appropriation of ten dollars in his favor. Yet another party from Pine Bluff, passing from Grand Prairie through Villemont and Old River townships, burned the residences, with their contents, of Thomas Farrelly, who was not nor had been in the Confederate service, and of Felix R. Robinson, who had died more than two years previous to this time.

After the adjournment of the county court on January 18th, 1864, Joseph H. Maxwell, clerk of the court and custodian of the records of the county, circuit and probate courts, fearful for the safety of these records, secretly, by night, removed them from the court house. He was assisted by Benjamin F. Quertermous and the place of hiding for these papers was a log cabin owned by W. S. Quertermous, located about two miles northwest of DeWitt. This cabin was situated in the prairie and was built on blocks two or three feet from the ground. There were no openings and the records were passed under the walls and then placed in the loft, one man standing on the ground and passing them to the other in the loft. The house was watched and protected by W. S. Quertermous, who kept the grass cut about the house, to avoid danger of fire. Here these papers remained in safety until some time after the close of the war, when they were discovered by a citizen, who, while out hunting sought shelter from a shower of rain in the cabin. He reported his discovery to others and it became known to the Federal authorities at St. Charles, who sent wagons to the cabin and had the books and papers taken to a place of safe keeping, where they remained until the re-establishment of civil rule in the county. Upon the re-establishment of civil authority Clerk Maxwell demanded possession of them and they were delivered to him and returned to their proper place in the court house with but little loss or damage.

Another incident of the times, worth noting, was the burning of bridges across the larger streams flowing through the county. This was not the work of Federal soldiers as they were of great convenience to them in their raids through the county, but of parties residing near them, who ignorantly supposed their destruction would prevent such raids. The destruction of these bridges caused great inconvenience to the citizens and heavy expense to the county in rebuilding them.

CHAPTER XVII.

From the Year 1865 to the Year 1870.

After the close of the war, in the spring of 1865, the surviving soldiers in the service, and the families of refugees returned to their homes and resumed their various avocations in civil life. On their return, all saw that the hand of destruction, incident to war, had been ruthlessly laid on their homes, farms and stock—in fact, on all their possessions—but, with the same indomitable courage and perseverance with which they went into and through the hardships of war and the deprivations following in its wake, all went quietly to work to rebuild their homes, repair their farms and gather around them such comforts as their means and industry might enable them to do.

In the summer of 1865 Governor Murphy, influenced by a spirit of liberality, notified the citizens of the counties without local government, that he would commission and recognize such officers as might be recommended to him by the citizens of these counties. In response to this liberal offer, the citizens of Arkansas county, in a public meeting held in DeWitt on the —— day of ————, 1865, recommended the following men for the offices named: Robert C. Martin for sheriff, Richard K. Gamble for county judge, Pleasant G. Tyer for treasurer, and Watkins A. Davis for assessor, with the names of gentlemen to be appointed justices of the peace. Joseph H. Maxwell claimed the office of clerk of the courts by virtue of his election in March, 1864, and this claim was recognized. So far as the writer remembers, all the men whose names were submitted to Governor Murphy were commissioned, qualified and remained in office until their successors were elected and qualified under the general election held in August, 1866.

It will be remembered by the reader that the last term of the county court held under Confederate authority, was in January, 1864, the adjourning order, on January 18th being signed by A. H. Almond, presiding judge, and G. C. Crosson and R. P. Ware, associates. From that date until the 2nd of October, 1865, there were no proceedings in any court of records in the county. On October 2nd, 1865, the county court convened, this being the first court held in the county under the Murphy government and after the close of the war. The opening order of court was signed by Richard K. Gamble, presiding judge, with John P. Butler, Perry Haynes, S. M. Crump, Robert Scanland, John B. Ritchie, William B. George, John B. Thetford, and Terence Farrelly, justices of the peace.

At this term of court, overseers on the various roads in the county and judges for each township, to hold the congressional election, were appointed. The grand and petit jurors for the November term of the Circuit Court were also appointed, under the law then in force. The names of these jurors are given, as follows: For grand jurors, Alfred

ARKANSAS COUNTY.

H. Almond, Barefoot D. Armstrong, Rice Dulin, Lewis Gacio, James T. U. Hawkins, Quinton D. Neck, Charles W. Olds, William B. Pool, John Roach, William H. Ransdale, Reuben Dollahide, Charles A. Brent, Asher H. Stillwell, Samuel W. Vittiton, William Word and George W. Goff; and for petit jurors, James T. Allen, Charles W. Belknap, Charles Bogy, John H. Bell, Jackson Davidson, Richard H. Graves, William D. Geavett, William R. Lear, Peter P. Luckado, John R. Maxwell, Azariah Mitchell, Richard L. Pearson, John W. Simpson, John W. Spratlin, Thomas J. Turner, Thomas J. Thompson, James M. Price and Thomas J. Sparks.

Of these thirty-four gentlemen, who were personally known to the writer, there is but one, Richard H. Graves, who is alive at the time of this writing, July, 1904, a great number of them having died fifteen or twenty years ago.

The first term of Probate Court after the establishment of the Murphy government convened on October 13, 1865, Judge R. K. Gamble, presiding.

The first term of Circuit Court in Arkansas county after the close of the war convened on November 13th, 1865, and continued in session five days. This court was presided over by the Hon. William M. Harrison, with C. C. Gadden as prosecuting attorney, Joseph H. Maxwell clerk, and Robert C. Martin sheriff.

The total amount of the assessed value of real and personal property in the county, as returned by the assessor for 1865, was $1,173,573.

Near the bridge crossing Long Point or Mill Bayou on the road from DeWitt to Brownsville, in Prairie county, three mysterious deaths have occurred. The first of these occurred in the fall of 1865, and was that of John Jelks, an old gentleman who had, for a number of years, lived on the east side of Big LaGrue. At the time of his death he was on his way from his home to Pine Bluff, where he was going to pay his taxes due the Federal government. His body, when found, was leaning against a tree, near the road, a short distance north of the bridge and there were no visible marks of violence on his person or disturbance of his money or other possessions.

The second of these deaths was that of Alpheus R. Bunfill, in the spring of 1866, who, at the time resided on Big Bayou Meto, some twelve or fourteen miles northwest of DeWitt. Bunfill had been to DeWitt on business, and was on his return home. His remains were found on the bridge and as in the case of Jelks, there were no visible marks of violence on his person or other evidence of disorder.

The third was that of ——— Crawford, a young man whose dead body was found lying across the fence around a horse lot on his mother's place, in the summer of 1901. His body was found by a friend passing the place, but a short time after his death. In this case, the only evidence leading to a surmise as to the cause of his death, were his tracks and those of a horse which he had led into the lot, which appeared as if there had been a struggle, but no marks or bruises were found on his person. The fence across which he was found, had been partially pulled or let down.

The point at which young Crawford was found is within half a mile of the bridge on which Bunfill was found, and near which Jelks met his death.

RECONSTRUCTION OF ARKANSAS COUNTY.

1866.

After the re-establishment of civil government in this county, under the constitution of 1864, and the inauguration of the Murphy Government, peace and good order prevailed throughout the country. The citizens, generally, returned to their homes and usual occupations. All seemed to accept and to recognize the results of the war that had raged in such fierce conflict for the past four years; all, apparently, resolved to build up and re-establish their homes and fortunes. Business in mercantile, agricultural, mechanical, professional, and other lines was being rapidly restored.

The courts, as heretofore stated, were established and the internal affairs of the county were provided for by courts created under the laws of the state (which had Federal recognition) and under the Federal laws, directly.

(The reader will please bear in mind that all the civil officers exercising jurisdiction or authority in this county at that time, were either elected at the March, 1864, election, or were appointed to their respective offices by Governor Murphy.)

The circuit judge, prosecuting attorney, and clerk of the courts were elected in March, 1864. The other officers of the county were appointed and commissioned by Governor Murphy in the fall of 1865. These officers exercised the functions of their respective offices until August, 1866, when their successors were elected and qualified under the general election laws then in force.

At this election, the following were chosen: W. M. Galloway, of Pine Bluff, Senator for the district composed of Arkansas, Desha, and Jefferson Counties; Elisha G. Abbott, Representative; Alfred H. Almon, County Judge; Robert C. Martin, Sheriff; William F. Gibson, Clerk of the Circuit Court; Pleasant G. Tyer, County Treasurer; J. W. McKewen, Coroner; A. G. Withers, Surveyor; and J. M. Price, Assessor.

This being the first election after the close of the war, under the Murphy Government, there was but little excitement in the public mind on the subject. All seemed anxious to elect men of intelligence and efficiency. There were no local or political issues involved. All of the officers elected were ex-Confederate soldiers or those in sympathy with them.

It may be said, with propriety, that there were few others in the county, at that time, eligible to office, who were competent to fill these positions of trust. The highest number of votes cast at this election was for sheriff, who received 569.

The predominant spirit may well be illustrated by the following incident growing out of this election. The contestants for the office of Circuit Clerk were, Captain Wm. F. Gibson, and Lieut. Benjamin F. Quertermous, both ex-Confederate soldiers. Gibson was elected, and as soon as commissioned, he appointed Quertermous his deputy. Mr. Quertermous was retained in this position until the summer of 1867,

ARKANSAS COUNTY.

when Mr. Gibson was removed from office by Military Authorities, under the Reconstruction Act of Congress, to make room for a "Carpet Bagger."

At the January Term of the County Court (1866), Watkins A. Davis, who had been appointed by Governor Murphy as Assessor for Arkansas County, made a report of his assessment for the year 1865, which showed the aggregate value of taxable property to be $1,173,514. At this term of the Court, a levy of One-half of One per cent was ordered for county purposes, also an order allowing Mr. Davis the sum of $158.60 as fees due him for his services (County Court Record "C", pp. 97-103). This was first Assessment under Murphy Government.

As commemorative of the incidents then transpiring in this county, I relate the following, which occurred at the May Term (1866) of Circuit Court, Judge Wm. M. Harrison presiding. The incident is mentioned for a two-fold purpose; first, to show the foreshadowing of Military Despotism; second, to memorialize the patriotism and integrity of Judge Harrison in upholding the majesty of the Civil law over that of the Military.

A suit was pending in the court, with Charles W. Belknap as plaintiff and H. H. Hennant, of St. Charles, with W. S. Oliver, of Little Rock, as defendants. The late Chief Justice English, then a partner with Judge Wilshire (Oliver's Attorney), appeared as counsel for Oliver. At the morning roll call for motions, etc., Judge English responded by asking privilege to make a statement, and it was granted him. He declared that he had recently become a partner with Judge Wilshire, Oliver's attorney, and was there to represent the defendant.

That previous to his departure from Little Rock, Judge Wilshire had obtained an order commanding the judge of the court to grant an order transferring the suit to the Military Authorities at Little Rock. After making this explanation, he asked Judge Harrison if a motion to that effect would be entertained if made. After thanking the attorney for the courtesies shown him in presenting the motion, Judge Harrison very promptly answered in the negative in terms that could not be easily misunderstood, saying: "Rather than entertain such a motion, I will adjourn my court. If that is not sufficient, to prevent such an order being made of record in my court, I will resign my Judgeship."

Judge English did not make the contemplated motion, but filed a preliminary one and obtained a continuance of the case. Oliver went into bankruptcy before the next term of court and Belknap ordered his suit dismissed. The writer was Belknap's attorney and present at the time, and can, with propriety, say: "All of which I saw (and heard) and part of which I was."

This was done more than a year after the surrender of General Lee, and the cessation of hostilities on the part of the Confederate States; and that, too, before a judge of known and acknowledged loyalty to the Union who was elected under the constitution of 1864.

The reader will bear in mand that, under the constitution of 1864, the legislature of the State in April, 1865, by unanimous vote, ratified the Thirteenth Amendment to the Federal Constitution. This action on the part of the State (Recognized by the Federal authorities as necessary for the ratification of said amendment), proclaimed to the world that Arkansas was at that time a State and a Member of the Federal Union. But we are assured that "Coming events cast their shadows before", so we may regard this action on the part of the Military Authorities as one of the dark shadows preceding the events of Reconstruction.

That the reader of these pages may have some idea of the impoverished condition of the citizens at this time, your attention is called to the fact that two hundred and sixty-one taxpayers of the county were returned as delinquent in taxes for the year 1865, the amount due aggregating the sum of $1,143.10. (County Court Record "C", pp 117-124).

During the war, all Post Offices and Routes in the county were either abolished or abandoned and there were no postal facilities until late in the year 1866, when several Post Offices were re-established, but no regular routes, nor were any contracts let for carrying the mails. The citizens were dependent upon such services as they could secure, and upon such as would carry the mail matter from the home offices to the regularly established postal lines operating on the Arkansas and White Rivers, and on the railroad between DeVall's Bluff and Little Rock.

1867.

In consequence of the short crop of 1866 and the impoverished condition of many of the citizens who were unable to plant and cultivate crops without pecuniary assistance, the County Court, at the instance of many of the taxpayers of the county, granted the following order at the April term, 1867.

Appropriation.

"Now, on this day, on motion and upon the representation of many citizens present in court, it is ordered that the sum of Five Thousand Dollars be, and the same is hereby appropriated, for the purpose of purchasing corn for the use of those in need who will execute a deed of trust, or Mortgage, on real estate, or a sufficient amount of personal property to secure the payment for the amount of corn received by them;

"And it is further ordered that John G. Quertermous be, and he is hereby appointed as a commissioner of this court, and that he enter into bond to the State of Arkansas for the use of Arkansas County in the sum of Ten Thousand Dollars, conditioned according to law, with security to be approved by the County Court, or the Clerk, in vacation;

"And that the clerk of this court be, and he is hereby authorized upon the filing of the Bond of said commissioner, to issue Two Thousand Dollars of said appropriation, and to deliver the same to said commissioner, and that he proceed immediately to negotiate for the purchase of as much corn as he can buy with that amount of scrip; and that he have Three Hundred Bushels of corn shipped to Arkansas Post, on the Arkansas River, and the balance of said purchase be shipped to Crockett's Bluff on the White River; and it is left to the discretion of the said commissioner to draw whatever other amounts remaining of

ARKANSAS COUNTY.

said appropriation from time to time as he may find necessary to meet the wants of the people, to be expended in like manner. Said scrip to bear Six Per Cent interest from date until paid, and payable on the 1st day of January, A. D., 1868."

Commissioner Quertermous found a purchaser for the scrip in his hands in the person of the late James H. Lucas, a citizen and a native of St. Louis, Missouri, whose name recalls incidents in his life that would "Point a moral and adorn a tale".

After Lucas had furnished Commissioner Quertermous the means with which to purchase the corn, he was directed to buy, and upon learning from Quertermous, who was acquainted with the citizens of Arkansas Post and vicinity, that certain of the older residents were still living, and that they, and their neighbors, generally, were impoverished by the results of the war, he ordered a shipment of Three Hundred Dollars' worth of supplies to be forwarded them at his expense. In addition to this, he donated a large portion of the County scrip purchased from Quertermous, to Mrs. Morton, a grand-daughter of Frederick Notrebe. These acts of kindness from Mr. Lucas were prompted by recollections of the kindness and liberality shown him in former days by the citizens of Arkansas County, and Mr. Notrebe, grandfather of Mrs. Morton. Mr. Lucas resided at the Post for a number of years, married there in 1832, Miss Emilie Derrisseaux, and from 1833 to 1835 he was County and Probate Judge.

The generosity of Mr. Lucas is a striking illustration of the maxim: "Kindness never goes unrewarded", for, after a period of more than thirty years, he repays the friendship shown him with compound interest.

The appropriation by the County Court mentioned, was a great relief, and all who received a benefit, promptly paid their indebtedness at maturity; thus enabling the County to redeem the scrip at maturity.

Returning the narrative to the events that foreshadow reconstruction, the reader's attention is directed to the frst act of Congress regarding reconstruction, passed March 2nd, 1867.

By the provision of the second section of this act the president was required to appoint a Military commander for this district to detail military force sufficient to compel an observance of his authority in the district; the third section declared:

"It shall be the duty of each officer assigned as aforesaid, to protect all persons in their rights of person and property; to suppress insurrections, disorder and violence; and to punish, or cause to be punished, all disturbances of public peace, and criminals; and to this end he may allow local civil tribunals to take jurisdiction of, and try, offenders; or, when, in his judgment, it may be necessary, he shall have power to organize military commissions, or tribunals, for that purpose; and all interference under color of State institutions with exercise of military authority under this act shall be null and void."

The reader is asked to note how completely the civil was subordinated to the Military authority. This Military dominated all the proceedings of the reconstruction in this county from start to finish.

FROM 1865 TO 1870.

Under the Reconstruction Act, the commanding general of this district issued his general order No. 31, Sept. 26th, 1867, entitled:

"Qualification of electors, and appointment of delegates to represent each county in the Convention ordered to be convened to formulate a new constitution for the State." The eleventh section of that order designated the number of delegates from the state as seventy-five, and from Arkansas County, two. This Convention was to meet in Little Rock at the state capitol on the first Tuesday in November, 1867.

The active movements by friends of Reconstruction, during the time intervening between the passage of the Reconstruction Acts and the meeting of the Constitutional convention, show plainly the events foreshadowing Reconstruction. Among the first of these, was the calling of a union state convention to meet in Little Rock, April 4th, 1867. Arkansas County was represented there by John McClure, Dr. A. Rice, A. D. Sheets, Thomas Quinn, and C. M. Burns.

Influenced by the spirit of Militarism, among the first motions offered was one by John McClure, that they confer with General Ord, then in command at Little Rock, regarding the qualifications of voters. On the second day of the convention, Mr. Redman, of Pulaski County, offered the following resolution, viz.: "Resolved, that this convention asks all citizens of the State who have been identified with the late Rebellion, and who heartily and in good faith acquiesce in the Reconstruction measures of Congress, and have wholly renounced the detestable theories of Secession and State Sovereignty, as opposed to national Union, to join us in our deliberations to harmonize the political conditions of the State."

"Resolved, that the union men in Arkansas, in convention assembled, declare and announce to those who have been engaged in the late Rebellion and who do not politically agree with us, that we desire no proscriptions, no confiscation, no laws that interfere with any of their rights to life, liberty, or property; that we desire to enhance the prosperity and happiness of every citizen of the State, and to procure unity of feeling, and, as soon as possible consistent with the safety of the Union men, we wish to obliterate the use of the words "Traitor" and "Rebellion", in this State."

These resolutions showed a disposition on the part of the mover to bring about reconciliation and restore the harmony once existing in the minds of the discordant elements of the country. But this disposition was not in accord with Congressional Reconstruction and, of course, met prompt and strong opposition. Among others, John McClure, the leading delegate from Arkansas County, is quoted as saying: "I am opposed to that part of the resolutions which declares there shall be no confiscation, etc., etc." Meeting with so much opposition, Mr. Redman consented to withdraw his resolutions. This action of the convention, regarding these resolutions, is sufficient index to the sentiments of the Union Loyal Republicans at that time. (Arkansas Daily Gazette, April 4th and 5th, 1867.)

As we are now about to enter the period of active Reconstruction in Arkansas County, the leading incidents will be given, as a rule, by copying, or by referring to date, page, etc., of the Journal of the Con-

ARKANSAS COUNTY.

vention, to Legislative acts, Orders of Court, and Military Authorities.

On the 5th day of July, 1867, Governor Issac Murphy issued a commission to Mr. Joseph H. Maxwell, as follows:

The State of Arkansas.

To all whom these presents shall come; Greeting.

Know ye, that in accordance with instructions from Brevet Major General E. O. C. Ord, commanding the fourth Military District, composed of Mississippi and Arkansas, Joseph H. Maxwell is hereby appointed Internal Improvement Commissioner, in and for, Arkansas County in the State of Arkansas, therefore, I, Isaac Murphy, Governor of the State of Arkansas, by virtue of the authority in me vested by the Constitution and laws of said State, and instructions as aforesaid, do hereby commission him, the said Joseph H. Maxwell, Internal Improvement Commissioner in and for the county aforesaid, for and during the term provided by the laws of the State.

He, the said Joseph H. Maxwell, is therefore, hereby authorized and required to do and perform, all, and singular, the duties incumbent on him as such Internal Improvement Commissioner in and for the County aforesaid, according to law and the trust imposed in him.

In testimony whereof, I have hereunto set my hand and caused the seal of the State of Arkansas to be affixed, at Little Rock, the Fifth day of July, in the year of Our Lord, One Thousand Eight Hundred and Sixty-seven.

(Signed) ISAAC MURPHY.

By the Governor,

(L. S.) Robert J. T. White, Secretary of State.

Headquarters of 4th Military District.

Vicksburg, Miss., July 11th, 1867.

Approved and confirmed by command of Brev't Maj. Gen'l.,

E. O. C. Ord,

D. Barin, Bvt. Maj. Gen'l.

U. S. A., Act. Inspector Gen'l.

The foregoing commission was copied, by the writer, from the original found on file in the Clerk's office of Arkansas County, and is referred to as evidence of the manner in which offices were dispensed in the County by the Military Authorities, preliminary to Reconstruction, and as the probable means used to remove Capt. William F. Gibson from the office of Clerk, and the appointing of his successor. It will be remembered that at the general election in August, 1866, Captain Gibson was chosen to be Circuit Clerk, and under the civil law then in force, he was commissioned by Governor Murphy, and entered upon the duties of his office about the 30th of October of that year. He continued in that office, to the satisfaction of the public, until some time between the 10th and 18th days of October, 1867, when he was summarily ousted by a military order commanding him to surrender his office with the records and files therein to Edmund R. Wiley, late Colonel commanding a regiment of colored soldiers in the United States Army.

The date of Wiley's commission is not known, as no record or file of such has been found in the Clerk's office. Circuit Court record "F",

p. 1, shows that Wiley was present and acting as Clerk of the Court on the 4th day of November, 1867. At this term of the Court, Judge Harrison granted a certificate of allowance to Wiley for ex-officio service during the court, for the sum of $31.25, on this certificate of the County Court, as appears of record in County Court Record "C", p. 273, allowed and ordered it paid. The reader's attention is called to this allowance for the purpose of exhibiting the difference between the ruling, or orders, of an Un-reconstruction and a Reconstruction Judge in this: At the November Term, 1868, Judge Morse, The Reconstruction Judge, allowed Wiley the amount of $210.15. At the November Term, 1867, Judge Harrison, the Un-reconstruction Judge, allowed him $31.25, showing a difference of $178.90. Further on in these pages, other like differences will be shown to exhibit the contrast in allowances before and after the inauguration of Reconstruction.

At this point of our narrative, another dark shadow of the coming events of reconstruction crosses our pathway as shown by the following order, made by the County Court at the October Term, 1867, viz.:

"Settlement with D. S. Cannon, late Common School Commissioner. Now, on this day, comes before the court said Daniel S. Cannon, late Common School Commissioner, and presents his accounts with the receipt of Edward Johnson, successor in office, for the bonds and notes for the money due the School Fund, which account being audited and examined by the Court, and the sum of Four Hundred and Sixty Seven Dollars and Seventy Nine cents being found to be due said D. S. Cannon, it is ordered that Edward Johnson, Common School Commissioner, pay over to said D. S. Cannon the said sum of Four Hundred and Sixty-seven Dollars and 79-00, and that the Clerk settle and balance the account of the said D. S. Cannon, late School Commissioner."

(See County Court Record "C", p. 279.)

At the January Term, 1868, of the County Court, the following order was made, to-wit:

"Daniel S. Cannon, as late School Commissioner in and for said County: Now, on this day the court having been called to the attention of General Order No. 13, issued from headquarters Fourth Military District, dated October 29, 1867, it is ordered that the order heretofore made in relation to the settlement in his behalf at the last term hereof requiring Edward Johnson, School Commissioner in and for said County, to pay the said Daniel S. Cannon the sum of Four Hundred and Sixty-seven Dollars and Seventy-nine cents be, and the same is hereby revoked and set aside in pursuance to the requirements of said Order No. 13. (Ib. p. 290.)

Edward Johnson, at whose instance and for whose benefit Order No. 13 was granted, in current phrase of the time, was a "Scalawag" from Mississippi, who came to DeWitt in 1860, was a good "Secesh" during the war, and a loyal Union Republican during the days of Reconstruction.

By provision of Section 1, of an Act of Congress, passed the 23d day of March, 1867, it was ordered that before the 1st day of September, 1867, the commanding general should cause a registration to be made of the male citizens of each county in the State, and under the

ARKANSAS COUNTY.

provisions and in obedience to command thereof, O. D. Green, Assistant Adjutant General, on the 13th of May, 1867, issued a memorandum of instruction, the fourth section prescribing the qualifications of voters thus: "Any person who has held an office under the general government prior to entering upon the duties of which he was required to take an oath of allegiance to the United States, and who afterwards engaged in and gave aid and comfort in the Rebellion, or Secession, is disqualified as a voter. Any person who has held an executive or Judicial office under the State government, and who afterwards engaged in or voluntarily aided rebellion or Secession, is disqualified to vote."

Acting Assistant Adjutant General, under the provision of the Reconstruction Act and Military Orders, reported the following named persons as Registrars for Arkansas County:

G. M. French, John McClure, and Andrew Rice.

The first two named, were "Carpet-baggers", the other one was an old citizen of the State, but of recent citizenship in Arkansas County.

The abstract of the returns of voters in Arkansas County as shown on page 769 of the Journal of the Constitutional Convention, were 498 white and 1,030 colored, an aggregate of 1,528 voters.

The reader's attention is again called to the workings of Reconstruction by showing the effects on the elective franchise as will be seen by reference to the vote at the gneral election in August, 1866, when the greatest number of votes cast for any office was 569. These were all white voters, qualified under the laws then in force in the State, however, the above abstract shows an increase of 959 votes in one year, and a decrease of 71 white votes. The number of disfranchised citizens is not given, except what is shown above.

Section 7 of the General Green's order of the 13th of May, 1867, says: "Registrars will not be permitted to become candidates for election to the Convention for framing the Constitution of the State."

Notwithstanding this prohibition, John McClure was voted for and returned as one of the delegates from Arkansas County to that Convention.

On the 26th of September, 1867, General Green issued his Order No. 31, in which an election was ordered to be held: "For the purpose of establishing a constitution and civil government for the states loyal to the Union, etc., etc." Each ballot should have written or printed upon it, "For Constitution", or "Against Constitution", and also the correct name, or names, of the delegate or delegates voted for. Said election to be held on the first Tuesday in November, 1867. (See pp. 27—Journal of Constitutional Convention.)

One of the peculiarities of the elections in these days was their indefinite duration, as shown by Order No. 31, thus:

"Commencing on the first Tuesday in November next and continuing as hereinafter prescribed." This election was held at the time and in the manner prescribed, at which time John McClure of Ohio, and John Hutchinson of Canada, were returned as delegates from Arkansas County.

The registered votes of Arkansas County, as before stated, were

1,528, of this number 1,030 were colored and 498 were white. At the election held in November, 927 were for Constitution, and 109 against, while 492 of the registered voters did not vote at all.

After receiving the returns of the election from several counties in the State, General Green, by General Order No. 37, dated, December the 5th, 1867, designated: "The Hall of the House of Representatives in the State House in Little Rock, Arkansas, at 11 o'clock A. M., Tuesday the seventh day of January, 1868, as the place and time for the assembly of the Convention for the State of Arkansas." In obedience to said order, the delegates appeared at the time and place designated, and upon the roll call, McClure and Hutchinson from Arkansas County were present.

As to the proceedings of the convention, little new can be said, except as to votes and speeches of the delegates from this County.

1868.

"Pending the proceedings of the Convention, on the 1st day of February, 1868, Delegate McClure offered the following resolution:

"Resolved, that the committee on the Constitution, its arrangement and phraseology, be, and they are hereby instructed to report an article to the Constitution, disfranchising all persons who oppose Reconstruction, and that the act of voting against the adoption of the Constitution shall be conclusive evidence of the fact of such opposition." (See Journal—p. 452.)

On the fifth day of February, 1868, Delegate McClure, as chairman of the committee on Penitentiary, submitted a report on the subject of the contract between the State of Arkansas and Hodges, Peay, and Ayliff, which had been made between these parties in February, 1867, for the term of fifteen years, holding that said contract was binding as between lessees and the State. Thus virtually confessing that in February, 1867, the State of Arkansas was a State legally existing under a Constitution and laws, and as such, capable of entering into a legal contract.

In order that the public might know the Committee'd appreciation of said legislation, it preferred the following charges against it:

Ist, That it spent $10,000 in drunkenness and debauchery with Andrew Johnson;

2nd, That they attempted to legalize Confederate money;

3rd, That they squandered $269,000 in money belonging to the State in extravagant and lascivious manner; and,

6th, That General Ord forbade them assembling, thereby saving the State an unknown amount of money." (Ib. 467)

This extract is made from the proceedings of the Convention for two purposes:

First, to show the light in which the Committee viewed the members of the Legislature of 1867; and,

Second, to show how unjust were the charges of drunkenness, debauchery, and lasciviousness made against the members of the Legislature, consisting of such men as Turner, Cravens, Lyle, Grant, Gantt, Galloway, Reynolds, Hunter, Fellows, and Smith, in the Senate;

ARKANSAS COUNTY.

and in the House, Abbott, Sorrell, Bunch, Berry, Fletcher, Weatherford, Eakin, Kelly, Gause, Hughes, Newton, and Farrell. All of these men are personally, or by reputation, known to the writer, to be men of unimpeachable Character, of recognized ability, and of moral worth.

Another object in making the foregoing, as well as following, extracts from the proceedings of the Convention, is to draw a contrast between their expressions and actions on the subject of Economy.

It will be seen by reference to the third charge in the foregoing report, that the Legislature in 1867, squandered $269,000 of the State money, that no facts are referred to, or evidence prsented, to support this charge. One would suppose, reasonably, that conscientious, economical, and intelligent men, in view of the impoverished citizen taxpayers of the county, would, when voting their pay, act in a spirit liberality.

But what are the facts? let us see. Referring to page 822 of the Journal of the Convention, we find the following ordinance:—

"Be, it ordained by the people of Arkansas in Convention assembled,

First, That the compensation of the members of this Convention shall be eight dollars Per Diem during the actual sitting of the Convention, and the same amount 'per diem' for each day's travel in going to and returning from the said Convention, estimating thirty miles to be a day's travel, and in computing the same by the nearest and most practicable route furnished; public transportation; also mileage each way at the rate of twenty cents per mile by the same route."

Under the provisions of this ordinance, the delegates from Arkansas County received the following sums as shown by the certificates below.

State of Arkansas, } ss.
City of Little Rock }

    I, Avery E. Moore, Auditor of State, hereby certify that the original voucher on file in this office shows that J. H. Hutchinson received and receipted for the following mileage and per diem to the Constitutional Convention of 1868, to-wit:

Services as delegate, 39 days at $8.00 per day.... $312.00
400 miles travel, going and returning, at 20c per mile 80.00
Thirteen and 33-00 days service for each thirty miles at $8.00 per day 106.64

Witness my hand and seal the 10th day of May, 1907.

                    AVERY E. MOORE,
                          State Auditor.

State of Arkansas, } ss.
City of Little Rock }

    I, Avery E. Moore, Auditor of the State, hereby certify that the original voucher on file in this office shows that John McClure received and receipted for the following mileage and per diem as a delegate to the Constitutional Convention of 1868, to-wit:

Services as delegate, 39 days at $8.00 per day.... $312.00
300 miles travel, going and returning, at 20c a mile 60.00
Nine and 99-100 days service for each thirty miles travel at $8.00 per day.................... 79.92

Witness my hand and seal, this 10th day of May, 1907.

AVERY E. MOORE,
Auditor of State.

Thus it will be seen that the delegates from Arkansas County received the sum of Three Hundred and Twenty-six Dollars and Fifty-six cents, for traveling expenses from their respective homes to Little Rock and return. Hutchinson's home was about one hundred and McClure's was about seventy-five miles by land from Little Rock.

Before closing our references to the proceedings of the Constitutional Convention, I wish to call the reader's attention to a few more of delegate McClure's declarations, showing his opinions of the character of the citizens of Arkansas.

In his report on the finances of the State, referring to the action of the State Authorities, he says: "A system of financing, known only to thieves and robbers without conscience, prevailed to such an extent that operations now cost the State the neat little sum of $5,104,606.16.

"Not content with impoverishing the State, desolating the country, and causing mourning at every hearthstone, we find these selfsame men arrayed in hostility to the present reconstruction measures, hoping thereby to hide from public gaze and investigation the plunder and theft of thirty years." (Ib. 486)

In support of this report, he said: "I observe that in this Convention every reference to these and some kindred facts seems to touch upon a tender spot with some individuals; and every time we touch a tender spot, it winces. I say, sir, that no State in the Union ever permitted, that the citizens of no state ever were subject to debauchery and corruption on the part of its public officers, as the state of Arkansas. So far as the State is concerned, she stands head in the history of crime." (Ib. 543)

The foregoing extracts will give the reader an idea of Delegate McClure's opinion of the citizens of the state of Arkansas. He had opinions, and the courage to express them.

It will be observed that little has been written in these pages, referring to Delegate Hutchinson. The reason is, that but few of his remarks are reported in the Journal of proceedings, and, as a rule, that little is not offensive, nor in a spirit of condemnation toward the citizens of Arkansas.

By an ordinance of the convention, the counties of Arkansas and Prairie were designated as the 12th District entitled to one Senator and four representatives, and by the provision of Section 1 of the Schedule, ordered an election to be held on the 15th day of March, 1868, and such other days as were necessary for the purpose of electing all officers

ARKANSAS COUNTY.

made elective under the Constitution to the people for their adoption or rejection. It also appointed a Board of Commissioners empowered to appoint suitable persons to hold the election, and report the result thereof to the Board. The number of registered voters under the provisions of the schedule authorized to vote in this election was 1826. Of this number, 1233 voted for, and 169 against, the adoption of the Constitution.

At this election the following named parties were candidates for the various offices named, as appears from a printed copy of the Republican State Ticket, now before me, to-wit:

District Officers, etc.

For State Senate, 12th District, John H. Hutchinson.
For Representative, 12th District; George M. French, Wm. S. McCullough, Isaac Ayis, and Thos. M. Gibson.

County Officers:

Sheriff—Joseph M. Maxwell,
County Clerk—Edmund R. Wiley,
County and Probate Judge—Thomas P. Morrison,
County Treasurer—Michael Holt,
County Surveyor—Buford C. Hubbard,
County School Commissioner—Edward A. Douglass,
County Coroner—Isaac F. Chesher,
Internal Improvement Commissioner—Albert Maxwell,
County Assessor—John P. Hubbard.

All of these were returned as elected to the office for which they aspired. As the returns of this election were made directly to the Board of Commissioners, no particulars of the votes for each candidate can be given. At this election, John McClure was elected Associate Judge of the Supreme Court.

The reader will observe by reference to the County ticket, as reported above, the office of County and Probate Judge was regarded as a County office, and that Thomas P. Morrison was elected to that office. It will, also, be observed by reference to Section 52 and 53 of an act of the General Assembly, approved July 23, 1868, that the legislature, as well as the governor, at that time regarded the office as elective by the people, and a county office. Section 52 says: "It shall be the duty of the Secretary of State, in the presence of the Governor, within thirty days after the time herein allowed to make returns of the election to the Clerks of the County Court, or sooner, if all the returns shall have been received from any one Judicial Circuit; to cast up and arrange the votes from the several counties from which returns shall have been received for each person voted for as County and Probate Judge, as Judge of the Circuit Court, and as Prosecuting Attorney, when such Judge and Prosecuting Attorney shall be by law made elective and such persons as shall have received the highest number of votes for either of said offices within the his respective county, or district, shall immediately be commissioned by the Governor."

FROM 1865 TO 1870.

Section 53 had reference, also, to contested elections, or where there was a failure to elect.

During the summer of 1868, Hubbard, who was at that time a resident of the town of DeWitt, and who had been elected County Surveyor at the March election, and as current rumor at that time reported, had grown weary waiting for his commission as Surveyor, went in person to Little Rock to obtain the same. Upon his return, instead of qualifying as County Surveyor, he exhibited a commission from the Governor, and was sworn in under that commission, as County and Probate Judge of the county, and the rumor, true or otherwise, it is a fact that on the 3d day of August, 1868, his name appears of record as such a Judge, for, on that day, he caused the County Court to be opened—he presiding as Judge. (See County Court Record "C" p, 359). He held this office and executed the function of same until the County Court and the office of County Judge were abolished by an act of the General Assembly, April 3rd, 1873, as shown by Section 29 of that Act Creating the Board of Supervisors.

It will thus be seen that all the legal machinery of the County was in the hands and under the control of the Reconstruction officials.

Among the first of their acts in reference to the internal affairs of the County, was the reconstruction of the boundaries and changing the names of civil townships. This was done at a special term of the County Court in August, 1868.

Section 6 of an Act providing for the Registering of voters, approved July 15th, 1868, says: "The Governor shall cause to be prepared the form of books and certificates for the registration of voters on or before the first day of September, 1868, and shall cause copies of such books to be deposited with each Clerk of the County Court. The Clerk of the County Court shall deliver to the president of the Board of Registrars a sufficient number of books and certificates for the registration of all the voters in each precinct, district, or ward.

Under this Authority, the Governor sends out the following instructions to Registrars, signed and sealed, as the same now appears on file in the office of the Clerk of Arkansas County:

"The attention of Registrars is respectfully called to the following synopsis of their duties and powers. To give notice of the time and place you will register ten days before registration by three handbills posted in public places. (Section of Reg. Laws.)

To take the oath of franchise and of office before entering upon the duties of Registrar. (Sec. 4.)

To register the qualified voters in the precincts, districts, or wards, certified to by the clerks of the County Courts. (Sec. 5 and 7.)

To write the name of the person so registering. (Sec. 8.)

To examine, under oath, the party applying for registration before registering his name, and ascertaining whether he has been guilty of any of the acts specified in the Constitution as causes of disqualification, 1st, whether he took the oath of allegiance to the United States or gave bonds for loyalty and good behavior during the late rebellion and afterward gave comfort and aid to rebels, either by becoming a soldier in the rebel amy, or by voluntarily giving aid and comfort, or countenance to the rebels, either by becoming a soldier in

ARKANSAS COUNTY.

the rebel army or by accompanying any armed rebels whether belonging to their command or not; or, by giving aid and comfort in voluntarily entering the rebel lines after taking the oath of allegiance to the United States; or, by adhering to the rebellion in any way; or, by furnishing any supplies of any kind whatever to the rebels.

By Section 11 of the registration Act, the person applying for registration must, if he has ever taken oath of allegiance, etc., show that he has not done any of these acts; (and his own oath is not sufficient evidence to show that fact, if the Registrar desires other proof,) before he can be allowed to register. In short, he must show that after he took the oath of allegiance, he did not join the rebels; did not go with them voluntarily at any time; did not go into their lines; did not sympathize with, support, or encourage them; did not furnish them any supplies of any description whatever; or, in other words, he had, ever since he took the oath of allegiance, been a true, faithful and zealous supporter of the United States Government.

If the applicant fails to establish these facts, he cannot register, his oath to the contrary notwithstanding. Provided, however, if he can show that he voted for the Constitution at the late election, he can vote. This Proviso is applicable to the next two clauses. (Sec. 3, Art. 8—State Constitution.)

Second, Whether he was disqualified in the state from whence he came as an elector or from holding office? If so he cannot register.

Third, Whether he did during the late rebellion violate the rules of civil warfare? If so, he cannot register.

Fourth, Whether he is disqualified by Article 14 of the Constitution of the United States, which has been ratified and proclaimed as a part of the Constitution of the United States, and is now in full force.

Fifth, Whether he was disqualified by the late registration? If so, he must be rejected.

Many persons voted, or were allowed to register at the last registration who were disqualified under the 14th Article of the Amendment to the Constitution of the United States, and by the registration Acts. They should have been rejected. To register anyone who has taken the Franchise oath, if the registrar is satisfied or thinks he ought not to be registered. (Sec. 9—Reg. Law.)

To sit with other registrars as a Board of Review six secular days next preceding the tenth day before each general election. (Sec. 12.)

To make out and certify two copies of each election precinct, to deposit one with the Clerk of the county, the other with one of the judges of the election. To deposit with the clerk as soon as possible. the original book. (Sec. 13.)

To appoint, while registering, three qualified electors as judges of election in each precinct, and notify them of their appointment. (Sec. 19.)

All evidence of any person offering or threatening violence to any person engaged in registering, or to any voter, etc., the names of the parties and witnesses should be carefully noted and one copy sent to the Prosecuting Attorney of the Court, and one copy to the Governor. (Sec. 19.)

FROM 1865 TO 1870.

Powers of Registrars.

To administer oaths in regard to registration.

To administer oaths to parties coming before them as witnesses.

To examine every person who applies to register, to learn whether he is entitled to register.

To reject anyone he may think is not entitled to register, although the applicant has already taken the oath.

The power of the Circuit Court for the preservation of order at and around the place of registration.

To issue subpoenas and commitments.

In all cases where registrars are illegally hindered or obstructed in the performances of their duties, or have reason to believe that it will be dangerous to proceed with registration in any locality without the presence of a posse, or Military force, they are hereby authorized to call upon the Sheriff of the County for a sufficient number of armed men to act as a posse to protect them in the performance of their duties. In case the Sheriff fails to furnish said men, the Registrars are then authorized to call upon the commanding officer of any troop, company, or detachment of State Guards who is hereby authorized and directed to furnish promptly the required number of men. In such cases they are required to report promptly, all the facts to this office.

(Signed) POWELL CLAYTON,
Governor of Arkansas."

The closing paragraph of the foregoing instructions shows the dominant spirit ruling reconstruction; that is, to resort to the Military power of the State to compel obedience to their dictation.

Under these instructions, the Registrars appointed under the election laws of 1868, caused the registration of the voters of this County to be made, commencing on the 11th day of September, and closing on the 15th day of October, 1868, and filed their report in the Clerk's office in Arkansas County the 31st day of October, 1868. By this report, it appears that there were 1618 registered voters in the County, 969 of whom were illiterate and unable to write their names.

Returning to a narrative of events transpiring in the county, I desire to call attention to the doings of our new County Judge, Mr. Hubbard; who, by way of introduction, was a native of Kentucky, a practicing physician, the soul of hospitality and good neighborship, but a devout worshiper at the shrine of "Mammon", and a lover of "The Almighty Dollar". He saw a prospect of increasing his store by adding the salary of County Judge to the fees of a physician, as will fully appear by following him through his career as Judge. Among the first of his acts as County Judge, is the following order, granted at the January Term, 1869.

Support Of Paupers.

Now, on this day, on motion, it is ordered that Robert C. Cheny be and he is hereby appointed as commissioner to advertise and let out the keeping of the paupers of Arkansas County for the year, 1869, on the 25th day of January, A. D., 1869, and that at the same time Medical

ARKANSAS COUNTY.

attention for the year 1869, be let by said commissioner to the lowest bidder. (County Court Record "C", p. 379.)

On Saturday, the 9th day of the same month, the following order was granted:

Medical Attention To Paupers.

Now, on this day, on motion, it is ordered that so much of an order of this Court of January 7th, 1869, as requires the medical attendance upon the paupers of Arkansas County to be let out to the lowest bidder for the year A. D., 1869, be and the same is hereby revoked and annulled. (Ib. 385.)

At the April Term, 1869, this order was granted, to-wit:

Employment Of County Physician.

Now, on this day, on motion, it was ordered that Buford C. Hubbard, M. D., be and he is hereby appointed County Physician to attend the paupers in the poorhouse and furnish them all necessary medicines and medical attention during the year 1869, also, all pauper practice outside the poorhouse in the vicinity of his residence, and that he be allowed for such service the salary of Four Hundred Dollars per year.

Whereupon, comes said B. C. Hubbard, M. D., and accepts such appointment upon the terms proposed, and takes in open court the oath of offices prescribed by law, which is administered by Fred K. Lyman, Esqr., a member hereof. (Ib. 420.)

At this term of the court, and before the granting of the above order, Hubbard presented two claims for medical attention to paupers, one of twenty Dollars, and the other for twelve. Both of these were allowed, and ordered paid. (Ib. 404.)

At the time of Hubbard's appointment to the Judgeship, the salary was Five Hundred Dollars per annum, but by an act of the Legislature approved the 12th of April, 1869, it was raised to One Thousand Dollars, and by another Act, March 27th, 1871, it was increased to Twelve Hundred. This salary was continued until the Court was abolished.

At the April Term, 1869, John P. Hubbard, a brother of Judge Hubbard, was allowed One Hundred Dollars for; "Services of self and horse, as coroner, in posting notices for registration in September and October of the previous year." The reader will bear in mind that at the March, 1868, election, Isaac F. Chesher was elected Coroner, and Jno. P. Hubbard Assessor, the latter qualifying as such as will more fully appear later.

At the March Term, 1869, of the County Court, it being the time appointed for filing and adjusting the assessment list for the year 1868; which, when filed, showed an aggregate of One Million, One Hundred Sixty-seven Thousand Dollars and Sixteen Cents of taxable property in the County. (Ib. 391.)

On this assessment, the County Court, on the 7th day of April, 1869, allowed Jno. P. Hubbard the sum of Seven Hundred, Eighty-three and 5-100 Dollars fees as Assessor. (Ib. 412.)

FROM 1865 TO 1870.

And, here again, is another object lesson presented to the reader, showing the contrast between this allowance to Hubbard and the one previously allowed to Price for the year 1867. Price's assessment showed One Million, Seven Hundred Thousand, Three Hundred and Twenty-six Dollars. (8 Ib. 184.) On this assessment the County Court allowed Price, Four Hundred, Thirty-five and 42-100 Dollars. (Ib. 203 and 312.)

This contrast is plainly shown by the figures as stated below:

Price's Assessment $1,773,326
Hubbard's Assessment 1,194,467

Excess of Price's Assessment.........................$ 578,859
Fees Paid Hubbard $783.05
Fees Paid Price 435.42

Excess of fees paid Hubbard............................$347.63

And this is not all; the County Clerk in issuing scrip, issued and delivered to him, the sum of Eight Hundred Eighty-three and 5-100 Dollars. (Scrip Book "H", p. 65.)

In this connection, I desire to call the reader's attention to the fact that James H. Price, the regularly elected Assessor, made and filed assessment of taxable property in the County for the Year 1868; That the same had been adjusted by the County Court, and the rate of taxes levied at the April Term, 1868 (County Court Record "C", p. 330); That these proceedings were ignored by the Reconstruction Authorities; or, in the language of the Legislature (July 23d, 1868), "Said assessment is held for naught". At a subsequent session, however, ordered the payment of the fees due.

On the 12th of April, 1869, the legislature passed an act fixing the salaries of the Probate Judges, and, by Section 2, authorized: "The County Court of the several counties in the state to determine the pay of the Associate Justices for their respective counties."

Under the provisions of this act, the County Court of Arkansas County, passed the following order at the October Term, 1869, to-wit:

Salary of Associate Justice.

Now, on this day, on motion, it is ordered that the salary of Associate Justices of this County, be, and the same is hereby fixed and established at the rate of Three Hundred Dollars per annum, for the year 1869. (County Court Record "C", No. 2, p. 70.)

Under this order, the sum of Two Hundred and Thirty Dollars was allowed Edward Johnson, as balance due him for the first, second, third, and fourth terms of said Court, ending in October, 1869; and Richard K. Gamble was allowed One Hundred and Fifty Dollars for two quarters, ending with the October Term, 1869.

The reader's attention is especially called to the fact that the Act of the Legislature, empowering the County Court to fix the salaries of the Associate Justices for the County, was approved April 12th, 1869; that the January Term of the County Court had passed, and also the April Term, which lasted from the 5th to the 8th, and on this latter day, the court adjourned until the 14th of April; that Johnson was not present during the January Term, but was present two days in March. These facts are taken from the County Court Record, now before me. Johnson received for his services, as a salary, Three Hundred Dollars, and Fifty Dollars at the October Term, 1870. (County Court Record "C", No. 2, p. 261.)

To meet the extravagant appropriations, it was necessary to have revenue. The statements following will show the means resorted to to obtain this. Section 84, of an Act to assess and collect taxes and for other purposes, approved July 23rd, 1868, reads:

"The County Court shall levy the amount of taxes necessary for the current expenses of the County for the Year; but not to exceed One and One-half per cent upon the appraised value of taxable property of the County." (Acts 1868, p. 284.)

Under this law, the County Court of Arkansas County, passed the following order on the 10th of September, 1869.

Levying of Taxes for County Purposes for the Year 1869.

And now here it is ordered by the Court, that there be levied for all County purposes, a tax of three per cent upon each One Hundred Dollars ($100) of the valuation of all taxable property, real and personal, in the County of Arkansas, as returned and equalized for the Year 1869. (Ib. p. 50.)

To prevent the collection of this unlawful tax, certain taxpayers in the County caused proceedings to be instituted on the chancery side of the Circuit Court before Judge Morse, to restrain the collector from collecting this tax. The hearing was had at the October Term, 1869, and the court dismissed the suit at the cost of the applicants, on the ground that the parties' remedy was on appeal from the order of the County Court.

At the hearing of this cause, John A. Williams, Associate County Attorney, assisted in the defense and support of the unlawful tax, and received for his services, by order of the Chancellor, a fee of $50.00, to be paid out of the County revenue. (Ib. 146.)

Before closing the reference to these events, will direct the reader's attention to another object lesson by exhibiting the contrast between certain salaries of 1869 and those of later date, for the same purposes.

The Constitutional Convention of 1868 created the office of Superintendent of Public Instruction, and his salary was fixed by an Act of the Legislature, passed July 23d, 1868, at Three Thousand and Five Hundred Dollars per annum. By another act of the same Legislature (passed July 23d, '68), the office of Circuit Superintendent of Public Instruction was created, to be filled by appointment of the governor, and the salary fixed at Three Thousand Dollars. The state was divided into ten circuits, thus making eleven offices created by the Constitution and the Legislature of 1868. Contrasted with this, we now have one Superintendent of Instruction whose salary is $2,500 per annum.

FROM 1865 TO 1870.

Table of Contrast.
1868.

Superintendent of Instruction	$ 3,500.00	
Ten Circuit Superintendents	30,000.00	
Total	$33,500.00	$33,500.00

1908.
Under the laws of 1875,

One Superintendent	$2,500.00	
Total	$2,500.00	$ 2,500.00

Difference in favor of the present law....... $31,000.00

The reader's attention is called to this from the fact that John H. Hutchinson was one of the delegates from this County to the Constitutional Convention, the first Senator, from this District, to the Legislature, and was one of the Circuit Superintendents of Education, having resigned his seat in the senate to accept this office.

As senator, he was supposed to represent the wishes of his constituents. He was at that time a respected citizen of Arkansas County, a highly respected Physician, and a leading, Loyal Union-Republican or Reconstructionist. He remained a citizen of this County until his death.

After Hubbard's appointment to the Judgeship of Arkansas County, he moved from DeWitt to Silver Lake Township, south of the Arkansas River, where he remained until that township was detached from Arkansas and added to Lincoln County. He returned to DeWitt before the new County was organized, thus retaining his citizenship in Arkansas County and his office as Couny Judge. But he lost none of his power as a leader of the Reconstructionist as will hereafter be seen.

CHAPTER XVIII.

From the Year 1870 to the Year 1875.

1870.

Pursuing our investigation of the actions and doings of the Reconstructionists within Arkansas County, we find that the County Court granted Mr. E. R. Wiley $513.10 for his services as Clerk of the Court, from the 5th of April to the 6th of July, 1870. This allowance was made at the July Term, 1870, and for future reference, it is itemized as follows:

Settling with the sheriff, ten days @ $5.00 per day.............$ 50.00
Two boxes of matches...................................... .30
Recording thirty-three orders of Board of Equalization at 25c ea. 8.25
Sixteen days attending Equalization Board @ $5.00........... 80.00
Copying Delinquent Tax List for Auditor..................... 87.00
Issuing 133 warrants, from No. 290 to 424................... 33.25
Filing 1,190 pieces of cancelled warrants at 10c.............. 119.00
(Ib. 240.)

There are several facts connected with this exhibit to which the attention should be directed:

First, the number of days and fees per day, for settling with the sheriff.

Second, the number of days, and fees for attending the Equalization Board.

Third, his calling attention to the issuance of warrants by referring to their numbers, "290 to 424".

Fourth, the number of warrants filed.

Under the law, as it now exists, twelve dollars is the maximum that a clerk may charge for settling with the sheriff. Under the law in force at that time, the Clerk was allowed 25c for entering an order of allowance, and issuing a warrant therefor.

On examining the Register of Warrants, Book "H", pp. 62 to 64, the covering dates of the preceding issue, there are but Seventy names to whom allowances were made. It is true that 133 names appear on these pages, but several of them, as the record shows, had several warrants on one allowance. According to this showing, the clerk received Fifteen and 75-100 Dollars more than the law allowed. Another mode of increasing fees, was the issuing of a number of warrants on the same allowance, because of the fee of 10c made for filing each warrant.

At the time of the event in question, an allowance of Eighty Dollars for Sixteen day's services on the Equalization Board was made to F. K. Lyman, as assessor of the County; and, One Hundred and Twelve Dollars was allowed to W. R. Lear, the county surveyor, as a member of the Equalization Board. This shows that it cost the County Two

FROM 1870 TO 1875.

Hundred and Seventy-two Dollars to equalize the taxable property of Arkansas County for the year 1870. (County Court Record "C", No. 2, p. 207.)

At the general election held on the 8th day of November, 1870, the following named parties were returned as elected to their several offices.

A. Hemingway, Arkansas County, Senator. (To fill vacancy caused by resignation of Hutchinson, who had been appointed Circuit Sup't. of Instruction).

Edmund R. Wiley and George H. Joslin, Representatives from this County, 12th Representative District.

The Governor appointed Alexander C. Wiley County Clerk, to fill the vacancy made by the election of his brother, E. R. Wiley, as Representative. Mr. A. C. Wiley had been Deputy Clerk under his brother.

Under an order made at the October Term of the County Court, 1870, a vote was taken at this election, as to whether the County should subscribe the sum of Two Hundred Thousand Dollars Stock in a certain Railroad proposed to be built through the County. The result was in favor of the Subscription.

The population of the County as shown by the Federal Census for 1870, was 8,268—a decrease of 576 since the Census of 1860.

When the ravages of the Civil War, together with the blighting influences of Reconstruction, are considered, the reader will not be at a loss to account for the deficit. The only wonder is that the loss was not greater.

1871.

It will be observed by reference to the proceedings of the County Court, at its first term in the year, that the Judge had lost none of his financial ability so far as he, individually, was concerned. At this Term an order was granted as follows:

B. C. Hubbard,
    vs.   Claim for $263.50.
Arkansas County.

On this day is present, the claim of said Hubbard for the sum of Two Hundred Sixty Three Dollars and Fifty Cents, for one quarter's salary as County and Probate Judge, and for acting as Judge of election at Silver Lake precinct on the 8th day of November, 1870, qualifying judges of said election and bringing up the returns thereof; which claims being audited and examined by the Court, are allowed and ordered paid. (Ib. 292.)

This order was made on the 4th day of January, 1871. On the 2nd of February, at an adjourned term of the Court, the following order was granted:

B. C. Hubbard,
    vs.   Claim for $6.00.
Arkansas County.

On this day is presented the claim of said Hubbard for clerk of election held November 8th, 1870, in Silver Lake Township, for Six Dollars, which claim being audited and examined, by the Court, is allowed and ordered paid. (Ib. 348.)

ARKANSAS COUNTY.

In these two orders the fact is shown that Hubbard, as County Judge, administered the necessary oath to himself and others, to hold the election; that he acted in the two-fold capacity of Judge and clerk of the election; and that he brought the returns of this election to the County Authorities; and, that he charged and was allowed pay for these services.

Alexander C. Wiley, who had been appointed County Clerk, took possession of the office about the 16th of November, 1870. January 11th, 1871, E. R. Wiley, the retiring clerk, filed a claim against the County for $746.70, for fees due him up to the 11th of November, 1870. On the same day of Court, A. C. Wiley, the new Clerk, filed a claim for $576.80. Both claims were allowed, and ordered paid. (Ib. 301.)

The last account is mentioned that the reader may know that the new clerk was adept in counting and charging fees as his brother had been, he, having obtained an allowance of $576.80 for less than two months' services. (Ib. 301.) One other allowance by the County Court for the year 1871, and we will close. On the 2nd day of May, 1871, the County Court granted the following order, towit:

Fred K. Lyman,
vs.   Claim for $1,322.00.
Arkansas County.

On this day comes up the claim of said Lyman for publishing the Delinquent List of lands for the years 1869 and 1870, for $2,322.00, Twenty Three Hundred and Twenty-two Dollars, on which claim the sum of One Thousand Dollars was allowed at the last term of this court, leaving a balance of $1,322.00, Thirteen Hundred and Twenty-two Dollars, which claim being Audited and examined by the court, is allowed and ordered paid. (Ib. 394.)

Under the election laws then in force, the 12th Representative District, consisting of Arkansas and Prairie Counties, was entitled to four representatives. Two of these were E. R. Wiley, and G. H. Joslyn, who were elected from Arkansas County, at the general election of 1870.

During the session of the Legislature of 1871, through the influence of these men, mainly, all that portion of Arkansas County lying south of the Arkansas River, an area of about 175 square miles and a population of 2,933 Souls, was stricken off from Arkansas County and made a part of the new County of Lincoln.

Lincoln County was created by an Act of the Legislature approved March 28th, 1871, and as soon as organized, the Governor filled all the offices that could be filled by appointment. Among those receiving appointments were: Representative Joslyn, as County and Probate Judge; Alfred Wiley, brother of Representative Wiley, Clerk of the Circuit Court; and J. J. Joslyn, brother of the new Judge, as County Treasurer.

Now, that I am writing about the changing of the boundaries of the County, I will show that all of Desha County that was lying north of the Arkansas River; and the cut-off connecting Arkansas and White Rivers; also, that part east of White River, was, by an Act of the legislature of 1885, detached from Desha and added to Arkansas County. This territory embraced an area of about 72 square miles, and had a

FROM 1870 TO 1875.

population of about 400. At the session of the Legislature of 1889, all of Arkansas County lying west of Big Bayou Meto, and south of a line running east and west, one mile north of the line dividing Townships 5 and 6, south; from the channel of said Bayou to the Range line dividing Ranges 6 and 7 west; was detached from Arkansas County and annexed to Jefferson. This territory embraced an area of about Eighty-five Square miles, and a population of about Two Thousand; these changes leaving the boundaries as described in topographical description of the County.

The reader is reminded, that at the October Term of the County Court, 1870, an election was ordered to ascertain the will of the voters on the subject of subscribing Two Hundred Thousand Dollars in County Bonds to assist in building certain Railroads that were proposed as about to pass through Arkansas County. The effort failing, the County Court at the October term, 1871, made another attempt in the same direction as is shown hereafter.

Petition for Railroad, Submitted.

On this day, it appearing that the President and Directors of the Grand Prairie and DeWitt and Chicora, Railroad Companies, have applied to the County Court of Arkansas County for a subscription of One Hundred Thousand Dollars to the capital stock to each of the said roads, by the County; and that more than One Hundred voters of said County have petitioned said Court for the submission of the question of such subscription to the voters of said County, it is therefore ordered by the Court that an election be held on Saturday, the 28th day of October, 1871, at the usual voting places in the County of Arkansas, and in the manner and form as required by law to determine the question of the subscription of One Hundred Thousand Dollars by Arkansas County, in Coupon Bonds of said county, to the capital stock of each of said Railroad Companies, in manner and form as provided by law, and on the following terms and conditions to-wit: That when the railroads intended to be constructed by said companies shall be located and surveyed within the County of Arkansas, as soon as the directors of the respective companies shall file with the County Clerk, their report in writing, of the entire length of the lines of the respective roads within said County, attested by the affidavit or oral sworn testimony of the engineer making such survey, and, thereupon, whenever any portion of the grading of said road within said county shall be completed, upon the filing in the County Clerk's office of the written application of the Directors, and the affidavit of the engineers of the respective Companies, or the County Surveyor, as to the length of such graded portions of said road; that there shall be issued to said respective companies an amount of bonds aforesaid, bearing the same ratio to the entire subscription which the length of that portion of the respective roads graded, as aforesaid, shall be to the entire length of their respective lines within said county; and so on from time to time, as the work progresses, until all the grading within the county shall have been completed, and the entire amount of bonds issued. That such bonds shall be of such denomination as shall hereafter be agreed upon between the directors of said Railroad companies and the said County Court, and shall have those of the DeWitt and Chicora Company twenty years, and those of the Grand Prairie Company fifteen years to run to their maturity, and bear six per cent per annum interest from the date of issuance. Said interest to be paid semi-annually at such banking house or office as may be hereinafter before the issuance of said bonds agreed upon, between the County and the Directors of the respective companies; that said bonds shall be denominated, respectively, Chicora Railroad bonds, and Arkansas County Grand Prairie Railroad bonds, and shall be signed by the presiding Judge of the County and countersigned by the County Clerk of this Court; and the interest Coupons thereunto attached, signed by the County Clerk; and the bonds and coupons attested by the seal of Arkansas County. And that the bonds, when issued, shall be accepted by the said Railroad Companies at their par value for the stock of said companies; and the clerk is hereby ordered to make out, forthwith, the Poll Books of said election, and the Sheriff to forthwith, post notices of said election in each Township of said County." (County Record "D", pp. 23-24.)

At the January Term, 1872, of the County Court, presumably upon the election held on the 28th of October, 1871, the Court granted the following order, to-wit:

Appropriation.

On this day it is ordered, that the sum of Eight Hundred Dollars be, and the same is hereby appropriated for the purchase of blank Bonds for the issuance, by Arkansas County, to the DeWitt and Chicora and the Grand Prairie Railroad Companies; the bonds heretofore subscribed to the capital Stock of said Companies upon the fulfillment by said Railroad Companies of the Conditions in said subscription contained and it is ordered that the clerk hereof draw his warrants on the Treasurer in favor of Buford C. Hubbard, who is hereby made a special commissioner for carrying into effect the powers of this order in such amounts as may be required by said commissioner to the aggregate amount of Eight Hundred Dollars, and that said commissioner, sell said warrants for cash, for the greatest price which can be obtained, but not a greater discount than Ten per cent; and hold the proceeds in trust for the purpose of this appropriation, until the further order of this Court. And that he report at the next meeting of this Court after the sale of said warrants, his acts and doings in this behalf and the amount then in his hands as the proceeds of the sale aforesaid. (Ib. 66.)

The Legislature of 1873, by an act approved April 3d, abolished the County Courts and established a Board of Supervisors for each County in the State, empowering the Governor with authority to appoint Three supervisors in each county.

Under the law, the Governor appointed Erastus Inman, John Matley, and Joseph Helm (the latter a negro), as the Board of Supervisors for Arkansas County. This Board at its July Term, passed the following order regarding the Railroads referred to:

"In the matter of voting the stock of Arkansas County, which has been voted to the Grand Prairie & DeWitt, and the DeWitt & Chicora Railroads:

FROM 1870 TO 1875.

Now, on this day, it is ordered that John Matley be, and he is hereby ordered and authorized to vote the Stock now taken by the County of Arkansas in the above mentioned Railroads, and that he is hereby fully authorized and empowered to represent the interest of the County of Arkansas in said Roads so far as the Stock in his hands will enable him so to do." (Ib. 323.)

These three orders are grouped together as all refer to the same subject matter, and that the reader may understand them.

It will be observed that the first order, required that an election be held, the second made an appropriation for the purchase of blanks for bonds; and, the third, a member of the Board of Supervisors was ordered to vote the Stock of the County.

On the margin of Record "D", p. 66, ordering the appropriation, the following note is made: "Issued, No. 45 to 56". Register of Warrants, page 97, Book "H", shows that on the 6th of January, 1872, warrants from 45 to 56, inclusive, were issued to B. C. Hubbard as Commissioner; that Hubbard acknowledged the receipt of said warrants by signing his name to the same; and, that on the 3d day of July, 1872, all of these warrants had been redeemed and interest charged on each, the interest ranging from 52 cents to $2.90. All of these warrants were issued the same day and redeemed the same day, but the record fails to show who returned these warrants to the Clerk whose duty it is to make such record as they are redeemed.

This record shows that on the same day as mentioned in the preceding paragraph, a large amount of money—running into Thousands of Dollars in County Warrants—was redeemed. Page 137, Record "D", shows that on the 9th day of July, 1872, that on settlement with the County Court, Michael Holt, County Treasurer, turned over to the County Sixteen Thousand Four Hundred and Three Dollars and 14 cents in "Arkansas County Warrants which have been redeemed by him and now have been severally cancelled in open court, it is, by the court ordered, that said warrants be filed."

There can be little, if any, doubt that these Eight Hundred Dollars in County warrants, with others, were paid to Holt, the Treasurer on the 3d of July, and he turning them over to the Court, which cancelled them on the 9th day that month.

Now the question is, who received the value of these warrants, and to whose credit did they pass?

It is a notorious fact that not one dollar of this sum was expended for the purpose designated in the order of the Court making the appropriation, and no bonds were issued for the reason that none of the conditions mentioned in the order, were complied with—not one foot of either road was ever built in the County.

One of the remarkable coincidents connected with reconstruction in Arkansas County was the presence and official actings of the three brothers: Alex. C., Edmond R., and Alfred Wiley.

Edmund was Clerk, first by Military appointment, later by election; representative in the legislature, justice of the peace, by appointment; and, Sheriff by election from 1867 to 1874.

Alexander Wiley was Deputy Clerk under his brother Edmund,

ARKANSAS COUNTY.

later Clerk, and afterward, deputy under E. P. G. Tackett, all of these positions obtained by appointment.

Alfred was appointed Justice of the Peace in 1868.

These facts are presented to the reader to show that at a majority of the sessions of the County Court from 1868 to 1874, two of these three men were present in an official capacity, participating in the proceedings.

The appointment of Alfred Wiley to the office of County Clerk in Lincoln County (1871), vacated his office as Justice of the Peace in LaGrue Township, however, he was present and acting as one of the Court, April 3d, 1871.

After the adjournment of the Legislature (1871), Edmond R. Wiley was appointed Justice of the Peace in LaGrue Township, and was a member of the Court on the 7th of July, 1871.

It will thus be seen that the principal actors in controlling the internal affairs of the County from August, 1868, to 1873, were the three Wileys, B. C. Hubbard, and Edward Johnson.

1872.

In presenting the official acts of the Reconstruction authorities, during the year 1872, I shall note only the most pronounced acts of theirs, for, as time progresses, they grow in ability to devise ways and means of appropriating the public moneys, as will fully appear by referring to the data given below.

At the April Term of the County Court, an appropriation was made to A. C. Wiley, as Clerk, for the sum of Four Hundred and Twenty Dollars and Twenty-five cents (E. R. Wiley appearing as a member of the court.) (Ib. 103.)

At the July Term of said Court the sum of One Thousand and One Dollars and Five Cents was allowed to A. C. Wiley as Clerk, the same parties constituting the Court as at the April Term. (Ib. 134.)

At the October Term of the same year, the same officials, the Court allowed Mr. Wiley Six Hundred and Eighty-three Dollars and Fifty Cents for his services. (Ib. 175.) The total allowance to Mr. Wiley for the year's services was Two Thousand One Hundred and Four Dollars and Eighty Cents, and the various allowances do not include fees due the Clerk from litigants in Circuit Court, nor those as Clerk of Probate Court and Recorder of the County.

On the 23d of December, 1872, before B. C. Hubbard as Judge and J. M. Barker and H. M. Shad as Associates, the salary of the County Attorney, R. E. Puyear, was raised from Five Hundred Dollars to Seven Hundred and Fifty per annum. (Ib. 203.)

At the General election held in November, 1872, the following officers were elected for the County and District.

P. C. Dooley, Senator.
J. F. Preston and D. J. Hinds, Representatives.
E. P. G. Tackett, Clerk.
E. R. Wiley, Sheriff.
Samuel McCarty, Treasurer.

FROM 1870 TO 1875.

L. S. Fields, Coroner.
Joe Webster, Surveyor.
J. W. Johnson, Assessor.

Immediately upon the Installation of Tackett, he appointed A. C. Wiley his deputy. The election of E. R. Wiley as Sheriff made the office of Justice of Peace in Lagrue Township vacant, and Geo. Kealhoffer was appointed to fill the vacancy. Kealhoffer was from Ohio and did not remain long in the County.

As an evidence of the burdens imposed upon the tax-payers of the County by the Reconstructionist, I will show that by the official report of the Commissioner of State Lands, made in 1876, there were forfeited to the State for non-payment of taxes, between the years of 1865 and 1872, 247,849.34 acres of land. (Commissioner's report, 1876, p. 41.)

1873.

The following order will show that the new Court, Organized at the January Term, 1873, maintained the reputation of its predecessor for liberality to its friends and members.

"The salary of Associate Justice for 1873."

"On this day, on motion of Edward Johnson, esquire, it was resolved that the salary of the associate Justices of this court be fixed at the sum of Three Hundred Dollars for the year 1873.

Salary of Justices of Peace attending Court this day. It is ordered by the Court that the sum of Ten Dollars be allowed each of the Justices of the Peace who have this day attended this Court." (Ib. 206.)

There were twelve Justices present at this term of court, and it will be seen that it cost the county One Hundred and Twenty Dollars to organize the first term, and that in addition to the annual salaries allowed the Judge and Associate Justices.

Further investigation reveals that at this term of Court, A. C. Wiley presented a claim against the County for the sum of $2,354.41, with a credit of $156.90 for taxes on seals collected by him, this leaving a balance in his favor of $2,197.50 which was allowed and ordered paid. (Ib. 230.)

On this allowance, the Clerk issued to Wiley Four Hundred and Fifty Warrants, all bearing the date of January 11th, 1873. All but seven or eight of these warrants were redeemed on the 10th of October, 1873, and so noted in red ink in the handwriting of A. C. Wiley. (Register of Warrants Bk. "H" pp. 121-131.)

If the same fees were charged and allowed by the Court on this allowance, as were to E. R. Wiley, it cost the County the sum of One Hundred Fifty-seven Dollars and Fifty Cents to authorize the Clerk to pay himself the amount of this allowance.

No itemized account covering these charges has been found, but when it is recollected that there has been no record showing an abatement of fees or allowances, but on the contrary, in many instances, an increase—it will be no violence to the ordinary mind to conclude that "Like begets its like" when manipulated by the same parties as was in this instance.

ARKANSAS COUNTY.

By an act of the Legislature, approved April 3d, 1873, the county courts of the State were abolished and a Board of Supervisors created instead. The last term of the County Court presided over by Judge Hubbard, assisted by George Kealhoffer and L. W. Barker, as Associate Judges, began on the 6th and closed on the 10th of January 1873. The Board of Supervisors, consisting of Erastus Inman, John Matley, and Joseph Helm, was convened and organized on the 9th of May, Mr. Inman being elected president under the law creating the Board.

The first act of this Board after its organization, was to abolish the office of County Attorney, but at the same term allowed R. E. Puyear Two Hundred Seventy Dollars and Eighty Three Cents fees due from the 1st of January to May the 10th of that year. But before the adjournment of the term, the Board annulled their first order and elected C. B. Brinkly County Attorney for one year and fixed his salary at Five Hundred Dollars. (Ib. 273.)

Heretofore, the references have, generally, been to the doings of the County Court or Board of Supervisors, but the following scene transpired in the Circuit Court at the March Term, 1873. It was in an action of Replevin by Jerry Willingham, a negro, against John Bigham, a white man and was brought before Judge H. C. Morse. Both litigants resided in Old River Township.

Several of the Jurors selected to try this case were negroes and were so arranged on their seats while the trial was in progress that they could be reached by persons who passed the ends of the benches on which they sat.

While the writer, Bigham's attorney, was presenting his argument in defence of his client, Willingham, who was seated near the Jury Box, rose from his seat and deliberately passed the seats of the Jurors, and as he did so, patted each negro Juror on the shoulder and in a voice loud enough to be heard through the court room said, "Stand firm, stand firm" and returned to his seat without one word of censure or reproof from the Court, the jury, or the attorney for Willingham.

The result was a verdict for Willingham, for, all the jurors did as they had been requested, stood firm for Willingham.

Before closing an account of the passing events in the County, for the year 1873, will invite the reader's attention to the following matter regarding the subject of taxation. This will show the contrast between that of 1865 and 1873 and between 1873 and 1888.

The first illustration shows the taxes as they were the first year of Democratic rule after the war and before reconstruction, and the last year of Republican rule since the War.

In 1865, the taxes on the N½, Sec. 1, T 4S., R 3 W. was $2.40 and the same tract without One Dollar's worth of improvements was taxed in 1873, $29.70, upwards of twelve times the taxes of 1865.

The second illustration shows that six lots with the improvements on them, had been assessed by the County Board of equalization for 1871, at Two Thousand and Nine Hundred Dollars, which was raised by the State Board of Equalization—the State Senate—to Four Thousand Six Hundred and Forty Dollars. These lots were taxed at the latter figures for that year, and the taxes, exclusive of school tax, were Ninety Two Dollars Eighty Cents.

FROM 1870 TO 1875.

The member of the State Board, from Arkansas County, was A. Hemmingway, a "Carpet Bagger" who resided on the Arkansas River and was comparatively unknown to a majority of the Citizens of this County. He had but limited knowledge of the value of real estate in this county, yet as our representative on that Board, he raised the valuation of all real estate in the county sixty per cent above that placed by the County Board.

On these lots, with six others, the taxes, including the local school tax, was, in 1888, $14.60.

The Contrast.

No. 1.	Taxes for 1865.............................	$ 2.40
	Taxes for 1873.............................	29.70
	Increase	$27.30
No. 2.	Taxes for 1873.............................	$92.80
	Taxes for 1888.............................	14.60
	Decrease	$78.20

These facts can be verified by referring to the taxbooks for the respective years as are now on file in the Clerk's office of Arkansas County.

1874.

The first act of the Board of Supervisors at the January meeting, 1874, was an allowance to Tackett, the Clerk; "The sum of Seventy-five Dollars for going to Pine Bluff in advertising the Tax-list of lands for the year, 1872, * * * That the said Tackett be, and he is hereby allowed and paid the sum of Fifty Dollars for services rendered in settling with Michael Holt, late Treasurer of Arkansas County." (County Court Record "D" p. 377.)

For the latter charge there may be some authority, but for the former there is none. The law designates in what paper to present the delinquent tax list and fixes the price for same, and all that the Clerk had to do was to prepare the lists and send them to the printer.

At the meeting of the Board previously mentioned, a new order was made regarding the employing of a County Attorney, prescribing his duties, etc., the latter clause of this order reads as follows:

"The said Attorney shall receive for his salary the sum of One Thousand Dollars per annum, in Arkansas County Warrants on Scrip, and shall serve for the period of one year from date of his election."

The above conditions being agreed to and understood by the Board, they proceeded to the election of an Attorney by ballot, as evidenced by the following extract from the records:

"Whereupon, the vote stands as follows: E. Inman votes Jas. A. Gibson, and John Matley and Joseph Helm vote for G. J. F. Van De Sande and it having been found that in Court that said Van De Sande had received two votes, and it being a majority of the Board, he is declared duly elected." (County Record "D" p. 451.)

This is quite an upward movement financially, in the interest of

ARKANSAS COUNTY.

the County Attorney, from the first order on the subject, in this: that by their first order on the subject, they abolished the office as unnecessary: second, they assume that the office is necessary and increase his salary from Five Hundred to One Thousand Dollars.

One of the remarkable incidents connected with this order of the Board, is the election of Van De Sande to the Attorneyship for he was unknown to the greater portion of the citizens of the County, even as a resident, to say nothing of his qualifications as a lawyer.

Previous to his election, he had resided the greater portion of his time, in Old River and Villemont Townships, associating upon terms of social equality with the negro population of these Townships.

But when the facts are known, that one member of the Board voting for him was a Negro, and the other an associate upon terms of equality with the negroes of his vicinity, this event will be fully understood.

When the news was received of the breaking out of the Brooks-Baxter War, April, 1874, Van De Sande and his colored friend Helms left the County for the County's good "without standing on the manner of their going," and have prudently remained out of it.

The departure of Van De Sande from the County, left the office of County Attorney vacant. To fill this vacancy, the Board of Supervisors at the July Term, 1874, granted the order as given below:

"In the Matter of the Appointment of County Attorney"

On this day for good cause shown, it is ordered that the former order of this Board, appointing G. J. F. Van De Sande, County Attorney for Arkansas County, be, and the same is hereby vacated.

And it is further ordered that A. L. Freeman be, and he, hereby, is appointed County Attorney of Arkansas County in place of said Van De Sande, for the term of one year from this date and that Freeman shall be allowed for his services as such attorney, as compensation, at the rate of Seven Hundred and Fifty Dollars per annum, payable quarterly." (Ib. 460.)

At the October term, 1874, of said Board meeting, on the 22nd day of the month, just three and one-half months since granting the order of allowance to Freeman as County Attorney, this Board granted the following order, to-wit:

A. L. Freeman
      vs.   Now on this day is presented the claim of said
Arkansas County.   A. L. Freeman, for the sum of ($750.00) Seven Hundred and Fifty Dollars, salary as County Attorney as per contract as hereinbefore made and of record of which sum, the sum of ($195.00) One Hundred and Ninty Five is due and the sum of ($585.00) Five Hundred and Eighty Five Dollars which sums are hereby allowed and ordered paid out of the ordinary County funds." On the margin of the page of the Record where this order is recorded, this endorsement occurs:—"No. 51—Issued 978 to 991, both inclusive all issued." (Ib. 534.)

Referring to page 217, Warrant Record "H", we find that warrants No. 978 to 991, inclusive, were issued on the 23d day of October 1874 to A. L. Freeman, and were receipted for on that day.

Here in the face of and in express violation of its own order, within

FROM 1870 TO 1875.

less than four months, the Board of Supervisors ordered the payment of Five Hundred and Fifty Dollars for services which were never performed.

The foregoing order of allowance to Freeman was made on the last day of the last term of the Board of Supervisors and was the last Record made by Tackett as clerk, except the note of filing and recording the names of the Judges appointed to hold the general election in October, 1874, under the new Constitution. This record was the 25th of October of that year.

The third section of the Schedule to the Constitution of 1874, declared, that; "An election shall be held at the several election precincts of every County of the State on Thursday the 13th day of October, 1874 for * * * all county and township officers provided for in this Constitution."

Under the authority of this section an election was held on the day designated, and the officers named were elected. At this election, the vote of the county on the adoption of the new Constitution was had, and an aggregate of sixteen hundred and forty-one was cast.

By the provisions of the new Constitution, the State election was separated from the Federal, the former being held this year on the 13th day of October, the latter, on Tuesday after the first Monday in November.

The Federal election of 1874 was held on the 3rd day of November in Arkansas county, for the sole purpose of electing a representative to Congress. The returns of this election were made to the County Clerk who held office under the laws of 1868, (The newly elected Clerk had not then been commissioned.)

These facts are mentioned that the reader may more fully understand the "Actings and doings" of the old and outgoing officials.

At the election held in this County on the 3rd day of November, to elect a representative to Congress—the only office elective by the voters of the County under the law then in force—nevertheless, votes were received, counted and returns made from four of the Townships of the County, for every office that had been elective under the Constitution and laws of 1868, notwithstanding the fact that every office from Governor down to Township constable had been elected, returns made and these returns certified by the same officers to the proper authorities, as the election held on the 13th of October, 1874.

The County Clerk, in certifying to the proper authorities the vote cast on the 3rd day of November for Representative, added to this the vote polled in four precincts of the County for four representatives to the State Legislature, County Treasurer, Surveyor, one member of the Board of Supervisors, Justices of the Peace and Constables. Abstracts of these were made and filed in the office of the County Clerk. This abstract is now before me and from this these facts are taken.

In addition to this, a copy of the certificate of election issued for the benefit of the four persons voted for as Representative in the State Legislature, is given.

ARKANSAS COUNTY.

State of Arkansas }
County of Arkansas } ss.

Be it remembered, that, at an election began and held in, the County of Arkansas, aforesaid, on the third day of November, 1874, at the several places of voting established according to law, for the election of four representatives in The General Assembly of said State, from the 12th Senatorial and Representative District; the following named persons received the number of votes set opposite their respective names, to-wit: M. B. Billingsly, One hundred and Nineteen (119) votes, D. B. McFarlane, One hundred and Nineteen (119) votes, Stephen Bilheimer, One Hundred and Twenty (120) votes, Thomas Kersh, One hundred and Twenty (120) votes.

I, E. P. G. Tackett, County Clerk, and ex-officio Clerk of the County Court in and for the County of Arkansas aforesaid, do hereby certify that the foregoing is a true copy and complete abstract of the whole number of votes cast at the election aforesaid, in all the precincts of the County of Arkansas aforesaid.

In testimony whereof, I have hereunto set my hand and affixed the seal of my office, at the County of Arkansas aforesaid, on the 6th day of November, 1874.

E. P. G. Tackett, Clerk.
By A. C. Wiley, D. C.

Filed November 6th, 1874.
E. P. G. Tackett, Clerk.
By A. C. Wiley, D. C.

Billingsly and McFarlane were citizens of Arkansas County; Bilheimer, of Prairie; and Kersh, a negro, was from Lincoln—it then forming a part of the 12th Representative District.

Were the facts as shown in the foregoing certificate prompted by a secret understanding between the old, or outgoing county officials and the Brook's faction, backed or encouraged by the Federal Authorities to overturn the new—or Garland Government—and install the Brook's faction?

For an intelligible answer to this question, let the following statement of facts be fully considered and understood.

After the formation of the Constitution of 1874, and pending its adoption by the State, the leaders of the Republican Party held a political convention in Little Rock, September 15th. That convention adopted and published an address, and passed resolutions expressing the political sentiments of the Republicans of the State.

In the address mentioned above, we find the following paragraph:

"Has the North changed its mind in relation to Unrepentant Rebels? We feel very confident that Congress will, at an early date, take up the Arkansas case and reinstate its lawful authority, and we hope no man, professing to be a Republican, or who desires to perpetuate the existence of the party in this State, will do anything to embarrass the actions of our friends in Congress. We regard our triumph as certain, if the policy laid down in this address be strictly adhered to."

The resolution referred to is as follows:

FROM 1870 TO 1875.

"That we approve the timely movement, calling a convention, to be held at Chattanooga on the 13th day of October next, and have the utmost confidence that its deliberations will result in great good to the whole country."

What was the object of the Southern Convention, and why was it so heartily approved by Arkansas Republicans if they did not contemplate an effort to reverse the ruling of President Grant, and reinstate Reconstruction Republican rule in Arkansas?

Following the suggestion and recommendation of the September Convention, we see the reason prompting the actions of the election officers in the November election of 1874.

In this connection, take into consideration the appeal of V. V. Smith to President Grant, dated the 16th of November, 1874, asking the President to support him in his pretended claim to the office of Governor of Arkansas. The appeal was supported by Clayton and the following persons: Dorsey as Senator, Snyder as Representative, Wheeler, Page, Corbin, Gray and Warwick, five of the seven State officers under the election of 1872. It also was endorsed by Thomas, Brooks, Tuck, Casper, Dennison, Edgerton, Mills and Harrington, eight of the Federal office-holders in Arkansas.

The petition of Joseph Brooks to President Grant, dated the 2nd of February, praying to be recognized as the lawful governor of Arkansas, and last, but not least, the special message of General Grant, dated February 8th, 1875. Among other things, the message says:

"These proceedings, if permitted to stand, practically ignore all rights of minorities in all the states, also, what is there to prevent each of the States, recently readmitted to Federal relations on certain conditions, changing their conditions and violating their pledge, if this action in Arkansas is acquiesced in."

Why the president changed his mind and actions in this matter from that as shown in his proclamation of the 15th day of May, 1874, is left to the conjecture of the reader.

But for the action of Congress, under the President's recommendation by his special message of February 8th, 1875, in which he said, "I earnestly ask that Congress will take definite action in this matter to relieve the executive from acting upon questions which should be decided by the Legislative branch of the Government."

I think it highly probable that the President, if left to act in the matter, would have overturned the Garland Government, and reinstated the Reconstruction and that with the Constitution of 1868.

Fortunately for the rights of the people, and the maintenance of Civil Government in our County, Congress did relieve the Executive by ordering an investigation of "Affairs in Arkansas" and on motion of A. Pollard, chairman of the committee making the investigation, the House of Representatives of the National Congress, March, 1875, adopted the following resolution:

"Resolved, that the report of the select committee on the subject of 'Affairs in the State of Arkansas,' be accepted. And in the judgment of this house, no interference with the existing government of

ARKANSAS COUNTY.

that State (Constitution of 1874—A. H. Garland being Governor) by any department of the United States is advisable."

Referring again to the election held by the State in October, 1874, on the question of adopting the New Constitution, and the election of officers under same; it is shown that there were 1641 votes polled, and of this number, 1211 were for adoption and 430 were against it. The list below names the officers elected and their offices.

Robert C. Chaney, Representative to the General Assembly.
Richard K. Gamble, County and Probate Judge.
Benjamin F. Quertermous, Circuit Clerk.
William Stillwell, Sheriff.
A. B. Crawford, Treasurer.
Dixon Adams, Coroner.
E. J. Connelly, Surveyor.
Jesse Bass, Assessor.

Each of these officers were elected as their successors at the general election of 1876, except Dixon Adams, who declined a re-election, and Jesse Bass, who died before the election, thus showing that the people of the County were fully satisfied with the officials of the County and their actions.